Charles Ives
and the
Classical Tradition

Charles Ives
and the
Classical Tradition

: : : :

EDITED BY

GEOFFREY BLOCK

AND

J. PETER BURKHOLDER

YALE UNIVERSITY PRESS
NEW HAVEN AND LONDON

Chapter 1 is adapted from "Charles Ives the Avant-Gardist, Charles Ives the Traditionalist," © 1990 by Gustav Bosse Verlag. Reprinted in revised form from *Bericht über das internationale Symposion "Charles Ives und die amerikanische Musiktradition bis zur Gegenwart" Köln 1988*, ed. Klaus Wolfgang Niemöller, pp. 37–51, by permission.

Chapter 4 is © 1978 by the Regents of the University of California. Reprinted from *19th-Century Music*, vol. 2, no. 1, pp. 72–81, by permission.

Designed by Helene Wald Berinsky.

Set in Janson type by Rainsford Type, Danbury, Connecticut.

Printed in the United States of America by Edwards Brothers, Inc., Ann Arbor, Michigan.

Library of Congress Cataloging-in-Publication Data

Charles Ives and the classical tradition / edited by Geoffrey Block
   and J. Peter Burkholder.
      p.   cm.
   Includes bibliographical references (p.) and index.
   ISBN 0-300-06177-3 (cloth : alk. paper)
   1. Ives, Charles, 1874–1954—Criticism and interpretation.
  I. Block, Geoffrey Holden. II. Burkholder, J. Peter (James Peter)
ML410.I94C35 1996
780'.92—dc20   95-31915

A catalogue record for this book is available from the British Library.

The paper in this book meets the guidelines for permanence and durability of the Committee on Production Guidelines for Book Longevity of the Council on Library Resources.

10 9 8 7 6 5 4 3 2 1

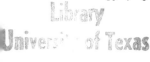

Contents

CONTENTS

Introduction:
"A Continuing Spirit"

J. PETER BURKHOLDER

From the first reviews of his music in the 1920s to the present day, Charles Ives has been viewed as a quintessentially American composer, one who rejected the European tradition and struck out on a new path. He has been hailed as "the Walt Whitman of American music" and as "our Washington, Lincoln and Jefferson of music," comparisons that imply his independence from European influences.[1] Music histories have emphasized the American character of his music, varying in their tone from describing him as "the first important distinctively American composer" to suggesting that the "pure Americanism" of his music was the result of a "bizarre unintegrated mixture of daring sophistication and homespun crudity."[2] Younger American composers have seen Ives as a forefather who broke with tradition, allowing them virtually unlimited freedom to explore new procedures, materials, and concepts for music; as John Cage wrote in 1964, "Now that we have a music that doesn't depend on European musical history, Ives seems like the beginning of it."[3]

For musicians and listeners who have absorbed this view of Ives, it may come as a surprise to read the composer's conception of what he sought to achieve, as recalled by his nephew Chester Ives:

> One evening, I talked with him about Beethoven, and I said that I felt what he [Uncle Charlie] was doing was what Beethoven would have done had he been able to keep on living. And he said that was the way he felt about it—a sort of continuing spirit.[4]

This sense of striving to continue the spirit of Beethoven and match his achievement is evident also in Ives's *Essays Before a Sonata*, in which he holds up Beethoven as a model of spiritual depth whose symphonies are "perfect truths."[5] He compares the Transcendentalist writers he discusses in the *Essays* and depicts in the *Concord Sonata* to Beethoven, proclaiming that certain of Emerson's revelations "approach as near the divine as Beethoven in his most inspired moments," that "both Beethoven and Thoreau express profound truths and deep sentiment," and that "the Concord bards . . . pound away at the immensities with a Beethoven-like sublimity."[6] Because much of Ives's praise for the Concord writers can be read as an assertion of his own philosophy and a defense of his own approach to music, by comparing their work to that of a composer he is implicitly comparing himself to Beethoven. In his later *Memos*, Ives asserts that Beethoven, along with Bach and perhaps Brahms, is "among the strongest and greatest in all art, and nothing since is stronger or greater than their strongest and greatest" even as he expresses his desire to move beyond their music to new sounds and ideas.[7]

In identifying with Beethoven, Ives was choosing as his model the most radical composer of the early nineteenth century, one who struck out in new directions, created a distinctive musical idiom, was attacked by some as bizarre or crude, and provided an example of freedom for composers to explore new ways of writing and thinking about music. Comparing him with Beethoven minimizes none of these aspects of Ives. But Beethoven did not reject tradition; he followed it, learned from it, and reinterpreted it. So did Ives. That, in brief, is the thesis of this collection of essays: that Ives placed himself in the classical tradition, drew on it heavily for his aesthetics and musical techniques, and extended it to create something new.

Following the example of Beethoven, Ives sought to absorb the central ideas and techniques of the European musical tradition and to develop them further, in order to give expression to musical and extramusical ideas that had never before been captured in music. To do this, Ives recast musical form and blended elements of disparate genres into single movements, as did Beethoven. He wrote sonatas, chamber music, songs, and symphonies that range from abstract musical argument to program music, as did Beethoven. And he assimilated into the idiom of art music a number of popular styles: not the peasant dances, Italian opera, and French revolutionary music of Beethoven's day, long since absorbed into the common musical language, but the hymnody, popular song styles, military music, and fiddle tunes of his native region. More broadly, Ives learned from and emulated not only Beethoven but the entire European pantheon of great masters as viewed in late-nineteenth-century New England, from Bach to such recent figures as Wagner,

Brahms, Dvořák, and Tchaikovsky. Yet his aspiration most closely matched that of Beethoven, and this was the spirit he sought to continue.

He had company, of course. No composer has had a more profound impact on his successors than did Beethoven, and the history of music for more than a century after his death is full of composers who sought to extend his ideas and to secure a place alongside him in the ranks of the great. This is particularly true of the Austro-German tradition in which Ives's teachers and mentors were trained. Moreover, Ives was thoroughly familiar with that tradition through concerts, his own playing and performing, and his musical education at Yale under the composer Horatio Parker, which included composing in the genres and styles of major European composers. Thus it is not surprising to find parallels between Ives's music and that of other composers of his time even when there is no question of direct influence. Ives was a man of his time, and his music reflects many of the same concerns and procedures as does that of his peers in Europe and America.

The essays in this collection contribute to our understanding of Ives as a composer committed to continuing the spirit of Beethoven and that of the classical tradition as a whole, and deeply immersed in the problems facing composers of his generation. The contributors illuminate his music through comparisons with that of other composers in Europe and the United States. The essays in part 1 trace possible influences on Ives by his predecessors and illustrate how much he absorbed of the language and aesthetic of his time. Part 2 discerns extensive parallels between Ives and his European contemporaries, whose music in most cases he did not know well, if at all. Their commonalities arise not from mere coincidence but from shared influences and concerns. Taken together, these essays demonstrate that even apparently strange or distinctively American aspects of Ives's music—from his penchant for quotation to his juxtaposition of disparate styles and concerns—have strong precedents and parallels among European composers. From these snapshots taken from different points of view emerges a picture of Ives as a composer at home in the classical tradition, exploring the issues that confronted composers of his generation on both sides of the Atlantic, and very much of his own place and time.

The first essay links Ives to those composers active in Europe during the second half of the nineteenth century whose works were best known in the United States, including Wagner, Brahms, Dvořák, and Tchaikovsky. After briefly considering the many ways in which German Romanticism is reflected in Ives's music and philosophy, the essay focuses on musical borrowing—seemingly one of the most unusual aspects of his music. Like most composers, Ives learned how to compose by imitating existing music, and this practice led to his first so-called quotations. His other early uses of borrowed material, from variation sets and new settings of familiar tunes to themes paraphrased from vernacular melodies, are equally common in the European tradition. Only in his mature music, after 1902, do we find innovative uses of borrowed tunes, such as cumulative setting and collage, and only then does borrowing come to be a frequent feature of his music. In this realm, as in others, he begins with materials and procedures common to most composers in the second half of the nineteenth century and only gradually evolves new and highly individual extensions of these ideas over the course of his career. That is, his roots are firmly in the European tradition of art music, the classical tradition extending from Bach through Beethoven and Brahms to his own time, and he develops his own recognizable idiom within that tradition by using some of its elements in new ways. This is the path taken by all of Ives's major European contemporaries, and in this respect Ives is typical of his generation.

Geoffrey Block's essay on Ives's relationship with Beethoven explores the ambivalence Ives felt toward the composer that he believed came nearest his ideal. Ives's reverence for Beethoven was tempered by competition, which is revealed both through his comments in *Memos* and in his music. Ives borrowed and reworked material from Beethoven more often than from any other classical composer, most significantly in the *Concord Sonata*. Block examines how these reworkings extend, reflect on, and "improve on" Beethoven's ideas. By the end of the sonata, the famous motive from Beethoven's Fifth Symphony has come to sound not like a borrowing but as an integral part of Ives's theme, just as Ives absorbed and ultimately transcended his greatest model.

Nicholas E. Tawa then draws our attention to the parallels in cultural heritage, musical training, philosophy, aesthetics, compositional procedures, and musical style between Ives and the most prominent American composers of classical music of the late nineteenth century, notably John Knowles Paine, George Chadwick, and Horatio Parker. The recognition of Ives as "the first distinctively American composer" has obscured the music of these and earlier composers, just as the notorious complexity and extraordinary individuality of his later music has obscured how deeply his earlier works are indebted to his American predecessors. The classical tradition was well established in the United States before Ives began to study it, and the connections that Tawa draws show that Ives was very much a part of this transplanted tradition.

The remaining essays consider parallels between Ives and his European contemporaries. Robert P. Morgan's essay, first published in *19th-Century Music* in 1978, was among the first extended comparisons of Ives with one of his European contemporaries and thus deserves reprinting here. Morgan finds significant parallels between Ives and Mahler. Both use familiar musical materials, from simple tonal gestures to standard musical types and outright quotations, yet transform them through fragmentation, distortion, and juxtaposition against different kinds of music, creating extraordinary effects. Both write stylistically heterogeneous music, interrupting the musical continuity to insert a radically different type of music, or combining different strands simultaneously, as if two pieces were being heard at once. Both create a sense of space and distance through contrasts of dynamic level, timbre, key, and placement of performers. Morgan finds these and other parallels springing from a common conception of the musical work not as something autonomous and complete in itself but as a reflection of the experience of life, in all its diversity, inconsistency, openness, and multiplicity. This conception, Morgan argues, is a shared response to the condition of European music and to ideas in the other arts. What seems peculiar in Ives's music is revealed through the parallels with Mahler to be a strong thread of the European tradition.

Keith C. Ward compares Ives with his almost exact contemporary, Schoenberg. The two composers knew of each other, perhaps even met, and may have known some of each other's music—but only late in their careers, making mutual influence unlikely. Their music is dissimilar in a number of respects. Yet Ward describes a remarkable affinity in their musical ideals. Both saw themselves as heirs of Bach, Beethoven, and Brahms, continuing and yet transforming that tradition; many similarities in their musical procedures result from this common heritage. Both relied on intuition rather than traditional prohibitions, conventional styles, the opinions of others, or other external guides to govern their artistic choices. Both articulated a central dualism between the inner core of musical thought and its realization through musical technique. Both sought new expressive means to convey the inner thought of their music, and both saw their innovations in technique as part of the constant development of new methods of musical expression. These similarities in their aesthetic ideals led Schoenberg and Ives to parallel, though different, solutions to the common problems faced by composers of their generation.

Philip Lambert explores similarities between the works of Ives and of Berg, whose opera *Wozzeck* established him as the most popular composer of the Viennese atonal school and whose Violin Concerto is perhaps the most widely played and best-loved twelve-tone work. Lambert's essay concentrates on compositional technique, demonstrating that procedures that may seem idiosyncratic or even bizarre in Ives have parallels in the music of Berg, one of the most significant modern composers in the central European mainstream. Once again, the similarities are no accident but arise from the common Romantic heritage of the two composers and the common concerns encountered by all composers of their generation.

Finally, Andrew Buchman links Ives with Stravinsky as composers born into nations that possessed both a strong classical tradition derived from Western Europe and a healthy native tradition of folk and popular music. Faced with similar problems as modernists and as outsiders to the central Western European tradition, they pursued parallel paths and achieved remarkably similar solutions. Familiar with vernacular music from their youth and trained in the forms and aesthetics of nineteenth-century Romanticism, they developed similar techniques of quotation, paraphrase, stylistic allusion, polyrhythmic layering, and bitonality in order to blend national or popular styles into their music. Surrounded, like other modern composers, by the enduring classics of the past, in their early works they emulated the music of Beethoven and Tchaikovsky, whereas their later works rework and critique their predecessors. Despite strong differences in style and aesthetic, both composers solved the common problem of their generation—that of achieving an individual voice within the received tradition—by writing music that reflects on the experience of music itself: music that is full of references to the music they heard and assimilated, yet which remains uniquely their own.

Other comparisons suggest themselves. Perhaps the strongest link between Ives and a European contemporary is with Debussy, whose music he knew perhaps as early as the first decade of the twentieth century. Debussy was a direct influence on several of Ives's works and on some of his characteristic procedures, such as the superimposition of independent layers, the creation of impressionistic washes of sound, and the composition of music that seeks to evoke real-life experience.[8] Like Richard Strauss, Ives preserves the fundamental polarity of consonance and dissonance but intensifies each one, to dramatic effect. Like Satie, Ives writes pieces that are both experimental and irreverent. Like Bartók, Ives blends indigenous materials with the procedures and aesthetics of the classical tradition to create a new synthesis, and he achieves new ways of establishing a tonal center and achieving resolution. The list could continue through Sibelius, Scriabin, Vaughan Williams, Ravel, and others. Each case shows striking similarities between Ives and his European contemporaries in musical procedures, aesthetic ideals, or both. Although the parallels differ in each case, they are more than interesting coincidences; they demonstrate how deep are Ives's roots in the attitudes and techniques of nineteenth-century European art music, how much he confronted the same artistic issues and problems as his European contemporaries, and how often his innovations and idiosyncrasies represent remarkably similar though independent responses to these common concerns.

Making this argument does not contradict but rather deepens and enriches our understanding of Ives as an American composer. To demonstrate repeatedly Ives's deep roots in the European tradition and parallels with European contemporaries illuminates only one side of his character: his desire to continue the spirit of Beethoven, extending the common musical language and giving expression to ideas never before expressed in music. What he had to say that was new was derived from his experiences within a certain place, time, and culture, as a white old-family Protestant from a small New England city in the late nineteenth century. Ives's Americanism is an instance of nationalism as it was understood in the realm of European classical music: an attempt to give voice to the distinctive culture of one's own region and people within the genres and broad aesthetic assumptions of the international tradition of art music. In that sense it is yet another example of his strong connection with that tradition. At a still deeper level it reflects Ives's desire to "express profound truths and deep sentiment," as did his heroes Beethoven and Thoreau;[9] the truths he had to express were those he knew from his own experience. Americanism, for Ives, is not a rebellion against the spirit of Beethoven, but part of its ultimate fulfillment.

There is no question that Ives has been a major influence on composers active in both Europe and America, especially after the Second World War, including Elliott Carter, John Cage, Luciano Berio, Karlheinz Stockhausen, Peter Dickinson, Louis Andriessen, John Adams, and many others. Ives's eclecticism, experimentalism, coordination of disparate elements, superimposition of multiple layers and tempos, complex textures, and use of quotation have all found echoes in post-war music, prompting Robert P. Morgan to argue two decades ago that Ives and Varèse "represented the true center of twentieth-century music history" as "the two composers who lead most directly to the musical present."[10]

The present volume also seeks to situate Ives in the historical mainstream of twentieth-century art music, but in a very different way. Like Beethoven, Ives has served as a model for younger composers who have taken what seemed new and fresh in his work and extended and reinterpreted it in ever-changing ways. But Beethoven never ceased to be a disciple of Haydn, Mozart, and Bach, reflecting their influences even in his last works. In a similar way, Ives remained devoted in many ways to the ideals and procedures he had inherited from Bach, Beethoven, Brahms, and Parker. While stripping away what he regarded as mere habit or convention, he emulated what he viewed as the heart of their music—its attempts to express spiritual truth—and continued many of their approaches. He shared with his European contemporaries a desire to continue the great tradition of art music at a time of crisis. Like them, he extended some elements, discarded others, and introduced new ideas,

PART ONE

: : : :

PREDECESSORS

: 1 :

Ives and the Nineteenth-Century European Tradition

J. PETER BURKHOLDER

C harles Ives is widely regarded as a uniquely American composer, one who turned his back on the European tradition of art music and struck out in a new direction. He is seen as a forerunner of the avant-garde whose music anticipated most of the important developments of the century. In his widely used textbook on twentieth-century music, Eric Salzman places Ives not with his European contemporaries but as the first composer in a section on the avant-garde, and calls Ives "the first important Western composer to stand essentially outside the mainstream of European culture."[1]

Yet this picture of Ives is incomplete and misleading. For Ives is not only an American but a composer working in European genres, using European procedures, and conforming to European ideas about the nature and purpose of art music; not only a radical experimenter but a writer of symphonies, sonatas, and art songs whose roots in the romantic tradition are very strong. Indeed, Ives was as much a part of the European tradition of art music as were Mahler, Debussy, Schoenberg, Bartók, Stravinsky, Berg, and the other progressive composers of his time. Like them, Ives sought to write music that would find a place in the permanent repertoire beside the masterpieces of the eighteenth and nineteenth centuries. Like his great European contemporaries, Ives understood that competition with the masterworks already in the repertoire required both emulation and innovation. His music must be on the same level as the classics, enough like them to be seen as belonging to the same noble tradition, while at the same time it must speak in a new and distinctive voice, one as personal, authentic, and deeply felt as the voices of the classical masters themselves.[2]

The late nineteenth century saw that music as great which was an authentic statement of the composer as an individual and as a product of his age and nation, yet able to speak to all people of any age or nation; original, yet capable of enduring for all time; innovative and forward-looking, yet well crafted, with deep knowledge of the tradition. This is how Beethoven's music was viewed, and it describes the aspirations of countless followers of Beethoven, including Ives. Ives's nephew Chester Ives once suggested to his uncle that what Ives was doing in music "was what Beethoven would have done had he been able to keep on living. And he said that was the way he felt about it—a sort of continuing spirit."[3] This Beethoven was not the mere mortal of recent scholarship but the titan of nineteenth-century myth. Ives sought to live up to these demands, casting himself in the role of composer-hero with Beethoven as his model.

This was not the aspiration of Henry Cowell, John Cage, or the avant-garde of the 1960s. Who among them was interested in creating classical masterworks, or indeed enduring art? Aleatorism, happenings, "pop" art, and most other recent trends with which Ives has been compared are focused in the present, not in hopes of immortality. Who among the avant-garde has sought to continue the spirit of Beethoven? Rather, composers from Cage to Mauricio Kagel have attacked that spirit, a spirit to which Ives was devoted.[4]

European Romanticism, and particularly German Romanticism, exercised an enormous influence on Ives, shaping his fundamental character as a composer. He absorbed this influence primarily through his composition teacher at Yale, Horatio Parker, who had studied at Munich with Josef Rheinberger. Parker has received more bad press than any other figure in Ives's life, and most of it is unfair. Parker is supposed to have been a musical conservative who ignored Ives's experiments and forced him to conform to a tired old routine of musical training. But Parker wrote many progressive works in addition to his music in a more conservative style, and the accounts of his studies with George Chadwick and Rheinberger show him to have been as a student at least as rebellious and interested in innovation as was Ives. Indeed, the deeper one explores Parker's character and opinions, the more parallels one finds with Ives.[5]

What Parker did for Ives was as important as what Schoenberg did for Berg a decade later, and strikingly parallel. Both teachers found a talented young man whose musical tastes and compositional habits had been formed by a popular tradition: Berg, by the sentimental *Lieder* of the salon; Ives, by the music for band, church, and parlor that he had already learned to compose skillfully. Both teachers schooled their students thoroughly in the classics, providing both the discipline that young talent needs and, even more importantly, an aspiration to write music that rose above sentimentality or entertainment. This was the Romantic ideal of music as an art for its own sake, one that should not be compromised for popular appeal or financial gain but rather should be motivated by the composer's need to create—an ideal both Parker and Schoenberg articulated in their writings.[6]

The results in both cases were spectacular and perhaps unexpected. Both students abandoned the popular forms they had practiced in their teens and devoted themselves to the genres of art music, but both Berg and Ives ultimately used their classical training and Romantic aspirations to return to their musical roots: Berg to write masterly atonal and twelve-tone music that makes frequent references to the waltzes, marches, songs, and harmonies of the popular tonal music of Austria; Ives to celebrate the vernacular music of America in symphonies, tone poems, sonatas, and songs.

Like Ives's adoption of European forms and genres, his acceptance of the ideal of music as an art practiced for its own sake, and his later predilection for program music, his nationalism also shows the influence of European Romanticism. Self-conscious nationalism was completely foreign to American vernacular styles and indeed virtually impossible, since nationalism requires an international style as a foil.[7] In the final analysis, Ives's music is no more and no less American than Berg's is Austrian or Bartók's Hungarian. All were nationalist composers working within an international tradition that esteemed national individuality, and each used music native to his region to address an international audience, offering (in Ives's words) "a local color that will do all the world good."[8]

Similarly, Ives's relentless search for new means of expression and his attempts to express in music what had never been expressed in music before are manifestations of the European Romantic tradition. So too are his moments of musical autobiography. So too is his turn to subjects drawn from literature; compare his "Thoreau" and his *Robert Browning Overture* to the *Faust* and *Dante* Symphonies of Liszt, Strauss's *Don Quixote*, and Schoenberg's *Verklärte Nacht*. So, too, is his celebration of national character, of events, places, and people; compare his *Thanksgiving* to Mendelssohn's *Reformation* Symphony, his *Housatonic at Stockbridge* to the Rhine music in *Das Rheingold* or Smetana's *Moldau*, the march music in Ives's *Putnam's Camp* and *The Fourth of July* to march movements in Mahler songs and symphonies. Romantic also are his excursions into philosophy and spirituality; his Transcendentalist "Emerson" is paralleled by Strauss's tone poem based on Nietzsche's *Also Sprach Zarathustra*, and the spiritual journey of Ives's vast Fourth Symphony has parallels in Mahler's Second and Eighth Symphonies.

Even Ives's penchant for quotation and allusion, once thought to be a peculiarity of his music (and much later an inspiration for collage compositions of the 1960s), turns out to have been part of the common currency of the nineteenth and early twentieth centuries. There is now a minor musicological industry devoted to ferreting out allusions, quotations, uses of models, and other forms of borrowing in composers from Beethoven, Schubert, and Schumann through Brahms, Elgar, Mahler, Debussy, Berg, and Stravinsky, and more articles on the subject appear every year.[9]

The aspect of Ives's music that most distinguishes him from his European contemporaries and makes him look like an avant-garde composer is his penchant for writing experimental music. From his mid-teens until his final years as a composer, Ives sketched dozens of small pieces or fragments in which he experimented with new or unusual musical procedures. In the 1890s he tried writing pieces based on two or more simultaneous keys, on a single whole-tone scale, on newly invented chords, on tone clusters, wedge formations, and parallel chords. Later he experimented with quartal and quintal harmonies, palindromes, rhythmic and pitch series, ostinatos, canons, layers of atonality superimposed on tonality or vice versa, quarter tones, and other devices. Almost without exception, these pieces are small, rigorously worked out, and completely private; rarely were they performed until decades later. But Ives later would often use techniques first tried out in these musical experiments in his larger, more ambitious compositions.

These small musical experiments are virtually unprecedented. No earlier composer of any nation so systematically researched new possibilities in musical composition by writing music to try them out. These pieces and studies have come to be seen as the fountainhead of the American experimentalist tradition, leading through Henry Cowell and John Cage to the radical experiments of the 1960s.

Do we have two composers here, one a musician trained in the European tradition, the other a Yankee tinkerer, one a traditionalist, the other an avant-gardist? No: each of these "experimental" ideas is in fact a response to the European tradition. Ives's experiments with novel musical techniques can be understood as a critique within music itself of the theoretical tradition in which Ives was trained, the German-influenced tradition of America's academic musicians.[10] This is clear from Ives's comments in *Memos* about his experimental pieces. For instance, he asks, "If you can play a tune in one key, why can't a feller, if he feels like [it], play one in two keys?"[11] And he cites examples of piano pieces written in the 1890s in which the two hands are in different keys. Over and over, Ives challenges the accepted rules of harmony and counterpoint and proposes alternative rules, typically by writing a piece that follows the new rules and demonstrates that they are just as logical as the old. Yet the challenge is always from *within* the tradition, not from outside it. Ives accepts the notion that music must follow logical rules, but he invents new ones; for example, he accepts the notion that music must have a tonic note and chord, but he devises a new way to establish them.

Ives's experimental music represents something new in music history, a trend that was to become increasingly important over the course of the twentieth century. But this does not mean that his music as a whole lies outside of the tradition. Even his experimental music grapples with the very core of the tradition, the procedures of tonality and counterpoint that underlie it.[12] In other words, even the avant-garde side of Ives is a direct outgrowth of Ives's engagement with the tradition. There is no conflict between Ives the avant-gardist and Ives the traditionalist; they are the same composer, reflecting the same concerns.

When one studies all of Ives's music in chronological order one sees a clear pattern in his development as a composer. He begins by imitating what has come before, proving his connections with the European Romantic tradition, and gradually asserts his individuality within and ultimately against that tradition.[13] One finds precisely the same pattern in the careers of Ives's great contemporaries in Europe. Debussy, Scriabin, Schoenberg, Bartók, Stravinsky, Webern, and Berg began by writing tonal, Romantic music, gradually extending and intensifying parts of their heritage while rejecting others, until each attained a unique personal voice. As an example of how this process unfolded in one aspect of Ives's music, I will trace the idea of allusion and quotation through Ives's career, showing how this device, at first a means of imitating European music and thus forging closer links with it, eventually became a means of differentiation, a characteristic of a unique musical personality. There is not space here to cover every aspect of Ives's uses of existing music, of course, but I will touch on several of his most characteristic procedures.[14]

Ives apparently learned how to compose through the centuries-old method of imitating existing music. Many of his earliest pieces are based on a particular model, and several incorporate elements from the model. One of these is a Polonaise in C for two solo instruments (probably cornets or violins) and piano, written about 1887–89 when Ives was in his early teens. Example 1.1 shows the opening measures of this short work as transcribed from the ink score prepared by Ives's father George.[15]

The Polonaise is modeled on the sextet from Donizetti's *Lucia di Lammermoor*, in particular on its opening eighteen-measure period, a duet for Edgardo and Enrico (ex. 1.2).[16] The only material Ives quotes exactly is the opening accompanimental figure, which he marks "stac-

EXAMPLE 1.1. Ives, Polonaise in C Major (ca. 1887–89), mm. 1–7.

cato" and "pizz[icato]" to simulate the pizzicato string accompaniment in the opera; perhaps he envisioned an orchestral performance. Yet the solo lines in the Ives work evoke the music of the singers at several points.

As shown in example 1.3, the opening phrase of the first cornet, imitated a measure later in the second cornet, is similar both rhythmically and melodically to Edgardo's opening phrase. (In this and all later examples, Ives's melodies are indicated by a vertical bracket in the left-hand margin next to the clef; staves lacking a vertical bracket are from the model.) The two opening phrases are aligned vertically in example 1.3 to show the similarity of melodic contour; Edgardo's rhythm is written just under Ives's opening motive to show the rhythmic similarity. The continuations are different, but the second melodic unit of the Ives parallels a later moment in Edgardo's vocal line, in mm. 16–17 of the sextet (or, more closely, the flute and clarinet at that point, which conclude with a descending fifth, as does the Ives). Ives transposes the long

EXAMPLE 1.2. Donizetti, sextet from act 2 of *Lucia di Lammermoor*, mm. 1–6.

EXAMPLE 1.3. Opening phrases of Polonaise compared with *Lucia* sextet.

EXAMPLE 1.4. Later passages from Polonaise compared with *Lucia* sextet.

note on the downbeat down an octave and uses as an upbeat the dotted figure from the opening phrase, which Enrico sings at this point in the Donizetti. The result is a very neat variation on the first two-bar unit of the Ives. As shown in example 1.4, measures 14–15 of the Ives copy from the Donizetti a descending scale in parallel thirds but substitute for its final flourish a dotted figure with a double chromatic appoggiatura to the tonic triad; this is borrowed from another spot in Donizetti's duet and is used once previously in the Ives (mm. 8–10). The continuations of the two passages (mm. 12–13 of the Donizetti, mm. 16–17 of the Ives) are also similar.

In addition to these specific correspondences, both Ives's piece and its model feature frequent movement in parallel thirds (or sixths, in the Donizetti) and a pervasive dotted figure on the third or first beat of each measure, especially at the beginning and end of melodic units. There is a wealth of similarities, from exact quotation and close allusion to these more general parallels, but the mix of elements in the two pieces is different, as if Ives had challenged himself to create a new work that simultaneously resembled its model as closely as possible, yet was as distinct from it as possible. This practice of imitating a model while varying it as much as possible is an ancient and effective method for learning composition. It may have been suggested to Ives by his father, who was at this time training the young Ives in theory and composition.[17]

Ives continued to use European music as models, but such overt melodic allusions soon disappear, at least temporarily. Instead, Ives borrows ideas of form, structure, procedure, and style. For instance, in writing his well-known *Variations on "America"* for organ in 1891, Ives borrowed techniques from the organ music he had studied and performed, including Johann Christian Heinrich Rinck's variations on "God Save the King" (the same tune as "America").[18]

Between the late 1890s and about 1902, Ives wrote over two dozen songs to lyrics famous in settings by European composers, including Schubert, Mendelssohn, Schumann, Franz, Cornelius, and Brahms, in most cases using the earlier setting as a model.[19] Several of these seem to have been written during Ives's studies at Yale with Horatio Parker, as Ives applied himself with greater depth and seriousness to learning the styles and techniques of European Romanticism, again through imitation. But part of Romanticism is individualism, and part of what every student composer of that era had to learn was how to write music that conformed to prevailing taste yet did not simply repeat what other composers had done. Comparing Ives's songs with the original settings makes clear both how assiduously he sought to absorb the language and spirit of the Romantic lied and how shrewdly he distinguished each song from its model.

For instance, in setting Heine's "Ich grolle nicht," Ives followed the model of Schumann's setting in *Dichterliebe*. Examples 1.5 and 1.6 show the opening passages of the settings by Schumann and Ives, respectively, with Heine's original text and the translation by John Sullivan Dwight that Ives most likely knew as follows:

Ich grolle nicht	I'll Not Complain
Heinrich Heine	*trans. John S. Dwight*

Ich grolle nicht, und wenn das Herz auch bricht,	I'll not complain, tho' break my heart in twain,
Ewig verlor'nes Lieb! Ich grolle nicht.	O love forever lost, I'll not complain.
Wie du auch strahlst in Diamanten-pracht,	Howe'er thou shin'st in diamond splendor bright,
Es fällt kein Strahl in deines Herzens Nacht.	There falls no ray into thy heart's deep night.
Das weiß ich längst. Ich sah dich ja im Traume.	I know full well. In dreams I saw thee waning,
Und sah die Nacht in deines Herzens Raume,	And saw the night within thy bosom reigning,
Und sah die Schlang', die dir am Her-zen frißt,	And saw the snake that on thy heart doth gnaw,
Ich sah, mein Lieb, wie sehr du elend bist.	How all forlorn thou art, my love, I saw.

EXAMPLE 1.5. Schumann, "Ich grolle nicht," mm. 1–12.

Schumann alters the original poetic form, shifting the break between the two stanzas to the middle of the fifth line, repeating the first line as a refrain at the beginning of the second stanza, and repeating the first three words twice at the end of the song. Ives follows Schumann exactly, and uses the same musical form as well: ABA'C. The two songs often feature a similar rhythm or melodic contour for the same words: the same intervals and similar rhythm at the first *grolle nicht*; similar rhythm and an inverted melodic contour at *und wenn das Herz auch bricht*; similar rhythm and contour in the repeated *ewig verlor'nes Lieb*; and virtually identical rhythm for the lines beginning at *Wie du auch strahlst*. Other parallels include the frequent use of repeated pitches in the melody and repeated chords in the accompaniment; a shift to minor at the second

EXAMPLE 1.6. Ives, "Ich grolle nicht," mm. 1–15.

Ich grolle nicht.
© 1933 by Merion Music, Inc.
Reprinted by Permission.

line; a change in character for the third and fourth lines of the poem, set in both songs as a rising sequence at a higher dynamic level than the preceding music; and a dramatic crescendo in the second stanza. In other words, the two songs are very similar in structure and in their treatment of the text.

Yet the two settings could hardly differ more in character. Schumann's is forceful and moderately fast, with a piano part consisting entirely of pounding octaves in the left hand and pulsing eighth-note chords in the right hand. Ives's setting is much more lyrical, slower, and softer, and features more varied figuration in the piano. A particularly striking difference is the treatment of the opening words: loud, defiant, and ultimately hollow in the Schumann, as if the speaker were feigning triumphant laughter that fails to hide his breaking heart and wounded pride; soft, almost tender, and full of an opposite but equally poignant irony in the Ives. This must have been part of the assignment from Parker: to write a song that closely follows the structure of Schumann's setting and is true to the text, yet achieves individuality in musical material and expression.

This song is typical of Ives's treatment of texts already famous in settings by European composers. Although he incorporates gestures or structural elements from the model, the mood and figuration of his songs are very different. This suggests a deliberate attempt not to repeat the same ideas, indeed to take a contrary path, seeking new interpretations of the familiar words. By using these texts and referring to his models directly, Ives publicly invites comparison with some of the masters and some of the masterpieces of the art song repertoire, asserting his right to a place in the European tradition; by taking a different approach to the texts, he asserts his individuality within the tradition.

So far we have seen Ives learning European styles and procedures through imitation—a European pedagogical technique of long standing. He begins by incorporating musical ideas from the model but seems quickly to learn that nineteenth-century expectations of originality require him to disguise his indebtedness. So it is striking when he returns in his First Symphony (ca. 1897–1902), the most ambitious work of his college years, to direct allusion to his models, including Tchaikovsky's *Pathétique* Symphony, Beethoven's Ninth Symphony, Schubert's "Unfinished" Symphony, and particularly Dvořák's "New World" Symphony. He does so in the spirit not only of emulation or homage but of competition, using the direct allusions as a signal that he aims to match or best these composers on their own ground.[20]

Signs of competition are abundant in Ives's treatment of the "New World" Symphony, then barely four years old. His choice of this work as his most important model is hardly surprising. Dvořák had just returned to Europe in 1895 after three years as director of the National Conservatory in New York; Parker had taught at the conservatory the first year Dvořák was there. The "New World" Symphony was premiered in New York in December 1893 and was an immediate success with both critics and public. As the newest European symphony known to Ives, as the most significant symphonic work composed in and identified with the United States, and as an enormously popular work, it was an obvious model for emulation, offering a clear challenge to Ives to write something as modern, as significant, and as potentially successful.

Throughout his symphony, Ives tries to match or outdo Dvořák. Both are cyclic symphonies, and both place themes from earlier movements in counterpoint with themes introduced in later ones; Ives's themes are often longer and the combinations more extensive. Both symphonies combine themes in diminution with themselves or with other themes; Ives carries this technique to greater length and complexity. In both first-movement expositions, an important element of the second theme is anticipated in the preceding transition, an unusual procedure that is not repeated in either recapitulation; in the Ives, the motive is longer and is stated more often in the transition. Both development sections begin with a dramatic diminuendo and ambiguous harmony based on symmetrical partitioning of the octave; Dvořák's approach is supremely simple, an augmented triad sustained for twelve bars, whereas Ives's is more interesting and unusual, a series of minor triads that rise in register (and change inversion) as their roots descend by step through the complete whole-tone scale. These and other similarities throughout the work show that Ives drew on Dvořák's symphony for many technical details while always seeking to outdo his model in some way.

The most direct allusion is in Ives's Adagio, which draws heavily on Dvořák's famous Largo. Both slow movements are in ABA' form, in a major key, with the middle section in minor. In both cases the principal thematic material from the first movement is recalled at the end of the B section and combined in counterpoint with a theme from the A section. This is extremely unusual, the parallel quite striking; once again, Ives's treatment is longer and more complex. The main idea of the A section in both slow movements is a lyrical English horn melody over sustained chords in the strings. In both cases, the English horn returns with its theme just after the climax of the movement; indeed, the deployment of the English horn throughout is virtually the same. As if to make the allusion as clear as possible, Ives paraphrases Dvořák's melody, changing the rhythm, eliminating repetitions, and omitting some notes, but preserving the general contour and effect.[21]

Ives's treatment of this theme is a small but neat example of how he sought simultaneously to imitate Dvořák and compete with him. Example 1.7 shows how the first five measures of Ives's melody almost exactly follow the pitch contour of the closing phrase of Dvořák's (mm. 15–18), beginning with the last two notes of the preceding phrase. Since the final phrase of the Dvořák is a variant of the first phrase (mm. 7–10) with the cadence transposed up an octave, these opening measures of Ives's melody can be seen as paraphrasing both the first and final phrases of the Dvořák (both phrases appear in ex. 1.7). The shape and internal stresses

EXAMPLE 1.7. Ives, First Symphony, second movement, opening of English horn theme, compared with Dvořák, "New World" Symphony, second movement theme.

of the Ives and of the final phrase of the Dvořák are very much alike, as are the articulation and dynamics.

Yet Ives is careful to differentiate his own melody from his source. He avoids the dotted rhythm that characterizes the Dvořák while creating a new rhythmic and melodic motive in m. 2 and repeating it in inversion in m. 4. This motive propels the melody through both the low point and the high point of the line—points at which Dvořák allows a break between melodic units. These elisions in the Ives contrast with the measure-to-measure segmentation of the Dvořák, making the two melodies sound less similar than they otherwise might. Ives also deemphasizes the point of articulation between the second and third measures, although there is still a sense of a breath just before the upward arpeggiation of mm. 3–4. By avoiding the dotted rhythms, the four-square phrasing, and the short-breathed melodic units of the Dvořák, Ives makes his melody more supple and less folk-like while preserving folk-like charm and simplicity.

The pitch material that Ives omits (from mm. 15, 16, and 18 of the Dvořák) is both highly recognizable as part of the Dvořák melody and melodically somewhat repetitive, emphasizing the same pitches as the surrounding music. By leaving these elements out, Ives tightens the melody and makes it more his own. As if to compensate for these omissions, Ives emphasizes in his opening gesture the same pentatonic set (a major second and minor third within a perfect fourth) that characterizes all three of the segments of the Dvořák melody that Ives omits or abridges.

The remainder of Ives's melody is derived from mm. 14–15 of the Dvořák (ex. 1.8). Here he repeats more than he omits, reiterating in m. 7 the descent of mm. 5–6. Having avoided throughout the first half of his melody the dotted rhythm so characteristic of Dvořák's tune, Ives

EXAMPLE 1.8. Continuation of English horn theme, compared with Dvořák.

finally states it once in m. 6. But unlike the dotted figures in the source, this one repeats the same pitch in its first two notes while the following note drops a third, so that the melodic effect is quite different. In the first four notes of m. 7, rhythm and pitch content are simultaneously like and unlike those of the source: the rhythm of the source is retained, but in diminution; pitches are paired as in the source, but their order within the pairs is reversed.

Taken as a whole, the Ives melody is an elegant condensation of the Dvořák, which at twelve measures of common time is three times as long as the Ives. The Dvořák melody is a tiny ternary form (ABA') containing significant repetitions within each phrase; every note in the Ives, is derived from the Dvořák and nothing essential is missing, but the repetitions within and between phrases are trimmed. Like his symphony as a whole, Ives's melody represents an act of homage to an important model and to one of the greatest modern symphonies, but it also be read as a challenge. Recognizing that the Dvořák theme is an elegant and famous tune, Ives cites it and attempts to improve on it. His recasting of Dvořák's repetitive melody in the musical equivalent of prose constitutes an implicit critique of Dvořák's theme as redundant and rhythmically uninteresting and an implicit assertion of Ives's superiority as a composer. I believe this was sincerely felt, for outside of his marches Ives never wrote a melody, paraphrased or original, that is as rhythmically and melodically repetitive or as predictable in its phrasing as this Dvořák theme. Ives's later writings emphasize the wealth of ideas and minimum of exact repetition in his music and complain of the repetitiveness and dearth of ideas in music by others.[22]

I have lingered on these early examples in order to emphasize how ordinary they are. Ives learned to compose through imitation, and by the end of his college years went beyond imitation to pay homage to or compete with his models. None of this is unusual. One finds such acts of emulation, competition, and homage in European music throughout the nineteenth and early twentieth centuries. In each case, Ives conforms to a traditional style and genre, seeking to match the achievement of his models and to contribute something fresh.

Having established his claim to a place in the tradition, Ives now tried to make it his own, to establish a unique identity as a composer. In the Second Symphony, composed around 1902–7 and revised in 1909, he claimed a distinctive voice in two ways: by using American material and by emphasizing allusion and quotation, taking what had been a commonplace of the tradition and intensifying it.[23]

Ives's principal models of symphonic writing—Brahms, Dvořák, and Tchaikovsky—all used national material within an international style. So it is not surprising that in asserting his own national identity Ives would do the same. Each of the themes of the Second Symphony is paraphrased from an American tune, typically a popular song or hymn tune. Ives does not simply quote these tunes unchanged but reworks them into well crafted symphonic themes, making the national material conform to the international style.

It is not that the tunes Ives uses are awkward or uncouth and in need of smoothing out. But the very traits that make them good popular tunes make them unsuitable as symphonic themes, at least for a composer as dedicated as was Ives to the Brahmsian tradition of musical prose and developing variation.[24] A characteristic example is the Civil War song "Wake Nicodemus" by Henry Clay Work, on which Ives bases the opening theme of the second movement. The first phrase of the verse, which is the same as its second and fourth phrases, is given as the top line of example 1.9.

The entire verse is based on a single rhythmic figure, the dotted figure that pervades mm. 1–4. That makes it easy to remember, but symphonic themes need much more rhythmic variety. The four-square phrasing and frequent tonic cadences make it easy to sing, but a symphonic composer cannot afford to kill the tonic at the outset or to stop the music dead in its tracks every four measures; the music should be gathering steam, not plodding along. In addition, the first, second, and last phrases of the tune are exactly the same. This is normal for a song, but boring in a theme; the material would be exhausted before the piece had even gotten underway. So Ives reduces the amount of repetition, varies the rhythm and the phrasing, spices up the harmony, and avoids coming to a close too quickly. He repeats the opening and closing ideas (the closing idea is designated with horizontal brackets in ex. 1.9), marking them as material for further development, and then proceeds to develop his theme in typical late-Romantic fashion. Yet, through all these

EXAMPLE 1.9. Ives, Second Symphony, second movement, opening theme, and Henry Clay Work's song "Wake Nicodemus," opening phrase.

changes, he preserves the American character of the original; the theme *sounds* American even to a listener who does not recognize the source tune.

At the same time that he asserts his nationality by paraphrasing American tunes in his themes, Ives shows his allegiance to European art music by adopting its elaborate forms—perhaps its most distinctive trait—and by referring overtly to his European models. Above all, he borrows transitional passages from Brahms symphonies and episodes from a Bach fugue and from the prelude to Wagner's *Tristan und Isolde*. Thus he emphasizes through his borrowings that European forms have transitions and episodes, whereas the simpler song-like forms of American vernacular music typically do not. If the First Symphony pays homage to the European symphonic tradition, the Second celebrates both European and American music and points out what is most characteristic of each. Although this symphony conforms to traditional symphonic style, the American tunes and the constant presence of borrowed material mark the assertion of an individual personality within the symphonic tradition.

This process of self-assertion continues in the Third Symphony, written around 1907–11.[25] The first and last movements are among the first instances of a new form that I call "cumulative form," in which the principal theme is not presented at the beginning but gradually accumulates over the course of the movement.[26] This borrows from sonata and variation forms the fragmentation and development of themes but establishes a new order of events. Ives takes as his theme an existing tune, adds a harmonization and an obbligato countermelody paraphrased from yet another tune, and places this complex near the end in the movement, like an apotheosis. This is preceded by fragments and paraphrases of both the theme and the countermelody, often including a statement of the complete countermelody and harmonization without the theme. The key is often vague or unstable until the theme appears near the end in the tonic. Thus, instead of beginning with a theme and developing or varying it, as is typical of traditional European forms, Ives begins with fragments and variants of his theme and gradually assembles the tune and its accompaniment. As Ives said of another piece in the same form, "The working-out develops into the themes, rather than from them."[27]

The last movement is based on the hymn tune *Woodworth* by W. B. Bradbury, usually sung to these words by Charlotte Elliott:

Just as I am, without one plea,
But that thy blood was shed for me,
And that thou bid'st me come to thee,
O Lamb of God, I come, I come!

Example 1.10 shows the beginning of the fourth and final section of the movement. This is the point where the hymn tune finally appears, complete, in the cellos, in the tonic, with a solo cello playing the same tune an octave higher (not shown). The violins play the main countermelody, which is paraphrased from the hymn tune *Azmon*, while the bassoon plays a subsidiary countermelody, which is not based on an existing tune.

Before this, at the beginning of the third section of the piece (about halfway through), we hear an almost complete but very distorted paraphrase of the hymn (ex. 1.11). Still earlier, at the beginning of the second section of the piece, we hear the countermelody with its harmonization as it will appear at the end, but transposed up a fourth and without the theme. At the very beginning of the movement we hear fragments of the hymn tune, tossed around like scraps of themes in the development section of a Beethoven symphony. Several instruments, one after another,

EXAMPLE 1.10. Ives, Third Symphony, third movement, beginning of section 4, showing *Woodworth* in cello and paraphrase of *Azmon* as countermelody in violin I.

play the opening three-note motive; meanwhile, the cellos, who will have the whole hymn-tune theme at the end, play its first phrase, stretched out and distorted (ex. 1.12). Other fragments appear, notably the peak of the hymn melody (its third two-measure phrase). Then, part of the

EXAMPLE 1.11. Third Symphony, third movement, *Woodworth* paraphrase at the opening of section 3.

EXAMPLE 1.12. Third Symphony, third movement, partial *Woodworth* paraphrase in opening measures.

main countermelody appears in the woodwinds, we cycle back to the opening idea, and the development of these fragments continues.

I have described these musical events in reverse order. The actual music starts with the development, with fragments of the theme and its countermelodies, and works toward the theme itself. What Ives borrows from the European tradition is not the form but the principles of development that underlie the form. The simple American tune is not reworked into a theme suitable for a sonata form, as in the Second Symphony, nor is it treated as the subject of a set of variations, as in the *Variations on "America."* Rather, it becomes the goal of symphonic development. When we hear the theme at last, we hear in it ideas that have been thoroughly developed in the preceding music, and it strikes us as something we have achieved only after an intense struggle. Through this process the simple American tune is raised to a level of seriousness that we associate with art music.

This technique reflects changes in Ives's own understanding of the music of his native land. In his teens, he participated in that music gladly, if naively, writing marches and playing hymns in church; in his twenties, he gained a command of European art music; then he returned to the music he had known as a youth and found in it riches he had scarcely suspected were there, riches he was able to find because of what he had learned from art music. If the Second Symphony shows Ives introducing the character of American melody into European form, the Third shows him investing American tunes with all the seriousness and profundity of the greatest art music. He has taken a decisive step away from European models, not only by abandoning sonata and other received forms but by placing American tunes at the center of his music. Rather than pay homage to Europe, he uses the techniques and ethos of European art music to pay homage to the music of America. Here, Ives does more than claim an identity as an American within the European tradition. He asserts the value of the American vernacular tradition in its own right through the methods of European art music.

After about 1908, Ives turned increasingly to American life as a subject matter, and he naturally used American tunes to evoke American life. A typical example is *The Fourth of July*, a symphonic poem sketched around 1913, when Ives was in his late thirties, and completed over the next decade.[28] This is a tribute to the celebrations of Independence Day, marked by parades, dancing, and fireworks. Not surprisingly, over the course of the movement we hear patriotic songs and dance tunes and, near the end, the fireworks.

This piece also uses cumulative form. At the climax we hear the complete verse of the patriotic tune "Columbia, the Gem of the Ocean," played by a brass band and accompanied by a great mass of sound that includes the principal countermelody, "The Battle Hymn of the Republic," and several other tunes. Prior to this we hear fragments of "Columbia" and its countermelodies, with other closely related tunes thrown in as well—more than a dozen different tunes all told. This kind of musical texture has unfairly earned Ives the reputation of a composer who quoted indiscriminately and was not quite in control of his materials. Fortunately, careful analysis and sketch study by several scholars is showing that Ives knew exactly what he was doing, and that this and other similar pieces are much more tightly organized than it would appear on first hearing.[29]

The Fourth of July captures an experience in music—not, in fact, that of a boy participating in the Independence Day celebrations in his home town, but rather that of a man approaching middle age, remembering the Fourth of July celebrations of his boyhood. For his pieces about life experiences, Ives developed a set of conventions, the most important being the presence of at least two simultaneous layers of music: the events themselves in the foreground, and in the background the noises of the environment. For pieces about recent experiences, these background noises are usually soft, dissonant ostinatos in complex rhythms, representing the sounds of nature in *Central Park in the Dark*, the rustling leaves and swirling river in *The Housatonic at Stockbridge*, or the traffic noises of New York's rush hour in *From Hanover Square North*. But the background to a memory is other memories, particularly those which are aroused involuntarily by their resemblance to the first. Ives signals this through quotation. When Ives is remembering, one tune will suggest another that it resembles in some way, and the result is a collage of half-heard and half-remembered tunes that constitutes a wonderfully true musical evocation of the way human memory works.

Ives's development as a composer is logical. He starts by emulating models, then gradually asserts his individuality. He ultimately claims an identity as an American, and in his mature music he celebrates the music closest to his heart, the music he knew as a boy. But this is the evolution of a composer evolving within the European tradition, not outside it. The quantity and complexity of quotation in *The Fourth of July* is truly extraordinary. Yet everything that brought Ives to that point has its roots in the European Romantic tradition, from the idea of musical borrowing to the nationalism and programmaticism that underlie this particular work.

Ives is unique. But so is each one of the great composers in his generation—Mahler, Debussy, Strauss, Scriabin, Vaughan Williams, Schoenberg, Ravel, Stravinsky, Bartók, Webern, Berg. This generation was marked by diversity, and Ives's uniqueness made him very much a part of it.

Ives is known as an avant-garde composer in part because of the history of the reception of his music. The first musicians to take a strong interest in Ives were, for the most part, members of the avant-garde. Ives's most important advocate and first biographer was Henry Cowell, an experimental composer who saw in Ives a forerunner for his own efforts. In promoting Ives's music, Cowell emphasized Ives's experiments with musical technique at the expense of his Romantic vision. Cowell was less interested in the early music, which showed so clearly Ives's allegiance to the European Romantic tradition, and thus he did not emphasize, perhaps did not even understand, Ives's development as a composer within that tradition, or the Romantic roots of his later sonatas and symphonies.

Ives certainly deserves his reputation as one of the first composers of experimental music and as a great influence on the later avant-garde. But he is also a composer whose music is rooted in the European Romantic tradition, which it reflects and extends. That is to say, he is a composer of international stature of the generation of Schoenberg, Stravinsky, and Bartók, a worthy peer to his European contemporaries.

:2:

Ives and the "Sounds That Beethoven Didn't Have"

GEOFFREY BLOCK

During his studies with Horatio Parker, Ives arranged the Adagio movement of Beethoven's Piano Sonata in F Minor, Op. 2, No. 1 for string quartet.[1] For the most part, Ives seems content to present a realization faithful to his model. Discrepancies are bound to occur in a transcription, however, and it comes as no surprise that Ives makes a number of departures from Beethoven's blueprint. In one four-measure phrase, the reprise of the second period of the opening section (mm. 39–43), Ives makes a significant alteration when he reassigns Beethoven's right-hand melody to the cello in order to reduce the melodic preeminence of the first violin (perhaps imitating Beethoven's own procedure in such slow movements as Op. 18, No. 1 and Op. 59, No. 1, in which the opening melody appears in the first violin and then in the cello). More radically, when this same phrase is introduced in mm. 9–12, Ives declares his independence by removing Beethoven's conventional Alberti bass and replacing it with a deliberately more distinctive chromatic obbligato line divided between the viola and the second violin (ex. 2.1, fig. 2.1).

J. Peter Burkholder interprets Ives's alteration as meaning that "both figures have the same function: to maintain a sixteenth-note pulse in an inner part while the melody moves more slowly. Yet Beethoven's simple arpeggiation was old-fashioned by 1890, and so Ives replaces the late-eighteenth-century cliché with a late-nineteenth-century equivalent. The result is stylistically coherent, as the new figuration recalls the chromatic touches in the first period of Beethoven's melody, whereas a direct transcription would have been pedestrian. Ives seems concerned to preserve

EXAMPLE 2.1. Beethoven, Piano Sonata in F Minor, Op. 2, No. 1, second movement, mm. 8–14.

Reproduced from
the Artaria edition,
Vienna, 1796.

EXAMPLE 2.1b. Ives, arrangement for string quartet of Beethoven, Piano Sonata in F Minor, Op. 2, No. 1, second movement, mm. 8–14.

FIGURE 2.1. Ives's arrangement for string quartet of Beethoven, Sonata in F Minor, Op. 2, No. 1, second movement, mm. 1–14. Ives Collection, John Herrick Jackson Music Library, Yale University, f7459/n1947.

the original effect. Paradoxically, this leads him to change some details to fit not only a new medium but a new age."[2]

Even if this modest collegiate rebellion cannot be interpreted as an attempt to improve on Beethoven's original keyboard version, reverence combined with a desire to surpass his model eventually evolved into a central dichotomy in Ives's attitude towards his musical and spiritual mentor. Although he revered Beethoven in his *Essays Before a Sonata* as "the best product that human beings can boast of," a composer worthy of eulogizing in a work as central to his output as his *Concord Sonata*, on more than one subsequent occasion, especially in the 1930s, Ives also conveyed feelings of pronounced ambivalence towards his spiritual musical father.[3] In fact, several statements by Ives support the conclusion that Ives viewed himself as the legitimate heir to Beethoven, a modern composer capable of successfully utilizing the "sounds that Beethoven didn't have."[4]

Ives integrated the symphonic writing of the late-nineteenth century Romantics Brahms, Wagner, and Tchaikovsky and even Dvořák's recently completed "New World" Symphony (in addition to Bach) into the transition sections of his Second Symphony.[5] Although he does not quote Beethoven, it is possible that the cyclic structure of Ives's symphony owes something to Beethoven's Ninth Symphony as well as to Dvořák's "New World" and other post-Beethovenian symphonies.[6]

After his youthful string quartet arrangement, Ives confronted Beethoven's music directly in three other works, the First Symphony, the Second String Quartet, and the *Concord Sonata*; no other classical composer is used as frequently or as extensively. Ives's scherzo borrows much of its theme and structure from the scherzo of Beethoven's Ninth, and "Arguments" from the Second String Quartet presents the opening twelve notes of the "Ode to Joy" melody in the second violin (mm. 96–97), before it is rhythmically absorbed by the first violin into Henry Clay Work's "Marching through Georgia" (mm. 98–99).[7]

Ives's principal use of Beethoven and his most single-minded tribute to any classical composer occurs in the *Concord Sonata*.[8] In his prose accompaniment to this magnum opus, *Essays Before a Sonata* (drafted in 1919 and published the same year as the sonata, 1920), Ives provides the central statement of his aesthetic position and devotes considerable attention to what Beethoven meant to him. For Ives, as for most of the musically educated nineteenth-century public, Beethoven represented the summit of musical achievement. In particular, the Fifth Symphony, on which Ives hangs his *Concord Sonata*, had been regarded by the *cognoscenti* as the crowning glory of the orchestral repertoire, ever since its first performances in the 1840s in New York and Boston.[9]

Thus, Ives made a fortunate choice when he asked Beethoven to speak musically for the Transcendentalists. No surviving evidence suggests that Ives had read John Sullivan Dwight's review in *The Harbinger* of a performance of Beethoven's Fifth Symphony, or Margaret Fuller's essays in *The Dial* on Beethoven and Goethe. But in his *Essays*, Ives demonstrates his kinship with these and other Transcendental writers in his evaluation of Beethoven's moral strength and in his reliance on Bettina von Arnim's spurious letters to Goethe and Beethoven.[10] This kinship is perhaps no more clearly illustrated than in Ives's interpretation of the famous incident at Teplitz, a story that illustrates "Goethe's confusion of the moral with the intellectual," whereas "there is no such confusion in Beethoven; to him they are one." Ives continues: "It is told, and the story is so well known that we hesitate to repeat it here, that both these men were standing in the street one day when the Emperor drove by. Goethe, like the rest of the crowd, bowed and uncovered— but Beethoven stood bolt upright, and refused even to salute, saying: 'Let him bow to us, for ours is a nobler empire.' Goethe's *mind* knew this was true, but his moral courage was not instinctive."[11]

Most of what Ives has to say about Beethoven in the *Essays* appears in the "Epilogue," the longest and most philosophical chapter.[12] Discussing musical progress, Ives tries to prove that the presence of "universal watersheds" explains why "a young man, two generations ago, found an identity with his ideals in Rossini; when an older man, in Wagner."[13] As he matured, this man's tastes evolved from Wagner to Franck and Brahms and then on to two musical conservatives, d'Indy and Elgar. Perhaps not coincidentally, Daniel Gregory Mason had praised this latter pair at length in his *Contemporary Composers*, a book that Ives read in 1919 in Asheville, North Carolina, where he drafted his *Essays*.[14] In Ives's words, "Wagner seems less and less to measure up to the substance and reality of César Franck, Brahms, d'Indy, or even Elgar (with all his tiresomeness); the wholesomeness, manliness, humility, and deep spiritual, possibly religious, feeling of these men seem missing and not made up for by his (Wagner's) manner and eloquence."[15]

Up to this point, Ives appears to embrace a theory of progressive musical evolution to explain why "something in us has made us flow past him (Wagner) and not he past us." But Ives quickly aborts this argument when he writes: "Something makes our hypotheses seem purely speculative if not useless. It is men like Bach and Beethoven." Ives thus questions the prevailing view "that the world's attitude towards the substance and quality and spirit of these two men . . . has not been affected by the flowing stream that has changed us."[16] After contradicting the notion of musical progress, Ives uses the examples of Bach and Beethoven to develop a new theory that dominates the final portions of the "Epilogue," a theory that might be described as one of "fundamental dualities"—

especially the duality of "substance" and "manner": "Here we shall have to assume, for we haven't proved it, that artistic intuitions can sense in music a weakening of moral strength and vitality, and that it is sensed in relation to Wagner and not sensed in relation to Bach and Beethoven. If, in this common opinion, there is a particle of change toward the latter's art, our theory stands—mind you, this admits a change in the manner, form, external expression, etc., but not in substance. If there is no change here towards the substance of these two men, our theory not only falls but its failure superimposes or allows us to presume a fundamental duality in music, and in all art for that matter."[17]

By the time Ives gets to the duality between "repose" and "truth" (also in the "Epilogue"), Beethoven stands alone at the top of his list of composers of substance. In comparing Beethoven to Strauss, for example, Ives writes: "A man may aim as high as Beethoven, or as high as Richard Strauss. In the former case the shot may go far below the mark—in truth, it has not been reached since that 'thunder storm of 1828' [sic] and there is little chance that it will be reached by anyone living today—but that matters not; the shot will never rebound and destroy the marksman. . . . This choice tells why Beethoven is always modern and Strauss always mediaeval—try as he may to cover it up in new bottles."[18]

The incompleteness of Ives's knowledge of the man Beethoven no doubt influenced his appreciation of the music, since Beethoven's moral rectitude was largely unquestioned until the publication of the fourth and fifth volumes of Thayer's monumental biography, published in German from 1866 to 1879, and Krehbiel's English version of 1921.[19] Since Thayer's third volume did not bring Beethoven's life past 1816, such controversial matters as his abusive behavior towards his nephew Karl and his sister-in-law Johanna and his unscrupulous dealings with publishers over publication rights to the *Missa solemnis* went unmentioned. The English version of Anton Schindler's *Life of Beethoven*, edited by Ignace Moscheles, goes so far as to place the less-than-exemplary characteristics then known in a favorable light.[20] Even Margaret Fuller, in her *Lives of the Great Composers*, accepted Beethoven's misogyny unquestioningly, asserting that Beethoven needed "to withdraw the boy from the society and care of his mother, an unworthy woman, under whose influence no good could be hoped from anything done for him."[21]

Like his nineteenth-century predecessors, Ives valued Beethoven for his uncompromising approach to music. Thus, in the following passage, Ives responds to the criticism, still frequently expressed, that Beethoven did not write sympathetically or idiomatically for the violin, the piano, or the voice (perhaps not incidentally, these same criticisms are often invoked in connection with Ives's works in these genres): "Some fiddler was once honest or brave enough, or perhaps ignorant enough, to say that Beethoven didn't know how to write for the violin: that maybe, is one of the many reasons Beethoven is not a Vieuxtemps. Another man says Beethoven's piano sonatas are not pianistic; with a little effort, perhaps, Beethoven could have become a Thalberg."[22]

In the concluding paragraph of his philosophical exploration of Emerson, Ives attempts to explain the extramusical significance of the four-note motive from Beethoven's Fifth Symphony that pervades Ives's *Concord Sonata*. Here Ives suggests a direct correspondence between Beethoven and Emerson and attributes a spiritual significance to the work of both men. In stark contrast to Stravinsky's adoption of Beethoven's motive in *Oedipus Rex* (1927), when Jocasta warns Oedipus that "Oracles always lie" (*Semper oracula mentiuntur, Oedipus, cave oracula*), Ives considers the oracular quality of Beethoven's motive as a means for man to approach God: "There is an 'oracle' at the beginning of the *Fifth Symphony*; in those four notes lies one of Beethoven's greatest messages. We would place its translation above the relentlessness of fate knocking at the door, above the greater human message of destiny, and strive to bring it towards the spiritual message of Emerson's revelations, even to the 'common heart' of Concord—the soul of humanity knocking at the door of the divine mysteries, radiant in the faith that it *will* be opened—and the human become the divine!"[23] It is fitting, then, that the central thematic material of the *Concord Sonata* includes this motive— since Henry Cowell's pioneering analysis commonly known as the "epic" motive— which bears the unmistakable rhythmic and melodic stamp of the opening of Beethoven's Fifth Symphony (ex. 2.2).[25] The Beethoven (or "epic") motive is frequently stated as a self-contained unit, appearing in descending major or minor thirds or as a variously pitched, often accented, rhythmic unit on many pages of the score.

It is clear from Ives's remarks in the *Essays* that his decision to use Beethoven's motive was to a large degree motivated by a genuine reverence for the master. Examples 2.2b and 2.2c demonstrate—literally and figuratively, respectively—that Ives intended, however, not only to praise Caesar but to bury him in an avalanche of new sounds. The next step for Ives was to go beyond his often radical transformations of the Fifth Symphony motive to make Beethoven his own in a new theme, the theme John Kirkpatarick and others have determined to be the "human faith melody" that Ives referred to in his essay on "The Alcotts." The "human faith melody" appears frequently (in various stages of completeness) in "Emerson" and more fleetingly in "Hawthorne" before it achieves its culmination in two passages in "The Alcotts," the second of which is shown in example 2.3.[26]

Clearly, Ives has placed Beethoven's central motive at the center of his theme. Less obviously, the first four notes of the "human faith mel-

EXAMPLE 2.2a. Beethoven, Fifth Symphony, first movement, mm. 1–13.

EXAMPLE 2.2b. Ives, *Concord Sonata*, "Emerson," p. 18.

EXAMPLE 2.2c. Ives, *Concord Sonata*, "Emerson," p. 12.

EXAMPLE 2.3. "Human faith melody" from Ives, *Concord Sonata*, "The Alcotts," p. 57.

ody" display the rhythmic profile of Beethoven's motive as well (ex. 2.4).[27] In two other passages, the final system of "Emerson" (p. 19) and the opening of "The Alcotts" (p. 53), Ives incorporates Beethoven's answer to the motive. In "Emerson" he even uses Beethoven's pitches (G–G–G–E♭, F–F–F–D) as well as the rhythm, although Ives thoroughly asserts his identity with a radical distortion of Beethoven's harmonic context.

In the second half of the "human faith melody," Ives combines material from Beethoven's Fifth Symphony with Simeon B. Marsh's hymn *Martyn* (1834) (ex. 2.5). Knowing of Ives's predilection for and skill in

EXAMPLE 2.4. Opening of the "human faith melody" from Ives, *Concord Sonata*, "Emerson," p. 1.

EXAMPLE 2.5. Marsh, *Martyn*.

EXAMPLE 2.6. Zeuner, *Missionary Chant*.

selecting and exploiting his musical borrowings for their common musical and programmatic properties, we can infer that the musical parallels to Beethoven's famous motive in the openings of *Martyn* and of another hymn published two years earlier, Charles Zeuner's *Missionary Chant* (ex. 2.6), were not coincidental.[28] In the light of Zeuner's extensive classical musical training in Germany, his certain awareness of Beethoven and the pervasive use of Beethoven's motive, including the opening descending sequence, in his hymn, *Missionary Chant*, it is possible that Zeuner too was paying homage to the master.[29] In any event, Ives noticed and then exploited the connection between both hymns and Beethoven's motive, incorporating the hymns into "Hawthorne," "The Alcotts," and "Tho-

EXAMPLE 2.7a. Beethoven, Piano Sonata in B♭, Op. 106, "Hammerklavier," first movement.

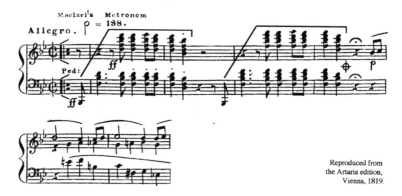

Reproduced from
the Artaria edition,
Vienna, 1819.

reau," and including recognizable portions of *Martyn* in his "human faith melody."

Beethoven's Fifth Symphony and *Martyn* do not tell the whole story of Ives's "human faith melody," Ives's indebtedness to Beethoven, or his attempts to borrow from and perhaps improve on Beethovenian models. At least once in each movement, most importantly in the "human faith melody," Ives paraphrases a second Beethoven theme and eventually makes it his own: the opening phrase of the Piano Sonata in B♭ Major, Op. 106, the "Hammerklavier" (ex. 2.7).[30] Since Ives does not mention this Beethoven work as a musical source for the *Concord Sonata*, the connection between the two works must be considered tentative, but a strong case can be made for it.[31]

Allen Gimbel provides four conditions that should be met before a pre-existing work can be considered to be quoted in a subsequent work: "(1) The pitch pattern corresponds to a preexisting pattern in the musical literature (rhythm need not reflect this correspondence). (2) The composer sets this pattern in relief. (3) It can be documented that the composer was familiar with the work or passage in question. (4) The extramusical context of the composer's work is reflected by that of the quoted work."[32] Does Ives's use of the opening eight-note theme in the "Hammerklavier" Sonata meet Gimbel's criteria?

(1) Pitch pattern: Ives adds a fourth D after the opening B♭ (transposed as E and C in ex. 2.7b)—no doubt in order to retain the rhythmic profile of Beethoven's Fifth Symphony—and he deletes Beethoven's second D (E in ex. 2.7b) after the E♭ (F in ex. 2.7b); otherwise the brief but strongly profiled melodies of Beethoven and Ives employ identical pitches. Furthermore, throughout much of "The Alcotts," as well as in its one appearance in "Thoreau," Ives places this theme in the key of

EXAMPLE 2.7b. Ives, *Concord Sonata*, "The Alcotts," p. 57.

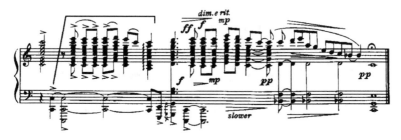

Beethoven's sonata, B♭. The C-major statement of the "Hammerklavier" theme still more emphatically resembles the distinctive opening chordal texture of Beethoven's sonata.

(2) Setting: It is easy to see how this quotation fits into Ives's sonata. The eight notes that comprise the quotation invariably appear as the beginning part of Ives's thematic extension of Beethoven's Fifth Symphony and thus conclude what is unquestionably the central extended theme in the sonata. By prefacing each statement of the "Hammerklavier" theme with that of the Fifth Symphony and its descending major third, and by concluding the "Hammerklavier" reference with the ascending major second of *Martyn*, Ives also makes a connection with the descending major third that concludes the "Hammerklavier" flourish (and the Fifth Symphony motive), as well as a connection between the "Hammerklavier" and a Concord hymn.

(3) Composer's familiarity: Although there is no direct documentary proof that Ives knew Beethoven's "Hammerklavier" Sonata, his transcription of the early piano sonata discussed at the outset of this essay establishes that he was familiar with at least one Beethoven sonata.[33] That Ives's familiarity with Beethoven's music extended beyond the piano sonatas is established by the organ arrangements—heavily marked up by Ives—of the Larghetto from the Second Symphony, the Adagio from the Fifth Symphony, and the *grande sortie* from the Ninth Symphony. Ives also had ample opportunity to hear Beethoven's orchestral works in his formative years. For example, while Ives attended Yale (1894–98) the New Haven Symphony Orchestra performed no fewer than five Beethoven symphonies (Nos. 2–5 and No. 7) in addition to the Romance in F for violin and orchestra, Op. 50, and the *Egmont* overture, Op. 84; the New York Philharmonic performed Symphonies Nos. 2–7 at least once, as well as the instrumental movements of Symphony No. 9.[34]

(4) Extramusical context: The "Hammerklavier" Sonata particularly

captured the imagination of musical connoisseurs throughout the nineteenth and early twentieth centuries and was emulated in youthful piano sonatas of Mendelssohn and Brahms.[35] Together with Beethoven symphonies, the piano sonatas of Beethoven exerted a powerful hold on the imagination of the Concord Transcendentalists as well as on the educated musical public of subsequent generations, a group that, of course, included Ives.[36]

Ives saves the apotheosis of the "human faith melody" for the flute entrance on the last two pages of "Thoreau," a gesture that may be construed as analogous to Beethoven's introducing the human voice in the last movement of the Ninth Symphony. Already by the end of "The Alcotts," but especially by the end of "Thoreau," Ives has succeeded in overcoming what Harold Bloom has called the "anxiety of influence" and has made Beethoven's themes sound like Ives's theme.[37] Example 2.8a shows the first complete appearance of the "human faith melody" in "The Alcotts," and example 2.8b reproduces the final statement of this melody in "Thoreau."

Having reverentially placed the master in the pantheon of artistic achievement in his *Essays* and in his acknowledged (Fifth Symphony) and unacknowledged ("Hammerklavier" Sonata) tributes to Beethoven in the *Concord Sonata*, Ives displays a surprisingly outspoken ambiguity in his *Memos*. In his final reference to Beethoven in the *Essays*, Ives provides a hint that his musical hero would not be impervious to criticism when he predicts and hopes for a "flowing stream" to come along and engulf Beethoven as well as Ives's most significant contemporaries: "In the history of this youthful world, the best product that human beings can boast of is probably Beethoven; but, maybe, even his art is as nothing in comparison with the future product of some coal-miner's soul in the forty-first century."[38]

By the early 1930s, Ives had completed the process of demythologization foreshadowed in the above passage from the *Essays* more than a decade earlier. The following passages from *Memos* in fact present a view of Beethoven in which reverence is contradicted not only by ambivalence but by disdain:

Even those considered the greatest (Bach, Beethoven, Brahms, etc.) have too much of it (i.e., emasculation), though less [than] the other rubber-stamp great men. They couldn't exactly help it—life with them was such that they had to live at least part of the time by the ladies' smiles—they had to please the ladies or die.[39]

I remember . . . coming home with a vague but strong feeling that even the best music we know, Beethoven, Bach, and Brahms (played at this

EXAMPLE 2.8a. First statement of the "human faith melody" from Ives, *Concord Sonata*, "The Alcotts," p. 55.

Second Piano Sonata (Concord Sonata).
Copyright © 1947, 1976 by Associated Music Publishers, Inc. (BMI).
International Copyright Secured. All Rights Reserved. Reprinted by Permission.

concert) was too cooped up—more so than nature intended it should be, or at least needed to be—not only in its chord systems and relations, lines, etc., but in its time, or rather its rhythms and spaces.[40]

Notwithstanding the above slants, which many would say are insults, it seems to me, as it did then and ever, that still today Bach, Beethoven, and Brahms (No) [*sic*] are among the strongest and greatest in all art, and nothing since is stronger or greater than their strongest and greatest—(not quite as strong and great as Carl Ruggles, because B., B., and B. have too much of the sugar-plum for the soft-ears—but even with that, they have some manhood of their own). I won't say that their

EXAMPLE 2.8b. Final Statement of the "human faith melody," from Ives, *Concord Sonata*, "Thoreau," p. 55.

Second Piano Sonata (Concord Sonata).

best is better or worse than any music before or since—I won't say, because I don't know—and nobody knows, except Rollo![41]

These "memos," in addition to what they reveal about Ives's obsession with masculinity, suggest that Ives had come to the conclusion that the stream he referred to in the *Essays* was now flowing past Beethoven (as well as Bach and Brahms) in search of more masculine and less compromising composers such as Ruggles and yes, Ives himself, long before the forty-first century. No "memo" better contradicts the hero worship for Beethoven that pervades the *Essays* than Ives's recollection of a concert performed by piano virtuoso Ossip Gabrilowitsch in 1915, the year Ives claimed to be that of the completion of the *Concord Sonata*. Here for the first (and only) time Ives actually accuses Beethoven of lacking substance, Ives's highest ideal in music:

> While we were living in East 40th Street (1915–16), Clara Clemens (Mrs. Osssssipy Gabrilowitsch) invited us to go with her to an all-Beethoven recital in Aeolian Hall, New York, played by Ossssssip. After two and half hours of the (perhaps) best music in the world (around 1829), there is something in substance (not spirit altogether) that is gradually missed—that is, it was with me. I remember feeling towards Beethoven [that he's] a great man—but Oh for just one big strong chord not tied to any key. I made some remark to that effect—that even two hours of Beethoven is quite enough—or something to that effect—but I was glad she misunderstood me and said, "Yes, an audience like this— an all-Beethoven program is a little too much for their musicianship." I meant just the opposite. The more the ears have learned to hear, use, and love sounds that Beethoven didn't have, the more the lack of them is sensed naturally.[42]

But if it was important for Ives to reinterpret Beethoven and to inject several chords "not tied to any key," it was also important for Ives to integrate Beethoven into the Transcendental world of Concord, Massachusetts, of the 1840s and 1850s. Just as he chose hymns in his First Piano Sonata and Fourth Symphony (and other works) for their common properties, Ives chose most of the pre-existent material in the *Concord Sonata*, especially the two hymns (Marsh's *Martyn* and Zeuner's *Missionary Chant*) but also David T. Shaw's "Columbia, the Gem of the Ocean" and the "Down in the Corn field" motive from Stephen Foster's "Massa's in de Cold Ground," for their musical or spiritual interconnectedness with the world of Concord, Massachusetts, 1840–1860, in which Beethoven occupied the place of honor.[43]

The Gabrilowitsch anecdote helps us to understand the *Concord Sonata* as a critique of Beethoven as well as a eulogy for him. It also suggests the possibility that, to Ives's ears, his sonata could be heard as the work that Beethoven would have composed had he been composing in 1915 rather than 1815. As Ives's nephew Chester recalled to Vivian Perlis in 1969, Ives "felt what he was doing was what Beethoven would have done had he been able to keep on living."[44] Just as Brahms delayed composing his First Symphony until he could meet Beethoven on a more equal footing, and as Beethoven himself, doubtless haunted by the specter of his teacher Haydn, delayed challenging his predecessor on his own turf—symphonies and string quartets—Ives needed to mature as a composer before he could confront the anxiety of influence and use Beethoven as a foundation that would not inhibit him creatively and cause him to sacrifice his own musical soul. From this perspective, Chester Ives's recollection that Uncle Charlie considered himself "a sort of continuing spirit" of Beethoven gains in credibility.

In his college years, Ives's emendations in his Beethoven arrangement are modest, his references to the scherzo of Beethoven's Ninth Symphony in his own First Symphony scherzo relatively humble. In the Second String Quartet, Ives satirically assigns a quotation from the "Ode to Joy" to the second violin, representing Rollo, Ives's musical symbol of excessive conformity (his Beckmesser). Finally, in the *Concord Sonata*, Ives effectively demonstrates his psychological and technical readiness to seriously challenge his predecessor. As a mature composer, Ives is sufficiently free to liberate Beethoven's four-note motif from a tonal center, and with his many big chords and other "sounds that Beethoven didn't have," Ives, the erstwhile student, now dares to improve upon the master with new sounds that Ives and others might consider more beautiful. In the process, Ives gives renewed meaning to Beethoven's stirring preface to Schiller's "Ode to Joy": *O Freunde, nicht diese Töne, sondern laßt uns angenehmere anstimmen, und freudenvollere* ("Oh friends, not these sounds, rather let us strike up more pleasing and joyful ones").

: 3 :

Ives and the
New England School

NICHOLAS E. TAWA

The relationship between Charles Ives and the New England composers of the previous generation has scarcely been addressed by music historians. Yet there is compelling evidence that the backgrounds, personalities, attitudes, and music of John Knowles Paine, George Whitefield Chadwick, Horatio Parker, and others of their generation reveal significant similarities in many essential details to those of Ives. Several layers of connection existed between Ives and these musicians of the preceding generation. First, there were strong cultural similarities, representing a common heritage. Second, there was a direct personal connection through Ives's studies with Parker. Third, Ives knew and was influenced by the music of Parker, Chadwick, Paine, and other New England predecessors. Finally, as a result of these influences, Ives resembled his forebears in his approaches to music and in his music itself.

The similar conditions surrounding ancestry, childhood, and youth could not help but contribute, at least to some extent, to the formation of a shared character, cultural disposition, and creative direction among these composers. All, including Ives, belonged solidly and willingly to the middle class for their entire lives. They never sought independence from their society and its mores. What freedom to create and to develop artistically they desired was not coupled with rebellion from their surroundings. Nevertheless, each was individual and unconventional in deciding on a career in art music at a time when such a pursuit was singular and usually disfavored. These musicians felt an attachment to their New England soil and treasured the cultural contributions of their region. None hesitated to depict New England places, history, and ideals in music. They built upon musical tradition and, although they began their creative careers composing in the styles of their mentors, they remained open to new possibilities. All remained loyal to the genres of symphony, string quartet, sonata, and oratorio. Programmatic pieces were more freely structured. The musical nationalism that they expressed remained true to their own Puritan-psalmodic and Anglo-Celtic Yankee past. Yet each yearned, as well, to achieve a music of boundless insight and universality, expressive of all humanity.

Like Ives, the most prominent members of the preceding generation of American classical romanticists were not only descended from old Yankee stock but also born in New England towns: Ives in Danbury, Connecticut; Paine in Portland, Maine; Chadwick in Lowell, Massachusetts; and Parker in Auberndale, Massachusetts. All four were truly religious, were church organists, and wrote utilitarian church music at an early age.[1] Each wrote sacred works that reflected traditional New England Protestant values: Paine's oratorio *St. Peter* (1872), his cantata *The Nativity (1883)*, and several hymns for chorus; Chadwick's *Three Sacred Quartets* (1885), *Three Sacred Songs* (1887), his oratorio-like drama *Judith* (1900), the psalm "Jehovah reigns in majesty" (1916), and numerous anthems; Parker's *Two Sacred Songs* (1890), his oratorios *Hora novissima* (1893) and *The Legend of St. Christopher* (1897), the psalm "The Lord Is My Shepherd" (1884), and many anthems; and Ives's anthems, psalm settings, and sacred songs, as well as his cantata *The Celestial Country* (1898–99).

Other conditions may have encouraged the development of similar cultural leanings. All four had the example of musicians in their families—certainly not a common phenomenon in the America of their day. Much has been written about Ives's influential father, George E. Ives, a bandmaster and a musical free thinker. Paine's father was also a bandmaster and helped direct his son's first musical steps. Chadwick's parents had received musical training in that distinctive Yankee institution, the singing school; his father was, for a time, a singing-school instructor, and his mother was active as a singer at church services. They passed on to . their son a love of New England hymnody, as Ives's parents did to him. Parker's mother, a keyboard player and music teacher, gave her son his first music lessons; in 1880, she engaged Chadwick to instruct him in composition. What Parker learned from mother and master informed his teaching at Yale (1894–1919), where Ives was his student between 1894 and 1898.

When the young Chadwick is described as following hand-organs about town, engaging in Sunday music at church, and participating in family get-togethers of parents, uncles, aunts, and cousins where hymn singing prevailed,[2] parallels to Ives's boyhood are apparent. Ives later entered the insurance business in New York City. Chadwick's father opened an insurance office, the Mutual Insurance Association, in Lawrence, Massachusetts, and the youthful George was engaged in the insurance business for a while, beginning in 1871.

The four composers had similar personalities. If Ives was self-reliant and intractable about what mattered to him most in music, so were the other three. Although this attitude did not cause them to write similar music, it did lead them to write music in which they firmly believed. Paine, Chadwick, and Parker surmounted serious economic or social obstacles, or both, in order to achieve the musical goals they had set for themselves. None of the four, when boys, took readily to advice or direction from others. Chadwick tells of giving musical instruction to an adolescent Horatio Parker who was little different from the young Ives: "As my pupil, he [Parker] was far from docile. In fact, he was impatient of the restrictions of musical form and rather rebellious of the discipline of counterpoint and fugues. . . . His lessons usually ended with his swallowing his medicine, but with many a wry grimace."[3] Chadwick, like Ives, delighted in his small-town origins, observing that both he and Whistler came from Lowell. "The difference," he said, "between Whistler and me was that Whistler was ashamed of his birthplace, and I was damn proud of it."[4] Chadwick's pride in his origins shows in his music, as is also true for Ives.

The older New England composers had inherited one especial philosophical viewpoint: Transcendentalism. Ives, too, has always been closely linked to Transcendentalism, a concept associated with Immanuel Kant and advanced in New England by Ralph Waldo Emerson, Bronson Alcott, and Henry David Thoreau. A romantic belief in the divinity immanent in man and nature, a hunger to transcend the finite self and aspire to the sublime, and a faith in humanity's inevitable progression toward a better existence were integral with the outlook of these men. John Sullivan Dwight, who was closely associated with the New England Transcendentalists, was a writer on musical subjects and publisher of *Dwight's Journal of Music* from 1852 to 1881. Throughout his life he promoted the works of Beethoven as supreme examples of Transcendentalism in music. Ives yearned to convey all these ideas through music, finding the latter the best means for expressing what might otherwise have remained ineffable—as heard, for example in the Second Piano Sonata, *Concord, Mass., 1840–1860*, and in *The Unanswered Question*.

Paine, who knew Emerson and Dwight personally and may have known Alcott, also aimed at Transcendental nobility in works like the *Mass in D* (1865), the oratorio *St. Peter*, the two symphonies (1875, 1879), and the prelude to *Oedipus Tyrannus* (1881, revised 1895). Chadwick's Second Symphony (1883–85), his *Melpomene* overture (1887), and the opera *Judith* (1899–1900) advance the same viewpoint. The most admired musical models for Paine and Chadwick were the works of Beethoven, whose exalted character and expression of universal humanism they found impressive. Paine's First Symphony, for example, shows several significant influences from Beethoven's Fifth Symphony. Both first movements are in C minor, with two pulses in a measure (alla breve and $\frac{2}{4}$, respectively), and have a similar rhythmic drive and a broad, integrated architectural structure. Both slow movements are in A♭ and in triple time. Both scherzo movements are in C (major for Paine, minor for Beethoven) and in triple time. Both finales are majestic statements in C major and alla breve. Paine's Mass tries to achieve the dignity of utterance found in Beethoven's *Missa solemnis*. The prelude strives for the same sense of grand tragedy as does Beethoven's *Coriolanus* overture. Both works are dramatic introductions to plays centered on the disaster that results from excessive self-esteem combined with dominion over others. Chadwick's Judith and Beethoven's operatic heroine Leonora are strong, noble women who struggle against oppression in order to lead a people toward a better existence.

New England composers of Ives's generation subscribed to these Transcendental beliefs—certainly Daniel Gregory Mason, Edward Burlingame Hill, and Frederick Shepherd Converse, all of whom had studied with Paine and Chadwick.[5] William Kearns and Macdonald Moore point out that music intended to embody Transcendental experience was endemic in Yankee composers from Paine and Parker to Ives and Mason.[6] But whatever Transcendentalisms Ives learned from his father were undeveloped and focused on the inherent moral excellence incipient in mankind.[7] The close connection with Emerson, Alcott, and Thoreau came later, beginning with Ives's years of study with Parker.

Indeed, many perceptions that Ives afterward claimed were his own may actually have come in part from Parker, among them Ives's concern for "substance" over "manner" and his belief that much of Europe's contemporary music lacked inner significance.[8] Parker, like Ives, championed "strong" rather than weak and maudlin music.[9] In 1902, during a talk at "The Club," in New Haven, Parker criticized contemporary German music, which was so overly "colored by externals that it has hardly a separate existence." French music sounded superficial, not coming "from deep enough," not going "deep enough." Italian opera suffered from severe limitations. English and American music, he said, is more impersonal and abstract than this, "and if it remains untainted by these (qualities)" will surely "bring forth results of great beauty and value." Modern European composers were striving to be original, to do something new at all costs [read Ives's "manner"]—"so much so that they frequently lose sight of form and substance." Parker had no objection to novel sounds, "but the new vocabulary must always remain a means, and never become an end of expression."[10]

Ives writes in the *Essays Before a Sonata* in similar terms, demanding music of "wholesomeness, manliness, humility, and deep spiritual, possibly religious feeling," not music that exhibited only "manner and eloquence." He questioned music that to him lacked substance, that was dominated by manner alone.[11] In a letter to John Tasker Howard, Ives objected to carving out a personal style and adhering to a unique idiom, which he perceived as tying himself down to a "definite brand," to something technical and not necessarily to an element of "man's general life experience." He continues: "I hesitate to use 'new' as a word by itself. If it isn't a relative thing, it isn't anything. The 'old' and the 'new' are either parts of the same substance or they are non-existent."[12]

Ives must never really have wished to break away from the guiding principles of his native New England. Transcendentalism, for instance, was translated into musical substance through the "romantic mysticism" that Chadwick detected in Parker's oratorio *Hora novissima*.[13] This work was a part of Ives's own student days and a manifestation of a way of thinking to which Ives was strongly drawn, however much he experimented with revolutionary musical techniques. A comparable romantic transcendentalism pervades the *Concord Sonata* and the Fourth Symphony (1910–16).

But there is a more direct connection between Ives and his immediate forerunners. Ives studied with Parker, met Chadwick, and knew the music of his New England predecessors. His formal music education at Yale University tied him directly to the musicians of the previous generation. In 1894, both Parker and Ives came to Yale University, the former as a new teacher, the latter as a new student; Ives would study music under Parker until his graduation in 1898. Parker guided his analysis of the scores of master composers, usually Central European. The older man was already a leading American composer, admired particularly for his sacred and secular vocal music, of which *Hora novissima* was the outstanding example.

Ives and many of his admirers took pains to conceal or deny Parker's influence on Ives. To understand it, we must take into consideration the emotional triangle in the mind of Ives formed by the student, the father, and the teacher. During Ives's first term at Yale, his much-loved and idealized father died unexpectedly and left behind a bereft son. In a letter later sent to John Griggs, Ives admits to having looked for someone "to help fill up that awful vacuum" and getting the "idea that Parker might." Yet, Parker had recently experienced painful deaths in his own family, was subject to intense and agonizing attacks of chronic rheumatism, and was heavily involved in teaching, conducting, and composing. He was in no position to substitute for the father that his student had lost. A possible result was a latent resentment of Parker. Ives later developed a fixation on his father as the bearer of all good things in the son's musical life. He also felt a nostalgia for a Yankee small-town way of life, into which he fitted himself and his father, that had scarcely ever existed and that countered the brash new American civilization gathering strength about him.[14]

Nevertheless, Ives must have valued Parker's instruction, since he studied with him for four years and surely learned to appreciate European masters like Beethoven, Mendelssohn, and Schumann through Parker's eyes. In addition, Parker thought enough of the undergraduate's talents to allow him to audit courses and receive personal attention during his first two years at Yale, when school rules prohibited the enrollment of freshmen and sophomores in music classes. Parker generously allocated some of his limited free time to examine and criticize works like Ives's song "At Parting" and the first movement of the First Symphony. In his junior and senior years, Ives enrolled in Parker's courses in instrumentation, counterpoint, and strict composition. He also took instruction in harmony, free composition, practical music, and music history.[15] Even a cursory glance at Ives's musical output shows that Parker's advice and compositions influenced to a considerable degree the music he composed between 1894 and 1902, including many songs, the cantata *The Celestial Country*, the First Symphony, the First String Quartet, and the early stages of the Second Symphony.

Henry Bellamann, who knew Ives from the early 1920s, states that Ives held his teacher in very high regard and was not as unhappy studying with him as some writers, including Ives himself, have suggested. Although the tonal experiments in which Ives engaged from time to time were not enthusiastically received by Parker, in general the student digested the instruction of his teacher and thereby acquired a thorough knowledge of a variety of compositional techniques. This knowledge is clearly manifested in the works from Ives's young adulthood.[16] Ives wrote, "I had and have a great respect for Parker and most of his music. It was seldom trivial—his choral works have a dignity and depth that many of [his] contemporaries, especially in the [field of] religious and choral composition, did not have. Parker had ideals that carried him higher than the popular, but he was governed by the German rule, and in some ways was somewhat hard-boiled."[17]

Like many skillful teachers, the older composer tried to teach the young Ives to discipline himself, to know the difference between genuine musical feeling and self-indulgence. He was concerned, and perhaps rightly so, that his student was showing signs of gratifying his whims to an excessive degree.[18] Finally, one recalls his father's admonishment: "If you know how to write a fugue the right way well, then I'm willing to have you try the wrong way—well. But you've got to know what [you're doing] and why you're doing it."[19]

Without Parker's guidance and training, Ives might have remained unaware of the possibilities of art music and of how to employ sophisticated musical techniques in the aid of expression. A fondness for using borrowed material, especially hymn tunes, began to develop while Ives was at Yale. His eventual employment of borrowings in early compositions like the First String Quartet and the first two symphonies would have been of limited usefulness if the means for developing this material and integrating it into a larger whole had not been made possible through Parker's tutelage. J. Peter Burkholder makes illuminating comments about how Parker freed Ives from "the limitations of both aspiration and genre imposed by Danbury's cultural life. Even Parker's pieces for church choirs and choral societies . . . asserted in their quality and complexity an ideal of music as an abstract art that was worlds away from the strictly utilitarian music of Danbury. Here is where Parker exercised his most profound and enduring influence on the young Ives."[20]

Moreover, Parker did not follow the "German rule" as assiduously as Ives claimed. Other students of Parker, like Douglas Moore, praised the training they received from their warmly regarded composer-teacher and were not oppressed by the Germanisms that Ives alludes to. Parker's biographer William Kearns insists that he did not promote Germanisms at Yale. Nor did Parker consider himself in the German fold. On the contrary, according to Parker his own study with Rheinberger involved "a development of the seeds sown by his American teachers [mostly by Chadwick] which contained most of the germs of art truth."[21] In Ives's First Symphony, composed under Parker's supervision, the secure mastery in the shaping and manipulation of themes is attributable to Parker's training. The competent handling of the orchestra, restrained but sure, and the mellifluous interweaving of simultaneously sounding melodies are Parker trademarks manifested in his student's composition. Much to Parker's credit, he allowed an individual style and a personal songfulness that hold one's attention to blossom forth in Ives's music.

Some thirty-five years after his sojourn at Yale, Ives grudgingly admitted Parker's influence, implying that he followed his teacher's suggestions, to some degree:

> The First Symphony was written while [I was] in college. The first movement was changed. It (that is, the symphony) was supposed to be in D minor, but the first subject went through six or eight different keys, so Parker made me write another first movement. But it seemed no good to me, and I told him that I would much prefer to use the first

draft. He smiled and let me do it, saying "But you must promise to end in D minor." (And also he didn't like the original slow movement, as it started on G-flat—he said it should start in F. Near the end, "the boys got going"—so at the request of Parker and Kaltenborn I wrote a nice formal one—but the first is better.[22]

The "original slow movement" later surfaced in his Second Symphony.

Although a Yale graduate and no longer Parker's student, Ives still took heed of his teacher's comments and revised it, as he says, "à la Brahms" (other writers have described them as à la Dvořák) seem to be slices of music cut from *Hora novissima* and other lyrically oriented works by Parker written around the same time as the oratorio. Later musicians only superficially acquainted with the actual sound of Parker's works would miss this significant teacher-student connection. They would also accept Ives's later contention that the influence of his teacher was meager.

Ives was also linked to Chadwick during his Yale years. He undoubtedly took into account Chadwick's high reputation as a composer and Parker's admiration for his compositions, which would have led Ives to become familiar with his music. An incident described in Ives's *Memos* might have encouraged him to feel grateful to and to become an admirer of Chadwick. In March 1898, Chadwick came to New Haven to hear a performance of his *Melpomene* overture. While in town, Chadwick attended Parker's class in strict composition. Ives describes the occasion in a marginal note appearing on a copy by George Price of his song "Ich Grolle Nicht":

> Geo. W. Chadwick came into class this afternoon (on [his] way back from Heiblein's), sat down behind me and Puss—Lord! [what a] beer breath! When Chadwick came in Parker [was] objecting to the too many keys in the middle [of Summerfields]—Geo. W. C. grinned at it and [at] H. W. P. Of this song, Prof. Horat[io] P[arker] said it ["Ich Grolle Nicht" was] nearer to the G[rolle] of Schumann than the Summerfields was near to Brahms.
>
> But Chadwick said the Summerfields was the best. C. said "the melodic line has a natural continuity—it flows—and stops when [rounded out]—as only good songs do. And [it's] different from Brahms, as in the piano part and harmony it takes a more difficult and almost opposite [approach] to Brahms for the active tranquillity of the outdoor beauty of nature is harder to express than just quietude. In its way [it's] almost as good as Brahms." He winked at H. W. P. and said "That's as good a song as you could write."

Ives adds a further comment: "[This was] written on the sides of the ms. of this and [of] the Summerfields sketch copy after I got back . . . as at that time (1897–8) Chadwick was the big celebrated man of American music."[24]

With a mind as inquisitive as his, Ives could not have been indifferent to the musical activities going on around him. One can logically infer that he at least looked through Chadwick's *Harmony*, published in Boston in 1897 and soon a highly approved text for musical-theory classes throughout the country, including those at Yale. In the book, Chadwick makes a remark that must have delighted and encouraged the young Ives:

> If, as has been repeatedly stated, the rules forbidding consecutive fifths, octaves, and augmented seconds and false relations, are broken with impunity, or even ignored altogether by modern composers, the question arises, why were these rules ever promulgated? To this we may answer, if the effect justifies the means, any rule may be disregarded. This usually involves considerations other than purely harmonic ones; orchestral color, rhythm, and the dramatic effect often give striking significance to harmonic combinations and progressions which would otherwise be offensive, or at least unsatisfactory to the normal musical ear.[25]

Every composer's music, however ardently its advocates tout it as absolutely original, has antecedents in past works. So it was for Ives. It is to be expected that Ives, especially as a student, would feel curious about the music that immediately surrounded him, constituting his usable cultural and artistic past. But what is the evidence that he knew the music of the other New England composers?

First, Ives owned some compositions by Chadwick and Parker and kept them to the end of his life, the most significant being the latter's *Hora novissima*. He also owned MacDowell's *Sea Pieces* for piano and Daniel Gregory Mason's Violin Sonata in G Minor.[26] Ives admired Mason's books, including *From Grieg to Brahms* (1902) and *Contemporary Composers* (1918), and praised Mason's "wholesome influence," which was "doing as much perhaps for music in America as American music is."[27] Mason was a musical conservative and a devotee of Thoreau and Whitman. He boosted an "Anglo-Saxon" Yankee orientation in American music and disparaged Amerindian and African-American musical nationalism.[28]

The young Ives played music of the New England composers for church services and in organ recitals.[29] While a student at Yale, Ives would have heard Parker conduct performances of several of his own compositions by the New Haven Symphony Orchestra: a portion of *Hora novissima*, the *Count Robert of Paris* overture (1890), and the *Ode for Commencement Day* (1898). He might also have attended the New York performance of Parker's oratorio *St. Christopher* in 1898. Chadwick's *Rip Van Winkle* overture (1879) and *Melpomene* overture were also performed by the New Haven Symphony during Ives's student years. Ives subscribed to a chamber music series featuring the Kneisel Quartet in New Haven that included a Chadwick quartet and Parker quintet. In addition, Parker conducted choral works with orchestra by him and Chadwick in concerts sponsored by the local Euterpe Society.[30] Furthermore, published scores of many works by the New Englanders would have been available to Ives in various library collections. When performed, especially for the first time, the music of the New Englanders was reviewed or discussed in music periodicals like the *Musical Courier* of New York, in the Boston and New York newspapers, and less often in general magazines like *The Atlantic*. Ives was not so incurious about contemporary musical life that he would have neglected to read publications such as these.

As might be expected, there are strong resemblances between Ives's music and that of the New England composers of the previous genera-tion. One resemblance involves the propensity for comic parody, the delight in incorporating commonplace matter from everyday life into a composition. Ives was a musical jokester and an inveterate parodist of the music and other sounds that he heard in Danbury. Fiddle tunes, Stephen Foster ballads, circus marches, and the styles of nineteenth-century European composers were grist to his mill. Employing music of this sort was a way of deflating the pontification of teachers and avoiding a "masterpiece" fixation. Other New England composers also had their moments of parody. The youthful Paine produced *Radway's Ready Relief,* written in 1863 and first publicly performed in 1883. A comic glorifi-cation of a patent medicine whose advertisement taken from a newspaper is sung by a bass soloist and men's chorus, it hilariously satirizes the styles of famous composers like Handel and Beethoven. Likewise, the youthful Chadwick, while a student at Munich, boldly introduced the American dance tune "Shoot the Pipe" into the third movement of his First String Quartet. Chadwick's staged spoof *Tabasco* (1893) lampoons all sorts of American musical styles, including the marches of Harrigan and Hart,[31] plantation ditties, sentimental ballads, and vaudeville song-and-dance patter. This musical comedy became sufficiently popular to be taken on tour by a travelling singing troupe. Ives might easily have heard it.

To be sure, Ives incorporated the melodies he fancied and the sty-listic peculiarities of prized compositions not only into his experimental musical jokes but also into works of notable worth, where borrowed tunes were reprocessed, transformed, developed, and reassembled in varying configurations. So did Chadwick in compositions like the *Symphonic Sketches* (1895–1904) and, simultaneously with the later stages of Ives's active composing career, *Tam O'Shanter*, a symphonic ballad (1914–15).

Parker did the same, although less obviously and only in passing. An observation of Rosalie Sandra Perry is pertinent here: "Ives applied in his music many of Parker's philosophical ideas. Parker's music with its occasional dissonances and Parker's use of borrowed tunes and musical styles possibly suggested to Ives the use that could be made of other composers' material."[32] In addition, Kearns observes that Parker introduced melodic phrases from Mendelssohn, Franck, Liszt, Gounod, Brahms, Wagner, and Dvořák into his own creations. For example, a snatch of Mendelssohn's Wedding March makes a cameo appearance at the end of part 1 of *Hora novissima*; Dvořák's "New World" Symphony haunts Parker's *A Northern Ballad* (1899); the slow English horn tune in Franck's Symphony sounds in *A Wanderer's Psalm* (1900). According to Kearns, these reminiscences at times appear amidst melodic and harmonic allusions to hymn settings and popular songs.[33] Nevertheless, we do not know whether such reminiscences were intentional or inadvertent.

Ives also incorporated incidents from his daily life into his works. Perhaps the most famous of these was a Danbury experience that found its way into compositions like *Putnam's Camp*: two bands approaching and then passing each other, each playing its own music.[34] Daniel Gregory Mason and Edward Burlingame Hill experimented with the same effect around 1893–94. Mason states that he and Hill often entertained their friends "with music, two-hand or four-hand—serious or frivolous." A favorite piece on these occasions was entitled *Between Two Bands*, "a graphic representation of one march (E. B. H. in the treble) beginning very near and loud, and gradually disappearing into space and *pianissimo*, while a different march (D. G. M. in the bass) would begin very far and soft and equally gradually approach into deafening *fortissimo*. There was a crucial moment when both bands were equidistant, supremely relished by us if not by our audience."[35] There was no attempt to reconcile the two marches harmonically. Unlike Ives, Mason and Hill chose to reproduce the effect only as a joke and not to employ it in music possessing "substance."

Ives reveals his musical connections with Parker, Paine, and Chadwick predominantly in the more traditional genres: the violin sonatas, piano sonatas, string quartets, and symphonies. In these genres, where control over structure is most necessary, Parker's guidelines are most in evidence. Even in Ives's later, more radical, compositions, we find evidence of the more customary ways of composing music represented by Parker and Chadwick: melodically centered writing, motivic development, repetition in order to articulate structure, moments of romantic eloquence, the rhetorical building of climaxes, and the cyclical return of ideas and passages from earlier movements.[36] Late as well as early works include traditional techniques: the Fourth Symphony, the Second String

EXAMPLE 3.1a. Chadwick, Second Symphony, first movement, introduction, mm. 1–7.

Quartet, the Third and Fourth violin sonatas, and the *Concord Sonata*. Ives revealed his thinking on this subject in his statement, quoted earlier, that the old and the new in music were parts of the same substance for him. John Kirkpatrick remarks that the more one disentangles "earlier and later states of Ives's [music] manuscripts, the more they reveal that the music did indeed fit into the [European-American] mainstream at the time of composition, before Ives later stepped up the level of dissonance." Commenting on the Third Violin Sonata, Kirkpatrick states that when Ives decided to tame down its music, he thought he had enfeebled the composition, "but actually its plain vocabulary reveals his musical character all the more clearly."[37]

While at Yale and in his first years in New York, Ives was already revealing his musical character in the First String Quartet, whose every theme is paraphrased from one or more hymn tunes. Ives's reprocessing of the tunes in order to fit them into traditional structures suggests the influence of Parker. Much the same thing might be said of the Second Symphony. Here the cyclical binding together of the symphonic movements through recurring motives and melodies points to a usage already solidly established not only in European symphonies such as Berlioz's *Symphonie fantastique*, Tchaikovsky's Fourth Symphony, and Dvořák's "New World" Symphony, but also in models closer to home, such as Parker's *Hora novissima*, Paine's Second Symphony (1879), and Chadwick's Second Symphony. For instance, the French-horn theme of the introduction to Chadwick's symphony provides motivic and melodic material that pervades the entire composition. Mysterious in the opening (ex. 3.1a), nervous in the main theme of the Allegro that follows, it becomes frolicsome and later songlike in the second movement, then a dignified processional melody laced with melancholy in the slow third movement, and a sprightly statement (ex. 3.1b) in the finale.

As Ives journeyed along his creative path, harmonic practices typical of the New England composers accompanied him, at least at first. For example, the second movement of Ives's Second Symphony (I–IV$^6_4$–I, repeated), the measured section of "The Alcotts" in the *Concord Sonata*

EXAMPLE 3.1b. Chadwick, Second Symphony, fourth movement, mm. 1–4.

Violino Primo.

(I–IV–I–IV–I), and the song "The Housatonic at Stockbridge" (opening I–VI–I–I–IV–III⁶–IV) feature the subdominant, submediant, and mediant harmonies, neglecting the dominant. A similar harmonic predilection characterizes the opening of the first movement of Paine's First Symphony of 1875 (I–IV–I–IV–I) and his *Commencement Hymn* of 1882 (I–VI–II–VI–III–I–II). One finds it also in Chadwick: at the beginning of songs like "Allah" of 1887 (I–VI–I–II–I–V of V–III–I–VI–III–II–VI), "A Bonny Curl" (1889), and "Love's Like a Summer Rose" of 1897 (I–II–I–II–I–II–I), the start of "Noel" of 1895 from the *Symphonic Sketches* (I–I–IV–V of VI–I–I–IV–I), and the beginning of the first movement in the *Sinfonietta* of 1904 (I–IV–I–VI–I–IV). Parker's *Hora novissima* contains harmonic progressions like those of the Ives pieces mentioned above: the choral entry of no. 4, "Pars mea, Rex meus," (I–IV⁶–I–IV–I–VI–III–IV), and the prelude to no. 11, "Urbs Syon inclyta," (I–I–IV–IV–I–IV–II–I). In short, H. Wiley Hitchcock's suggestion that Ives's harmony "is rooted in American hymnody with its relaxed subdominant emphasis"[38] does not tell the whole story, for Ives's procedures are just as deeply rooted in the practices of the New England classical romanticists.

All four composers frequently structured melodies within tetrachords, either as two interlocking tetrachords (for example, G–C–F) or as contiguous tetrachords (G–C, D–G). Examples of the first type occur at the start of Paine's *Commencement Hymn* and in all four movements of Chadwick's Second Symphony, all four movements of Ives's First Symphony, and the first unequivocally diatonic passage in the first movement of Ives's First Violin Sonata (mm. 40ff. of the Allegro). Parker's structuring of his main motive in *Hora novissima* into overlapping tetrachords (see ex. 3.4a) is also found in Ives's music, especially in works begun while he was taking instruction from Parker.

The Parker composition that seems to have made the greatest impression on the young Ives was *Hora novissima*, premiered in New York in 1893 and published in piano-vocal score that same year.[39] Throughout the work, Parker shows a special fondness for a dotted rhythm that normally occurs in the second measure of a half-phrase, at the barline (ex. 3.2). Ives does the same in his cantata *The Celestial Country*, completed in 1899 (ex. 3.3a), songs like "At Sea," No. 4 of *114 Songs* (ex. 3.3b), and the First String Quartet (ex. 3.3c). The overlapping tetrachords that gov-

Nicholas E. Tawa

EXAMPLE 3.2a. Parker, *Hora novissima*, part 1, no. 1, "Hora novissima," mm. 63–67.

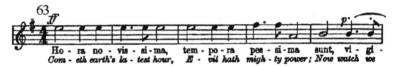

EXAMPLE 3.2b. Parker, *Hora novissima*, part 1, no. 5, "O bona patria," mm. 19–20.

EXAMPLE 3.2c. Parker, *Hora novissima*, part 2, no. 10, "Urbs Syon unica," mm. 1–4.

EXAMPLE 3.2d. Parker, *Hora novissima*, part 2, no. 11, "Urbs syon inclyta," mm. 41–44.

EXAMPLE 3.3a. Ives, *The Celestial Country*, no. 5, "Glories on Glories," mm. 1–6.

The Celestial Country.
© Copyright 1971 and 1973 by Peer International Corporation.
International Copyright Secured. All Rights Reserved. Reprinted by Permission.

EXAMPLE 3.3b. Ives, "At Sea," mm. 2–4.

Some things are un-di-vined ex - cept by love—

EXAMPLE 3.3c. Ives, String Quartet No. 1, second movement, mm. 32–41.

EXAMPLE 3.4a. Parker, *Hora novissima*, part 1, no. 1, "Hora novissima,"
orchestral introduction, mm. 24–28.

EXAMPLE 3.4b. Ives, "So May It Be," mm. 6–7.

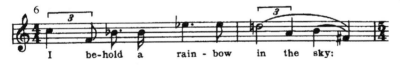

I be-hold a rain - bow in the sky:

ern the main motive of "Hora novissima" (ex. 3.4a) are reflected in those
of Ives's song "So May It Be" (ex. 3.4b).

Both Ives's *Celestial Country* and Parker's *Hora novissima* are ardently
romantic works. The Ives cantata has a text by Henry Alfred which, like
the text of Parker's work, extols a heavenly abode that men and women
aspire to attain. The melodic phrases or harmonies or both in several of

EXAMPLE 3.5. Ives, *The Celestial Country*, no. 5, "Glories on Glories," mm. 93–99.

the cantata's passages would not sound anomalous in *Hora novissima* (ex. 3.5). One finds no direct likeness to a Parker segment, yet the music comes from the workshop of Parker, though in somewhat elusive fashion. For instance, both this example and "Urbs Syon unica" in *Hora novissima* are for a cappella chorus and in C major. The melodies in both are stated quietly, beginning on the tones c'–e'–f '–g'; Ives briefly sounds f ' and g' before skipping to c'', whereas Parker immediately skips up to c'' (ex. 3.2c). It is not until mm. 77–81 that Parker, like Ives, has the line move up (g'–c''–d''–e'') before descending to b' (after sounding c''). Nineteen measures before the close of the oratorio's first number, the choral "Hora novissima," the dynamics become very quiet and the bass sounds a persistent tonic tone (in E major) while the sopranos twice rise to e" and the harmonic pattern I–VI–I–II–I is repeated. Eighteen measures before the end of the fourth number, "Pars mea, Rex meus," the chorus sings a majestic passage to the harmonies I–IV (or II⁶)–II–I. Both are comparable to Ives's I–II–I–II–I in example 3.5.

The most obvious parallels to the Parker work are found in the third number of Ives's cantata, where the music of the solo quartet "Seek the things before us" is indebted to the bass aria "Spe modo vivitur," no. 3 of *Hora novissima*. Both pieces begin in $\frac{3}{4}$ meter and in D minor, marked Moderato. The prelude in each number goes from a tonic harmony to the subdominant, back to the tonic, and then to the dominant (the aria after three intervening measures, the quartet immediately).[40]

Both numbers frequently change meter. "Spe modo vivitur" alternates between $\frac{3}{4}$ and $\frac{4}{4}$ with one measure of $\frac{5}{4}$ and one of $\frac{2}{4}$ (mm. 32–51). "Seek the things before us" alternates between $\frac{3}{4}$ and $\frac{4}{4}$ (mm. 1–5, 37–75, and 111–16). In his *Memos*, Ives remarked that in his *Over the Pavements* (1906–13) for chamber orchestra the concurrence of divergent rhythms and pulsations represented the motion of people and horses on Central Park West. However, John Kirkpatrick wondered, "Might Ives be forgetting how the beauty of the 7-rhythm in the 3rd movement of *The Celestial Country* is the clarity of its 4 plus 3?—and how well it illustrates . . . a possible indebtedness to Parker, whose *Hora novissima* (1891–92) explores the same rhythm in #3, the bass aria."[41] Perhaps there was as much concealment as forgetting in Ives's statement.[42]

The two preludes share running eighth-note figures, heard first in the bass, then in the bass and treble, beginning at m. 5 in each. Both numbers also feature two-measure half-phrases with a dotted rhythm in the second measure. The new melody that Ives introduces at m. 50 skips up a major third (f '–a'), moves up again by a half-step (to b♭'), then by a whole-step (to c"), and eventually curves back to a'. The melody in no. 7 of *Hora novissima*, "Urbs Syon aurea," behaves in the same manner.

The Celestial Country was apparently intended to suit current tastes and to appeal to the many music-lovers that had approved the Parker oratorio. Why else state the fact that Parker was his teacher? Although respectfully reviewed in the *Musical Courier*, Ives's cantata made little impression. The lack of success signaled the end of Ives's attempts at reaching a wide American public.[43] In addition, it marked the end of Ives's public acknowledgement of his debt to Parker.

Like his American musical predecessors, Ives put a great deal of emphasis on melody. John Kirkpatrick considers him "primarily a melodist, with a genius for melodic variation and eloquence."[44] He had a special affection for American hymns, quoting, paraphrasing, or reworking them

EXAMPLE 3.6a. Paine, Second Symphony, *Im Frühling,* first movement, mm. 1–9.

frequently or writing passages that sound hymnic. Henry Bellamann was the first to note how many movements in an Ives work proceed in the direction of a culminating rendition of a theme, which as often as not is hymnic.[45] At other times, Ives's tunes are pentatonic and have a kinship to Anglo-Celtic American folk melody, or they may resemble the melodies in sentimental American popular ballads. For example, "An Old Flame" and "In the Alley," two songs from 1896, belong in the latter category.

Similar proclivities occur among the other New Englanders. The compositions of Paine, Chadwick, and Parker reveal broad, dignified melodies that have ties to New England's psalmodic and hymnic tradition. At other times, their lyricism mirrors American folk song or their Celtic or Anglo-Saxon musical heritage. Often these two sources of inspiration are indistinguishable. Every now and again, particularly with Chadwick, a tune resembles popular song—the sentimental ballad or the minstrel ditty. Examples include Chadwick's songs "Before the Dawn" (1882) and "In Bygone Days" (1885).

Some of their compositions also progress toward a final grand hymnic statement, as do many of Ives's. In Paine's Second Symphony, the first large American orchestral work to be published in full score (in 1880), the concluding hymnic statement (ex. 3.6b) grows out of the germinal motive for the entire work that is first heard in the introduction to the first movement (ex. 3.6a). The contour of the first six notes of the motive is echoed, although not exactly, in notes 6–10 of the hymn in the finale; the raised tonic note in both passages occurs as tone 17. Chadwick's Second Symphony is based entirely on a motive heard in the introduction to the first movement; the finale's majestic restatement of the theme, in the trombones, is a culmination to the entire work. In Chadwick's Fourth String Quartet (1896), the first movement's subordinate theme and the second movement's main theme owe much to the style of hymnody. Moreover, the work is crowned by the finale, the lengthiest of the four movements, a set of variations on a solemn theme that is not far removed from the psalm tunes sung in seventeenth-century New

EXAMPLE 3.6b. Paine, Second Symphony, fourth movement, mm. 416–26.

EXAMPLE 3.7. Chadwick, *Judith*, act 3, finale, mm. 113–22.

England. The opera *Judith* has a chorus of Hebrews singing broad cho-
rales that emanate from the Yankee psalmodic tradition, culminating in
the sustained hymnody of the final act (ex. 3.7). *Land of Our Hearts*
(1917), for chorus and orchestra, includes a final melody also very much
in the vein of a hymn tune. Although this may be too late a work to have
influenced Ives, it does indicate their like thinking.

Although it is sometimes suggested that Parker was antagonistic to hymns, his statement, in 1899, before the Episcopal Club of Massachusetts, demonstrates otherwise:

> Music is the art which comes nearest to the people and the one to which they can get nearest themselves ... Musicians [today] look upon the making of hymn tunes as an amusement rather than a serious occupation. ... However, the simple nature of the Hymn Tune is nothing against it. There must be all kinds of musical as well as natural creations! A hymn *must* be simple ... but it ought not to be didactic, if it is for common use. What is true of hymns as poetry or literature is true in greater measure of tunes as music. They must be simple in rhythm, melody, and harmony, not merely on account of the difficulty of things not simple, but rather because nothing other than simplicity will serve as a vehicle of expression for the feelings of a mass of people.[46]

Parker goes on to say that some of the best hymn tunes are the old ones, like *Windsor*. He wants to reinstate them in place of more recent ones, including some of his own, which have felt "the enfeebling influence of the Anglican School."[47] Parker had been helping with the revision of the Episcopalian hymnal while Ives was still at Yale and the above talk was given a year after Ives graduated; therefore, teacher and student might have discussed this issue during the previous four years. Although Parker's sacred vocal compositions incorporate hymnic tunes, he wrote too few purely instrumental works to show whether he might have done likewise in them. Nevertheless, the introduction to *A Northern Ballad*, a symphonic poem, offers a main theme touched by folk hymn, out of which emerges all the thematic material. At the end, the theme takes the shape of a broad closing melody, which marks the summation of the piece.

Many of the melodic borrowings in Ives's compositions were taken from the music of older New England composers other than Paine, Chadwick, and Parker, among them Lowell Mason, William Bradbury, George Frederick Root, and Henry Clay Work. Some early anthems of Ives were modeled after the music of Dudley Buck, the Connecticut-born organist and composer who gave Ives organ lessons.[48] The *Variations on "America"* for organ, which Ives wrote around 1891, had its antecedents in similar organ variations by Buck and Paine, each of whom wrote variations on "The Star-Spangled Banner." The spirit of the Ives work may differ; the structural layout is certainly comparable.

Ives had a special affinity for Chadwick's music. One probable reason is that Chadwick's chamber and orchestral works, like Ives's music, are alive with sounds unique to America: hymns, marches, popular song, and dance of the past and present. They often boast exuberant melodies, syncopated rhythms, surprising turns of harmony, and smart instrumentation. Ives surely knew this music well. Many of the extraordinary effects

EXAMPLE 3.8a. Chadwick, *Rip Van Winkle*, overture, rev. ed., mm. 38–41 (Boston: Birchard, c. 1930; published for the Eastman School of Music).

EXAMPLE 3.8b. Ives, Second Violin Sonata, first movement, mm. 10–11.

that Ives achieves were also employed by Chadwick; for example, in the first movement of his Second Symphony, Chadwick recapitulates his subordinate theme in the muted trumpet, producing the impression of a New England summer band concert, an effect dear to Ives. Chadwick also does something similar in *Jubilee* (1895). The older composer not only dared to employ the American vernacular but also openly and frequently introduced humor into his works. *A Vagrom Ballad* (1896), for example, flippantly throws out a fragment of a Bach fugue and offers a version of a vaudevillian song-and-dance act. Ives would have appreciated its assault on genteel ears. Chadwick's concepts have frequent parallels in Ives's music, as in the *Four Ragtime Dances* for small orchestra, the Second Violin Sonata, with its second and third movements "In the Barn" and "The Revival," and the Second String Quartet, whose first two movements are labeled "Discussions" and "Arguments."

Chadwick at one moment writes short-breathed diatonic phrases whose harmony is deliberately plain and concordant, at another, long chromatic lines with complex chord structures, as in the Piano Quintet (1887) and the Fourth String Quartet. Somewhat similar writing occurs in Ives's Second Violin Sonata, Third Symphony, and *Putnam's Camp*. It is difficult to believe that Ives was not familiar with and influenced by more than a few Chadwick's compositions. Further evidence of a close connection between Chadwick and Ives is found in the extraordinary number of analogous tune-shapes, many of them based on pentatonic scales, in their works. Compare the main theme of Chadwick's *Rip Van Winkle* overture with the opening Allegro in the first movement of Ives's Second Violin Sonata (ex. 3.8), or the main theme of the third movement in Chadwick's Fourth String Quartet and the "Pig Town Fling" ditty inserted into Ives's Second Symphony, Fourth Symphony, and *Washington's Birthday* (ex. 3.9). Other parallels of this sort occur in Chadwick's songs "O Love and Joy"

EXAMPLE 3.9a. Chadwick, Fourth String Quartet, third movement, mm. 1–6.

EXAMPLE 3.9b. Ives, Second Symphony, fifth movement, mm. 56–61.

(1892), "Love's Like a Summer Rose" and "In Mead Where Roses Bloom" (both 1897), and Ives's songs "Over All the Treetops" (1901) and "On the Counter" (1920); the subsidiary theme, *largamente*, in the fourth movement of Chadwick's Third Symphony (1894) and Ives's song "Mists" (1910), a *largo sostenuto*; the subordinate theme in *Jubilee*[50] and the second movement of Ives's Fourth Violin Sonata (1916), whose tune is based on William Bradbury's *Jesus Loves Me*.

The many links between Ives and the New England composers who immediately preceded him demonstrate that they were not musicians against whom Ives was rebelling but ones to whom he owed a great deal. Their milieus, attitudes, aims, and creative efforts have so much in common with those of Ives that their influence cannot be ignored. The fiction that requires rejection is that Ives was an absolutely original creator, unbeholden to the music of the American art composers that came before him. No musician forms his creative faculties in a vacuum; neither did Ives.

PART TWO

EUROPEAN
CONTEMPORARIES

:4:

Ives and Mahler: Mutual Responses at the End of an Era

ROBERT P. MORGAN

Ralph Waldo Emerson once referred to himself as "an endless seeker with no Past at my back." In doing so, he adopted a perspective that has often supplied a framework for the characterization of American art and artists. According to this view, the most important examples of American art—its most characteristic and individual inventions—have been largely autonomous, independent of foreign influences. Relieved, above all, of the heavy burden of the European cultural tradition, our native artists have been free to develop in an atmosphere of almost limitless possibility for innovation and experimentation—without, as Emerson would have it, a Past at their back to hound them into submission and conformity.

Certainly this outlook has characterized much of the critical writing on Charles Ives that has appeared both here and abroad. Ives is commonly looked upon as a sort of innocent at home, a noble savage who, unencumbered by the strictures of inherited conventions, was able to create a radically new kind of music largely independent of the forces of European music history. It is not my wish to belittle this viewpoint, which supplies a useful means for focusing upon, and thus emphasizing, certain characteristic aspects of Ives's music. Taken in isolation, however, it leads to a greatly oversimplified picture of the composer. Ives's music represents as much a confrontation with the larger Western musical tradition as with his own vernacular traditions; and it can be properly understood only by considering both of these dimensions. Thus a view of Ives outside the context of the European tradition, especially that of the eighteenth and nineteenth centuries, is as one-sided and intellectually impoverished as a view of Ives divorced from the context of his native America.

There are several ways one might go about revealing connections between Ives and the European past. One could show, for example, that Ives's work represents an extension of European conceptions of tonal and rhythmic structure, or indicate how earlier European composers anticipate techniques that reappear later—usually in a more intensified and exaggerated form—in Ives. I have chosen a third possibility: that of comparing Ives to his European contemporary Gustav Mahler in order to indicate the extent to which these two composers shared common assumptions regarding the materials and techniques, as well as the underlying aesthetic, of musical composition. Mahler was a composer totally immersed in the European tradition—indeed, one sometimes feels that his music is almost overwhelmed by that tradition. And his similarities with Ives suggest that the apparent "idiosyncracies" of the latter were not simply those of a quirky composer working in isolation, but were rather a profound and articulate response to the critical situation in which the Western musical tradition found itself at the particular moment when both of these composers were active.

Although Mahler was some fourteen years older than Ives, and Ives lived some forty years after Mahler's death, the two were almost exact compositional contemporaries: their principal works were all conceived within a thirty-year period extending from 1888 to 1918. This period was, of course, one of extraordinary musical upheaval, characterized by an atmosphere of crisis brought on by the progressive deterioration of the pitch and rhythmic conventions of so-called "common practice" tonality. That Ives and Mahler should have reacted in certain similar respects to this crisis is a matter of considerable historical interest. It suggests that the obvious stylistic dissimilarities between their respective works may hide more fundamental underlying affinities, affinities which transcend both cultural and personal differences.

This raises an important point that should be clarified at the outset: the similarities between Ives and Mahler are almost never of a kind to make their music *sound* alike, at least in any significant sense. (One thinks, perhaps, of the last movement of Ives's Piano Trio, which has a slightly Mahlerian cast; but even here the similarities are minimal and superficial.) Rather, the correspondences pertain to their basic conceptions of what a musical composition is—how it relates to the surrounding world, the types of materials that are appropriate to it, and the way these materials are to be combined and organized. As Ives himself might have put it, the substance of their music is similar, while the manner—the specific form of its presentation—is altogether different. It is not, then, so much a matter of the musical surface as of the aesthetic interior.

The moment-to-moment succession of their music sounds very different, then; Mahler is as unmistakably Austrian as Ives is American. Yet both composers often cling to an historically regressive stage of the musical language of common practice tonality, a stage long since passed over by the currents of nineteenth-century evolutionary chromaticism. The chromatic saturation of the tonal field, so consistently evident in other advanced composers of the time, is often absent in Ives and Mahler, even in their later compositions. Clear examples are the largely diatonic opening sections of Ives's Fourth and Mahler's Ninth Symphonies. Moreover, the dominant retains its structural, key-defining role with surprising frequency—and not just in that elliptical, attenuated sense (as with Wagner) in which tonics are implied by their dominants but never explicitly stated. In both Ives and Mahler, tonality in the strict, functional sense remains an active force. Moreover, it is by means of its very retention that its transformed historical meaning is reflected in their works in such a remarkably pointed way.

Tonal and diatonic conservatism forms part of a more general shared characteristic. This is the blatantly "popular," even "low-life" tone of much of their work, which lends it a complexion quite different from the "elevated" character of most eighteenth- and nineteenth-century art music.[1] Folk and popular elements are no longer neutralized, as with earlier composers, but appear undisguised—in their own clothing, as it were. The sense of intrusion from a foreign musical realm becomes an essential component of the compositional statement and reflects a radically new conception of the nature and limits of serious musical language. It is probably this matter of tone, more than anything else, that accounts for the negative reaction that both composers have so often encountered and that persists even today in certain musical circles. The apparent ordinariness of the musical statements leads to charges of banality, and coupled with yet another shared attribute—the stigma of the part-time composer—fosters claims that neither was an artist of the first rank.

Significantly, Mahler, who was, of course, much more conscious of the weight of the European tradition, was himself beset by such doubts. It is well known that he was deeply troubled—and puzzled—by the intrusion of the commonplace in his work; and this seems to have been one of the reasons he felt a need to consult Sigmund Freud in the spring of 1910.[2] But Ives, too, had moments of self-doubt. One thinks particularly of his poignant remarks made after playing some of his works for an uncomprehending musician with whom he was acquainted: "I felt (but only temporarily) that perhaps there was something wrong with me . . . Are my ears on wrong? No one else seems to hear it the same way."[3]

Of course, in neither composer is the ultimate effect one of straightforward restatement, a point that again suggests an important correlation between the two. What is involved, I think, is a process of "defamiliar-ization," an idea that has been extensively developed in art and literature but less so, at least until more recently, in music.[4] It is grounded in the notion that as objects of perception become overly familiar, our experi-ence of them takes on an habitual and automatic character. We no longer perceive the real object at all, but only its vague shadow or outline. Although the object is recognized, it is not truly seen or heard; it has becomes neutralized and thus deprived of its expressive potential. Only by removing what Coleridge called the "film of familiarity" can this potential be re-established.

This process, which depends on both the use of recognizable, known musical objects and their placement in new and newly illuminating per-spectives, is of the utmost importance for both Ives and Mahler. One of the most characteristic features of their music is the way it transforms the familiar, distancing it so as to rekindle its affective force. The quo-tations and the relative simplicity of large segments of the music are both part of this process, as is the revolutionary way in which the materials are integrated into the larger musical context.

A related charge is that both composers were incapable of inventing their own musical materials and thus had to borrow ideas from external sources. The use of quotation, closely connected with the previously dis-cussed matter of tone, forms an essential aspect of their work. In Ives, of course, the hymn tunes, popular songs, and so on, are usually apparent and are often intended to be heard as quotations. In Mahler the matter is more complex, for his "quotations" are normally not so much literal borrowings as synthetic recreations of certain standard musical types. Literal quotations occasionally do occur: in the third movement of the First Symphony, where a minor-mode version of the song "Frère Jacques" provides the principal thematic material, or in the scherzo of the Third Symphony, which incorporates a fragment of Liszt's *Rhapsodie espagnole*. But more commonly there is an artificial reconstruction of a specific compositional type—the march tunes in the first movement of the Third Symphony, the Alpine folk song in its third movement, the Bohemian music in the third movement of the First Symphony, or the bugle calls in the Fifth. Yet in effect—and this is the essential point—all of these passages are as clearly representative of the real thing as are Ives's more literal borrowings.

What Ives and Mahler achieved in this regard represented a highly original reaction to the peculiarities of the musico-historical situation of their time. The hyperchromaticism and concomitant tonal decentrali-zation of musical language at the turn of the twentieth century produced a radical neutralization of materials. The basic structural functions of the tonal system became more and more equivalent, tending to level out all musical statements and thus render them increasingly interchangeable. Every advanced composer of the period faced this problem. Strauss, for example, countered the tendency by developing an ever more exaggerated range of musical gestures, straining the already weakened substructure to its breaking point. This was, of course, consistent with the historical evolution of chromaticism and represented a development that would ultimately "progress" to the twelve-tone system.

Ives and Mahler approached the problem from an entirely different direction. As if realizing that Western music history, at least as it had been known, had reached the limits of its own history—had become, that is to say, incapable of continuing to generate a consistently progressive evolution—they fashioned a new type of music based on older and simpler models largely neglected by the main tradition. They thus set about renewing musical prototypes that, from the point of view of most of their contemporaries, seemed outmoded and historically regressive. The twofold nature of the process required that the music be distinctly recognizable as a representative of its original source and yet appear to be reactivated in a new context. The ways in which Ives and Mahler achieved this are essentially the same. Borrowed material is fragmented and juxtaposed against other kinds of music, combined simultaneously with different music, distorted through the appearance of unexpected intervals and through complex and ambiguous phrase relationships, or distanced by means of elaborate orchestrations that contradict the material's true heritage. But in each case the materials are transformed in such a way as to acquire new expressive life.

It is these procedures of "defamiliarization" that refute the charges of banality, charges which take into account the isolated event but ignore the larger context that supplies the materials with their expressive value and justifies their presence in the work of art. Through their context they are transfigured and take on a new depth of meaning dependent on the complex system of references in which they participate. Thus the almost shocking simplicity of the music in certain passages, a matter touched upon earlier, is normally limited to a single dimension of what is actually a multi-dimensional process. The straightforward diatonic character of the opening of Mahler's Ninth is belied by the way the music gradually forms itself out of bits and pieces of melodic and accompanimental figures, each of which by itself might be heard as a stock item drawn from the standard catalogue of nineteenth-century musical effects. Taken collectively, however, they produce a collage-like continuum of extraordinary subtlety and ambiguity. Similarly, the hymn tune that dominates the opening of Ives's Fourth, *Watchman, Tell Us of the Night*, is transformed not only by its tonally obscure introduction but by its remarkable scoring (especially telling is the faintly heard harp and violin ensemble), its harmonization (which occasionally—though only occasionally—injects a foreign, dissociative element), and the deliberate truncation of its final cadential phrases.

It is sometimes said of both composers, and especially of Mahler, that their music sounds as if we have always known it. This touches upon an essential aspect of their work but leaves unmentioned the other, complementary side. What initially sounds familiar always ends up sounding very different from what we actually expected. The paradox implicit in this conjunction supplies the crucial point: what seems strange and extraordinary on one level does so only because, on another, it is so familiar and ordinary.

Perhaps even more characteristic than Ives and Mahler's use of quotation is their handling of form. A high degree of disjunction marks the music of both. The underlying continuity often appears to be cut off in midflight, rudely interrupted by the intrusion of heterogeneous elements. There are, of course, precedents for this kind of musical thinking—one thinks of late Beethoven or of Berlioz, where there is often an abrupt confrontation of radically contrasting musical units—but never before was this done with anything like the same frequency and exaggeration.

Formal disjunction can be understood as a necessary consequence of the reliance on foreign materials. Since the popular and folk elements are not "house-broken"—that is, not accommodated to the requirements of traditional symphonic structure (as they tended to be with the nationalist composers, for example)—it becomes necessary to "make room" for them in the musical structure. In Ives and Mahler this is often accomplished by a kind of *force majeure*: the structure is simply broken into, cut open to allow for the insertion of extraneous elements. As a result, forward motion is suspended, brought to a standstill so that a way can be cleared for the appearance of music drawn from another domain. Space is thus provided for elements that, quite literally, could "find no place" in earlier Western music.

This happens on various structural levels. On a small scale, Ives breaks into the highly dissonant, rhythmically driving music of the "Hawthorne" movement of the *Concord Sonata* to present a brief fragment of hymn music (which also pre-echoes the music of the "Alcotts" movement), just as Mahler intersects the trio of the third movement of his Seventh Symphony with occasional sudden bursts of faster music. In both cases, it is as if a curtain is drawn open, giving view to a different and totally unexpected musical landscape. Or on a larger scale, an established, ongoing continuity will be rudely severed, or radically dissolved, to allow for the interpolation of entire sections of extraneous music—as in the barn-dance episode of Ives's *Washington's Birthday*, or in the posthorn episode from Mahler's Third Symphony. Despite the length of these sections and their apparent independence and self-sufficiency—or rather, perhaps, just because of these characteristics—they sound like isolated moments that have temporarily broken through from an altogether separate sphere of musical activity.

Such juxtaposed components can occur not only sequentially but also simultaneously. The band music in the finale of Mahler's Second Symphony first appears as a momentary interruption of the prevailing musical continuity; but subsequently it recurs in simultaneous opposition with the latter, creating a multi-leveled structure made up of two independent but interconnected textural strands, each with its own rhythmic structure, tempo, instrumentation, and general character. In this latter form it provides a striking parallel to those moments in Ives—*Putnam's Camp*, the second movement of the Fourth Symphony, or *Decoration Day*—where two independent "musics" collide in mutual and simultaneous confrontation.

The notion of combining or crosscutting between two different tempi is conspicuous in both composers. It appears in its most radical form in Ives, when he actually notates two independent rates of speed—as in the second and fourth movements of the Fourth Symphony, *Central Park in the Dark*, or *The Unanswered Question*. And there are many other passages in his music which give the effect of multiple tempi, even though everything is notated within a common metrical framework—as in the scherzo *Over the Pavements*, where in the cadenza the wind instruments gradually accelerate against steady sixteenth notes in the piano.

But Mahler, too, will disengage one strand of continuity from another by having it maintain an independent metric pulse. A common indication in the symphonies is that an instrument is to be played "without reference to the prevailing tempo." In the opening section of the first movement of the First Symphony, for example, the cuckoo call (once again a "borrowed" idea with an independent existence outside the work) continues at its previous pace after all the other instruments have taken up a new tempo. An even more striking example is the recapitulation in the opening movement of the Third. Here the reprise does not provide, as classical connotations of the term might suggest, a "resolution" for the development section. The latter is not resolved at all, but is rather "dissolved"—gradually filtered out until it is finally represented by only a muffled snare drum figure in the distance. This figure is not completely extinguished at the return of the first principal section but overlaps with the latter, persisting with its own tempo in conjunction with the other music. Only then does it gradually sink into complete inaudibility. (Indeed, in both composers the independent levels often seem to relinquish their hegemony only with the greatest reluctance.)

This passage from Mahler's Third recalls one of his most striking parallels with Ives: an interest in exploiting space in their music. Mahler's snare drums sound distant, removed from the main locus of musical activity, not only because they are muffled; they are also placed off-stage and are consequently perceived as occupying a different physical as well as musical territory. This is one of many such placements called for in his scores. As early as *Das klagende Lied*, Mahler locates a wind band off-stage so that it can force itself upon the principal musical continuum from without. Later, when this band is heard simultaneously with the main orchestra, the distinct musical difference between the two combined layers is supported by an equally pronounced spatial one.

Several of Ives's scores—the Fourth Symphony, *The Unanswered Question*, the Second Orchestral Set—call for a similar spatial separation of instrumental forces. The famous "Conductor's Note" to the second movement of his Fourth Symphony includes a lengthy discussion of the effect of hearing music from different directions and spatial distances, in the course of which Ives mentions the special quality of a horn heard at a distance across a lake. This passage vividly recalls the footnote to the finale of Mahler's Second Symphony, in which the composer states that he conceived of the off-stage music as the "isolated sounds of a barely audible music, carried on the wind." And in the same movement, just before the entrance of the chorus, Mahler concerns himself with the varying distances and specific directions from which four off-stage trumpets are heard. Here the music is conceived literally as moving in space, approaching and receding according to such indications as "from a great distance," "somewhat nearer and stronger," "much nearer and stronger," "again more distant," and "losing itself" into inaudibility.

The most significant point to be made about these similarities is that they are not simply isolated correspondences, which, though perhaps surprising in number, could be passed off as merely superficial or coincidental occurrences. On the contrary, they are conjoined with and subsumed under a more general conception that touches upon the nature of the musical composition itself. The tendency in Western music of the common practice period was to treat each composition as an autonomous whole from which all elements foreign to the system of relationships defined within that whole were necessarily excluded. Emphasis was on internal consistency, with each contributing element justified by its role in a consistent and congruous structure. Extraneous material—material not actively participating in this process or, as analysts of this music like to put it, not fulfilling a "structural function" essential to the working of the entire system—was thus rigorously barred. In both Ives and Mahler there is a distinct shift away from this view of the work. The composition is opened up—made permeable, as it were, so as to be subject to outside influences. It becomes a more inclusionary whole, vulnerable to the ambiguities and contradictions of everyday experience, both musical and otherwise, and more truly reflective of the manifold conditions of human activity. Although the musical result may seem less consistent—and thus considerably more resistant to the kind of systematic analysis that even now many view as the only legitimate kind—it is both richer in possibilities and broader in perspective.

Quotations are perhaps the most forceful image of the work's surrender of its autonomy. One type of quotation that has not yet been mentioned, the self-quotation, is particularly suggestive in this regard. In both Ives and Mahler, the boundaries between compositions are often indistinct. Both are fond of quoting passages from their earlier works, and even entire movements may result from a reconstruction of previously used material. One thinks of those symphonic movements by Mahler, such as the first movement of the First Symphony or the third movement of the Second, that are to a considerable extent paraphrases of his earlier vocal compositions; or of the first movement of the Seventh, which, in a less literal sense, is an elaborate variation on the first movement of the Sixth.[5] In Ives the tendency is so developed that it frequently becomes difficult to say just where one work ends and another begins. Examples are the second movement of the Fourth Symphony, the "Hawthorne" movement of the *Concord Sonata*, and the piano fantasy *The Celestial Railroad*, all of which are closely interrelated and share common material, or the last movement of the Fourth Violin Sonata, which incorporates the music of the song "Shall We Gather at the River" in its entirety.

There is, then, a pronounced "biographical" dimension in the music of both composers. One is almost inclined to see their individual compositions as parts of, and variants on, a single aggregate work in progress which encompasses their entire output. The individual pieces provide their own particular comment on this aggregate work and make their own unique contribution to it.

More generally, one notes a desire to accommodate the contradictory and variegated components of a complex reality quite different from that of the period in which common practice tonality flourished. Ives and Mahler no longer see the world as a neatly ordered entity capable of being rendered into musical terms that are both consistent in content and syntactically logical. In this connection one recalls comments made by both composers on the effect of the simultaneous occurrence of two or more musical events, and on the importance of such multi-leveled textures for their own work. Ives's boyhood experience, reported by Henry and Sidney Cowell, of hearing a parade in Danbury in which a dissonant counterpoint was produced by two bands playing different pieces in different meters and keys, both at the same time, is widely known.[6] But it is perhaps worth quoting in full Mahler's extraordinarily Ivesian description of his own similar experiences, made in the presence of his friend Natalie Bauer-Lechner, who recalls:

> Mahler told us at table that, on the woodland path at Klagenfurt with W. (who had come to settle his repertoire) he was much disturbed by a barrel-organ, whose noise seemed not to bother W. in the least. "But when a second one began to play, W. expressed horror at the cater-wauling—which now, however, was beginning to amuse me. And when, into the bargain, a military band struck up in the distance, he covered up his ears, protesting vigorously—whereas I was listening with such delight that I wouldn't move from the spot."
>
> When Rosé expressed surprise at this, Mahler said, "If you like my symphonies, you must like that too!"
>
> The following Sunday, we were going on the same walk with Mahler. At the fête on the Kreuzberg, an even worse witches' sabbath was in progress. Not only were innumerable barrel-organs blaring out from merry-go-rounds, see-saws, shooting galleries and puppet shows, but a military band and a men's choral society had established themselves there as well. All these groups, in the same forest clearing, were creating an incredible musical pandemonium without paying the slightest attention to each other. Mahler exclaimed: "You hear? That's polyphony, and that's where I got it from! Even when I was quite a small child, in the woods at Iglau, this used to move me strangely, and impressed itself upon me. For it's all the same whether it resounds in a din like this or in a thousandfold bird song, in the howling of the storm, the lapping of the waves, or the crackling of the fire. Just so—from quite different directions—the themes must enter; and they must be just as different from each other in rhythm and melodic character. (Everything else is merely many-voiced writing, homophony is disguise.) The only difference is that the artist orders and unites them all into one concordant and harmonious whole."[7]

Excluding Ives himself, what other composer of the period could, or would, have said anything even remotely similar? Yet, paradoxically, just because the similarity between Ives and Mahler seems so personal, so intimately tied to the peculiar attributes of these two particular composers, one may hesitate to accord them more than coincidental value. That is, if the similarity does not embrace stylistic attributes generally characteristic of the period and thus equally attributable to other important composers of the time (and not just as isolated cases, but as essential features of an overall compositional approach), one may be inclined to see these correspondences as only idiosyncratic, and thus ultimately insignificant, "abnormalities."

I have tried to show, however, that the parallels between Ives and Mahler are comprehensible only when viewed within the context of the particular stage of Western music history during which both were active. So understood, the "abnormalities" take on a very different complexion. Moreover, their significance has become increasingly apparent in the light of more recent compositional trends. If the principal currents of musical evolution during the first half of this century tended to place Mahler and (especially) Ives outside the main stream, the compositional developments of the past half-century have forced them into its forefront. It would be difficult to name two composers who have had a more profound impact on the dominant compositional attitudes of the present age.[8] And it is no accident, surely, that among all those composers who can now be considered "historical" figures, Ives and Mahler have enjoyed the greatest increase of interest in their music during the recent past.

When viewed within a wider context, the complex of interrelated techniques and attitudes common to Ives and Mahler can be seen to represent an articulate musical response to some of the most important intellectual and artistic ideas of the nineteenth century. Already at the turn of the century, Novalis observed: "There must be poems that simply sound well and are full of beautiful words—but without sense and continuity—at most understandable as individual strophies—they must be like so many fragments of the most varied things." Coleridge spoke of a poetic imagination that "reveals itself in the balance and reconciliation of opposite and discordant qualities." Both Coleridge and Wordsworth were concerned with the idea of lifting the "film of familiarity." And later, in a modified form, this same concern reappears as an important component of the symbolist aesthetic. Finally, Hugo von Hofmannsthal, Ives's and Mahler's contemporary, formulated the matter in terms that get very close to the spirit of their music. Commenting on recent French poetry, he remarked:

> The creative individual, surrounded by all-too-restricted forms of expression, as though by walls, casts himself into language itself and tries to find in it the drunkeness of inspiration, and through it opens up new entries into life in accordance with those senses of meaning which are freed from the control of conscious understanding. This is, and always was, the Latin approach to the unconscious: it occurs not in half-dreamy self-indulgence . . . but through an intense self-removal, in intoxication . . . through a simultaneous, confused piling up of objects, a violation of order.[9]

Nor is this line of thought restricted to literature: the manipulation of fragments so as to achieve a reconciliation of "opposite and discordant qualities" is one of the most characteristic features of nineteenth-century architecture, in which the structural surface often reveals an eclectic, though mediated, conglomeration of heterogeneous details drawn from a wide range of historical sources.

Further elaboration on these more general correspondences would take me too far afield.[10] I mention them, in any event, only to indicate that Ives's and Mahler's procedures are in fact less peculiar than they may appear if considered solely within musical terms. They form close parallels with some of the main currents of nineteenth-century thought. Indeed, it is surprising that similar procedures were not more widely developed in nineteenth-century music. Of course, they were not completely absent, as I have suggested. But only with Ives and Mahler do they begin to be extensively and consistently (one might even say systematically) translated into musical terms, so that they assume a principal role in shaping the compositional statement and defining its aesthetic intent.

Finally, there is a well-known incident that, in light of these considerations, takes on particular interest. In 1911, when Mahler was in New York as conductor of the New York Philharmonic, he happened to see a score of Ives's Third Symphony in the office of his music copyist. Mahler was sufficiently interested to ask for a copy, which he took with him when he returned to Europe shortly before his death.[11] I like to think of this as more than just a pleasant anecdote, for it indicates that Mahler saw something in this extremely individual composition—which on the surface, at least, was worlds removed from all the music he knew and respected—that interested him and struck a responsive note. Ives was completely unknown, not only in Europe but in America; no other major composer of his time ever showed the slightest concern for his work. The similarities that have been pointed out above may help explain why it should have been Mahler, and Mahler alone, who was able to discern in his music something recognizable, something of interest and value.

:5:

Ives, Schoenberg, and the Musical Ideal

KEITH C. WARD

There is a great Man living in this Country—a composer.
He has solved the problem of how to preserve one's self-esteem.
He responds to negligence by contempt.
He is not forced to accept praise or blame.
His name is Ives.

This famous panegyric by Arnold Schoenberg, written presumably in 1944, was found among the composer's papers after his death. Sent to Ives by Schoenberg's widow, Gertrud, in November 1953, it is the most tangible shred of evidence of any admiration between these two composers.[1] Though Schoenberg provides no context or reference that tells us what inspired him, his laudatory words suggest that at least he knew of Ives as a progressive musical figure. He might have heard some of Ives's music in live performances, on radio, or on record, and he also might have known of Ives's reclusive nature and comfortable affluence, since he quips that Ives was "not forced to accept praise or blame," presumably for his highly controversial music. That Ives "responds to negligence by contempt" could be interpreted as praise for a kindred spirit, one who stayed the course of artistic integrity instead of acquiescing to the tastes and needs of another audience.[2] Certainly he viewed Ives as a sympathetic colleague.

Schoenberg's praise, however, invites closer scrutiny. Accolades from a voice as important as Schoenberg's should not go unheeded. What did Schoenberg know of Ives, and Ives of Schoenberg? What inspired

Schoenberg to write this acclamation? Did Ives at any time respond in kind? Could these words suggest that Schoenberg sensed a deeper connection to Ives than we have previously thought? Did Schoenberg find Ives's music noteworthy, and did Ives feel similarly about Schoenberg's creations? This essay will explore these questions and will attempt to show that these composers, born in the same year (1874), shared some concerns. Indeed, they approached creativity with remarkably similar aesthetic ideals. Though Ives worked largely in isolation during his creative years, his conception of the aesthetic issues raised by new approaches to musical syntax and expression paralleled that of Schoenberg, a leader of musical modernism. Though their creations may be dissimilar, free of influence from the other, their ideals and the way in which they espoused those ideals are strikingly similar and provide a rich illustration of the aesthetic dilemma fundamental to the early twentieth century. Both developed unique musical compositions that challenged the traditions in which they were so firmly rooted. Their appeals to spiritual truth as justification for music that questioned the primacy of codified structural and harmonic norms, like their resilience in weathering the criticisms of unreceptive audiences, attest to their shared concerns. Peter Yates, who befriended both composers, suggests a connection between Schoenberg and Ives when he contends that Schoenberg's tribute to Ives, no matter how each may have responded to the other's work, "speaks [aesthetically] a common language."[3] This essay will investigate the foundations of that common language and will show how each composer's noteworthy innovations, radical and different as they may be, take root from a common tradition and similar aesthetic. This commonality raises fundamental questions about the long-held notion that Ives was an anomaly in his day.

Schoenberg and Ives were not totally ignorant of each other. There are reports they even met on one occasion in 1933, the year Schoenberg immigrated to the United States. Ives is said to have attended a reception in New York City that was organized to welcome Schoenberg. Being in ill health, Ives did not stay for most of the party. He reportedly shook hands with the Austrian composer, spoke briefly with him, and then left.[4]

Their familiarity with each other's music is less tangible. Schoenberg was probably more knowledgeable of Ives's music than Ives was of his. He owned copies of *The Fourth of July*, *Lincoln the Great Commoner*, *Three Pieces for Theater Orchestra*, the *Concord Sonata*, and *114 Songs*.[5] Despite the small number of Ives pieces that had been published before his death in 1951, Schoenberg's collection is relatively extensive. Though possession of scores does not constitute intimate familiarity, the number of Ives's works that Schoenberg owned—significant works, at that—implies at least curiosity. Even if these scores were unsolicited gifts, they demonstrate at the very least Schoenberg's awareness of Ives.

Schoenberg may also have heard Ives's music. Peter Yates describes a conversation with Carl Ruggles in 1964 in which Ruggles said he and Schoenberg heard together a performance of Ives's *Unanswered Question*.[6] Another possible site for hearing Ives's music is the "Evenings on the Roof" concert series in Los Angeles, which began in 1939. In the first seven seasons, Ives's music enjoyed frequent performances. His *Concord Sonata* was performed ten times, the Third and Fourth Violin Sonatas three times, the First Violin Sonata once, and movements 1 and 2 of the Second Violin Sonata once. There were also seven performances of various groups of songs.[7] According to Hans Stuckenschmidt, Schoenberg did not hear any live performances of Ives's music at "Roof" concerts even during the 1943–44 season, which was dedicated to both Ives's and his music. However, since Schoenberg is known to have listened to broadcasts of these concerts, Stuckenschmidt suggests that Schoenberg probably heard some of Ives's music on the radio.[8]

Some scholars contend that Ives was ignorant of Schoenberg's music.[9] Indeed, there is no substantive discussion of Schoenberg in any of Ives's published or unpublished writings. In a letter to E. Robert Schmitz, dated 10 August 1931, he professed never to have heard or seen "a note" of Schoenberg's music.[10] Though he may not have heard Schoenberg's music before or after 1931, there is some evidence that he may have known of the composer Arnold Schoenberg before 1931. One suggestion comes from a letter to Ives from Elliott Carter, dated 19 February 1927. Carter writes: "I am sending you a very interesting magazine dealing with recordings entirely. In it, this month, has appeared an account of private recordings. I wonder if Pro-Musica could not have a department for recording its more popular modern works. *Pierrot Lunaire* and other things are waiting to be done as well as some Scriabine [*sic*]."[11]

In this letter Carter refers to Stravinsky, Scriabin, Beethoven, and Brahms, but he does not identify the composers of *Pelléas et Mélisande* (Debussy?), *Pacific 231* (Honegger), or *Pierrot Lunaire* (Schoenberg). Did Carter assume that Ives knew the composers of these landmark compositions? Ives attended concerts in the 1920s and, according to Carter, had heard compositions by Scriabin, Stravinsky, and Ravel.[12] Jeffrey Gibbens has demonstrated Ives's knowledge of Debussy, whom Ives discussed at length in the *Essays Before a Sonata* and whose *Prelude to "The Afternoon of a Faun"* he quoted in the song "Grantchester."[13] However, if we are to believe Ives's response to a review by Henry Prunières, Schoenberg was not among the composers whose music Ives knew. Was *Pierrot* mentioned in the magazine article Carter sent, making the reference self-explanatory? Did Ives read the magazine and thus become exposed to at least the name of Arnold Schoenberg?[14]

A likely source for information about Schoenberg would have been Ives's friend and advocate Henry Cowell, who had attended some of Schoenberg's private analysis classes in Berlin in the early 1930s. As Schoenberg was by then an internationally recognized musical figure, Cowell would have discussed with Ives his encounters with one of Europe's leading modernist composers. In turn, Cowell might have spoken to Schoenberg about the leading figures of the American modernist movement. Carl Ruggles, a friend of Ives and a composer he respected highly, might also have shared his enthusiasm for Schoenberg with Ives.[15]

Certainly Ives was not ignorant of Schoenberg after 1932. In April of that year, Cowell issued the first American publication of Schoenberg's *Klavierstück* Op. 33b, in *New Music*. Since Ives subscribed to (and subsidized) the magazine, he must have seen the piece.[16] Despite this, there is not a single reference to Op. 33b in Ives's published writings, and there are no copies of any works by Schoenberg in Ives's music collections at his West Redding home or at Yale University. It appears that Schoenberg's music did not leave an indelible impression on him.[17]

In their music, Schoenberg and Ives at first seem to have had few common concerns. They pursued their interests without knowing each other, in different directions. Schoenberg sought to convince the world in an uncompromising way that he had discovered the path that led to the future of music; he had found the way for which all conscientious artists groped. Ives, on the other hand, directed his search inward, hoping to find the inner inspiration to understand himself, his world, and his ideals. Schoenberg's music has an organic unity; whether it is tonal, atonal, or twelve-tone, traditional devices, such as imitation, developing variation, written-in rubatos, Brahmsian crescendos, and standard forms, are present. His performance directions are meticulous, especially in his later works. Ives's idiom, outside his student compositions, is less predictable, often diverging from Schoenberg's tendency toward stylistic homogeneity. Indeed, Ives positively sought heterogeneity of style, using it as a basic element of both form and expression.[18] Schoenberg sought a system in which to compose, whereas Ives did not search for an all-encompassing collective compositional method. Schoenberg was obsessed with organization, whereas Ives's approach to musical structure was less dogmatic.[19] Schoenberg made a determined effort to abandon tonality, whereas Ives continued to use it when it was needed for a desired effect.[20] Richard Middleton suggests that Schoenberg and Ives also had different audiences in mind, that Schoenberg believed art was meant for the intelligentsia, whereas Ives intended his music for the masses.[21]

Other differences lie in the roots and directions of their arts. Schoenberg clearly saw his art as based on historical development. As Charles Rosen has pointed out, Schoenberg considered himself an "inevitable historical force." He felt responsible for reconstituting and preserving the integrity of German music during the rise of French and Russian styles in the early part of this century.[22] Ives, on the other hand, was caught in an identity crisis: American music, other than popular song, did not seem to have the same rich and honored tradition. Some critics argue that Ives's music has a timeless character, a sense of discovery as it explores expressive possibilities. Schoenberg's, they contend, begins to sound dated; it can be pinned to a certain era.[23]

In their search for a new language, Ives and Schoenberg approached the problem from opposite poles. Middleton sees Schoenberg's art as that of rejection, of negation of the "horrors of bourgeois society," whereas in Ives he sees the affirmation of "not only a *new* vision but also of the *original* truth of that which is negated."[24] Ironically, Ives was instructed thoroughly in the German musical tradition throughout his education, beginning with studies with his father and ending with those with Horatio Parker at Yale University; Schoenberg was essentially self-taught, studying only briefly with Alexander Zemlinsky. Considering their respective educations, one might imagine that the conventional wisdom about their music, which regards Ives's as the product of a composer lacking sufficient training and Schoenberg's as intellectually conceived and formally executed, should be reversed.[25]

With so many differences, where do the significant parallels—even connections—between Schoenberg and Ives lie? One link that has been suggested is their supposed mutual exploration of twelve-tone composition.[26] Ives's experimentation with twelve-tone structures independent of and prior to Schoenberg is common knowledge, and Schoenberg's development of the technique of composing with all twelve tones related only to one another has influenced generations of composers. Certainly, both composers developed their techniques in response to a common stimulus, the increasing chromaticism and attenuated tonality of late-nineteenth-century music. However, their respective uses of twelve-tone technique are anything but similar. As Philip Lambert argues convincingly, Ives does not pursue Schoenberg's systematic goals. For Schoenberg, the technique was a compositional method. By contrast, Ives used the chromatic scale as only an aggregate structure in compositional experiments. With Ives's "experimental attitude," the scale was viewed as an "intervallic structure" in which pitch order could be manipulated and subsegments highlighted.[27] Though there are isolated examples in which Ives applies techniques that resemble those of Schoenbergian theory, such as *Study No. 5* for piano,[28] Ives's use lacks thorough and consistent application. It would be difficult to call Ives's varying techniques a method.

From his prose we learn that Ives looked on twelve-tone structures not as musical processes but as musical metaphors. Whenever identifying such structures, he describes them as experiments in sound; he even goes so far as to assign them extra-musical associations. One of his best-known references is found in a note he wrote on the pencil full score to *The Masses*. One verse of the song begins, "As the tribes of the ages wandered and followed the stars—whence come the many dwelling places of the world." The associated musical plan, Ives tells us, is to "have each [instrument] complete the 12 notes (each on a different system) . . . and hold the last of the 12 . . . as finding its star."[29] Here and elsewhere his use of the chromatic scale is not a solely musical one: it functions as a gesture to represent something beyond the music itself. In Schoenberg's case, this scale is used in a purely musical sense to construct a row. Thus, the attempt to draw parallels between the composers in their use of the chromatic scale as an aggregate structure becomes problematic, especially when Ives refers to such a method as an "artificial process without strength," a type of "wall-paper design music [that] is not as big as a natural, mushy ballad."[30] Lambert correctly posits that Ives's experiments are neither understood nor appreciated when they are viewed as failures to achieve the compositional objectives of Schoenberg's twelve-tone system.

The parallels between these composers lie elsewhere. Many scholars have explored other aspects of their artistic kinship. For example, there are at least forty-three citations linking the two in Geoffrey Block's bio-bibliography of Ives.[31] Most of these articles refer to Ives as a precursor, an independent thinker, or a counterpart of Schoenberg and other contemporary composers, or they place Ives's philosophy or works within the context of musical progressivism that includes Schoenberg. Others, while concentrating on analysis of Ives's music, refer to Schoenberg as a contemporary. Some allude to but do not explore connections between the two composers. However, two articles deal specifically with parallels between Schoenberg and Ives. Fred Fisher suggests that both composers developed a "credo of radicalism" as a reaction against early failures: Schoenberg as the director of an unsuccessful cabaret in Berlin, Ives as a young composer unable to draw any attention from the premiere of his cantata *The Celestial Country* (composed 1898–99, premiered 1902). Noting that both men admired Brahms, he suggests that their obsession with expressivity places them "irrefragably" in the great Romantic tradition. The essay by Richard Middleton cited earlier also contributes insightful comparisons. Acknowledging the importance of their "almost single-handed transformation of musical history," he draws three important "lines of correspondence" between Schoenberg and Ives: a quest for unity, a lack of concern for idiomatic writing, and a need to compose in whatever style each felt was necessary.[32]

To be sure, there are striking differences between the music of Ives and that of Schoenberg. However, stressing the unique results of their ideals would miss the point. They shared the common heritage of Austro-German music, one having lived the tradition (Schoenberg), the other (Ives) having learned and assimilated it through teachers who professed it (Ives's father, George, and Horatio Parker at Yale University).[33] Invoking the names of Bach, Beethoven, and Brahms throughout their writings, Ives and Schoenberg proceed from a reinterpretation of a compositional style whose character is based fundamentally on the organic development of themes and motives—in Schoenbergian terms, on the *Grundgestalt* ("basic shape") and developing variation. Instead of rejecting their past, Ives and Schoenberg continued what they viewed as best in it and discarded that which they saw as superficial. In their prose, they used many nineteenth-century aesthetic arguments to justify their compositions.

The consensus between their thoughts and aesthetic ideals is striking. It shows two composers struggling with questions about the content and process of musical construction in a way that was characteristic of their time. One (Schoenberg) expressed the dilemma publicly and vocally, the other (Ives) privately. As Fisher and Middleton infer, the correspondence between the two composers lies in the fundamental principles of their shared aesthetic. It encompasses an idealistic state of mind in which the discrepancies described above are a result, not the source. The connection lies in their mutual appeal to and trust in the power of the subconscious, the faith in intuition as a guide for artistic expression. This belief contains three elements: dualism; a need for expression without regard to the limitations of tradition, technique, or taste;[34] and an appeal to the artistic spirit of eternal, constant change as a vindication of their art.

Dualism is one of the basic aesthetic tenets of both Ives and Schoenberg.[35] Though the idea of a duality between the metaphysical and the material, phenomena and noumena, or subject and object is nothing new, the fact that both composers went to great lengths to explain its significance is noteworthy. They used it as a justification for their respective creations. Ives's most characteristic duality is that of "manner" and "substance," to which Schoenberg's contrast of "style" and "idea" is a close parallel.

According to Ives, substance, the "stronger" of the two elements, is the spiritual fabric of music. It suggests "the body of a conviction which has its birth in the spiritual consciousness, whose youth is nourished in the moral consciousness, and whose maturity as a result of all this growth is then represented in a mental image."[36] Substance deals with spiritual beauty, honesty of spiritual expression. For Ives, it reflects the inherent goodness of humankind and the artistic honesty of the individual; it has nothing to do with a composer's particular style. Music, according to Ives, is a vehicle not of personal but of spiritual expression. The nearer one comes to mere expression of emotion, the farther one is from art.[37] Manner, the less important and weaker of the two elements, is the means of expressing substance in the material world. Ives thought it came "as a kind of by-product of an intense devotion to a principle or ideal."[38] Ives felt that when one became preoccupied with musical manner (conventional principles of composition), whether by personal choice or by dutifully following rules of composition, one missed the true power of the substance behind the thought. Because Ives viewed sound as only the approximation of the idea, he believed an overemphasis on it would cause a listener or composer to overlook the substance of the idea, which in turn would limit what one could appreciate or express.[39]

Schoenberg's dichotomy between style and idea, what Middleton refers to as the "how" and the "what,"[40] is strikingly comparable. Schoenberg defined style as "the quality of a work [which] is based on natural conditions, expressing him who produced it. . . . He will never start from a preconceived image of a style [i.e., he will be led instead by intuition]; he will be ceaselessly occupied with doing justice to the idea. He is sure that, everything done which the *idea* demands, the external appearance will be adequate."[41] Here Schoenberg views style as a result of that "which the idea demands," or, as Ives put it, "as a kind of by-product of an intense devotion to a principle or ideal." Schoenberg did not allow past musical tastes—"a preconceived image of a style"—dictate his art, but instead concerned himself with "doing justice to the idea," or, as Ives thought, with translating as closely as possible the substance of an idea into expression. Later in the same essay, Schoenberg describes style as a mannerism, "an aspect or novelty not derived profoundly from basic ideas."[42] In their analysis of this, Allan Janik and Stephen Toulmin observe an Ivesian disregard of sound, noting that "nothing is said about *sound* itself . . . because Schoenberg . . . considered the question, how a composition sounds, as having no importance."[43]

Both Schoenberg and Ives laid the greatest importance on the idea and its origin in intuition. They also concurred on the limitations of musical sound and convention as means to express their ideas. Schoenberg and Ives speak a common language in the following outbursts:

> and art belongs to the *subconscious*! One should express *one's self*! Express one's self uncompromisingly! Not, however, one's tastes, one's [artistic]

training, one's [intellectual] understanding, one's knowledge, or one's ability—not all of these attributes which are not inborn, but rather the innate, impelling [forces of expression].[44]

My God! What has sound got to do with music! . . . Why can't music go out in the same way it comes in to a man, without having to crawl over a fence of sounds, thoraxes, catguts, wire, wood, and brass? . . . That music must be heard is not essential—what it *sounds* like may not be what it *is*.[45]

Schoenberg believed that the idea of a composition was the composition itself, the resulting work being a study of balancing elements used to construct it.[46] His interpretation may be more pragmatic than Ives's, but the fundamental similarities to Ives's dialectic are compelling. Traveling the street in both directions, he, like his friend Wassily Kandinsky, the painter and leading spokesman for *Der blaue Reiter* (the Munich-based association of progressive artists), was attempting to move from the material realm to the spiritual through a combination of abstract and real images.[47]

Though his interpretation is more pragmatic, Schoenberg's concept of the idea is expressed more abstractly than Ives's. There is something mystical about the "Idea." Schoenberg hints at this by referring to style as a mannerism that can become out-moded, whereas an idea remains eternal.[48] In turn, Ives's heterogenous musical idiom was not constrained by the tastes of his time. By borrowing melodies pregnant with meaning from his own experiences, Ives tried to connect what he saw as the spirit and strength of "local colors" with pigments of "the universal color" of substance.[49]

Like Ives, Schoenberg expounded on the importance of the idea through a scorn for contemporary musical preferences. He regretted seeing "many a great talent" perish "through a corrupt attitude towards the arts which aimed only for a sensational but futile success, instead of fulfilling the real taste of every artist."[50] Ives might have said that these great talents had become preoccupied with exercises on paper, that they were "trading an inspiration for a bad habit."[51] Both men lamented what they saw as a loss of idealism in a generation of composers.

Ives and Schoenberg held the mode of expression as unimportant; the idea remained the root of art.[52] Their interpretations of beauty were nearly identical, Ives expressing the transcendental ideal of spiritual beauty, Schoenberg concurring by recognizing the artist's unwilled attainment of beauty as he or she strives for truthfulness.[53] Schoenberg speaks of beauty in remarkably Ivesian terms: "But beauty, even if it does exist, is intangible; for it is only present when one whose intuitive power is strong enough to produce it, creates something by virtue of this intuitive power, and creates something new every time he exercises that power. Beauty is the result of intuition; when one ceases to be, the other ceases also."[54] One can understand why Schoenberg referred to Ives as "a great Man." Through whatever music by Ives he heard or studied, or prose by Ives he might have read, he must have recognized in Ives a kindred spirit, a composer who attempted to satisfy an inner compulsion without regard to the reaction or reception of the musical world. From his perspective, Ives would have relished Schoenberg's distaste for his critics.

Much more than dualism comprises their shared philosophy. They believed in the mystical aspects of music, the primacy and significance of—as well as devotion to—spiritual roots of inspiration, and in the measurement of aesthetic value free of sensual, social, or moral assessment. Their viewing of music as a direct, immediate expression of a higher, non-empirical realm arises from a tradition that reaches back to Emanuel Swedenborg (1688–1772) and Immanuel Kant (1724–1804).[55] The fact that both composers were addressing such fundamental questions similarly, simultaneously, and independently suggests the pursuit of a pressing dilemma common to their time.

Not only do the two composers share similar thoughts on the power of the idea or substance; they also intersect in the actual manner in which they treat musical material. Whatever disregard the composers expressed in both music and prose for methods of composition, and however lofty their ideals may have been, their innovations still arose out of a common heritage steeped in the works and methods of German and Austrian composers from the eighteenth and nineteenth centuries. As uniquely different as their outputs are, both were schooled in the same tradition, and its influence governed each one's sense of musical structure to varying degrees. In many of his writings Schoenberg describes his debt to this musical past, a past that Ives shared.

One technique common to both composers is the process of generating material from basic musical cells, particularly the procedure Schoenberg called "developing variation." According to Schoenberg, developing variation is the "variation of features of a basic unit [which] produces all the thematic formulations which provide for fluency, contrasts, variety, logic and unity, on the one hand, and character, mood, expression, and every needed differentiation, on the other hand—thus elaborating the *idea* of the piece."[56] This development begins with the most basic musical unit, the motive, which may be varied or combined with other motives to create the *Grundgestalt*, the basic shape or phrase that is the germ of all to follow. This basic shape is then varied to create the theme, and subsequent variation spawns the later themes, transitions, and other developments. Developing variation thus becomes a process

EXAMPLE 5.1. Schoenberg, *Klavierstuck*, Op. 11, No. 1, mm. 1–8.

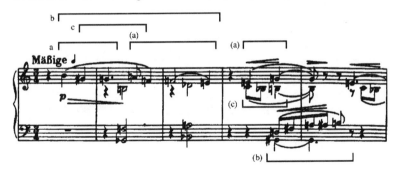

that occurs at many structural levels; it can entail the creation of motivic variations, phrases, phrase groups, or ultimately entire sections of a piece, each a logical development of what has come before.[57] It is a technique Schoenberg credits to his predecessors, especially to Bach, Beethoven, and Brahms.

The opening measures of Schoenberg's *Klavierstück* Op. 11, No. 1 (1909), provide one example of this technique (ex. 5.1). Nearly all the musical material of this composition is derived from the opening three pitches (the basic motive) and the first phrase (mm. 1–3, the *Grundgestalt*).[58] In the second phrase (mm. 4–8), the texture expands from two voices to four, and Schoenberg uses variations of rhythm and motive to construct the phrase. The rising minor third in the upper voice in m. 4 is an inversion of the opening interval (a in ex. 5.1); the motive in the alto voice is derived from notes 2–4 (c), and the tenor presents in inversion the shape of the basic melody, the *Grundgestalt* (b). Rhythmic development is particularly evident in the alto voice. In m. 4, this lower voice enters simultaneously with the rising minor third of the upper voice. In the second statement (mm. 5–6), it creates the allusion of an accelerando by entering after the upper voice and finishing with it. Finally, in the third entrance (mm. 7–8), the melodic gesture is elongated, beginning and ending after the upper voice. By the end of the second phrase, the basic melody has expanded by two beats. Its entrances have been varied rhythmically as well, creating phrase units that flow freely across bar lines. Had Schoenberg simply repeated the first unit of this

EXAMPLE 5.2. Ives, *Concord Sonata*, second edition (1947), "Emerson," p. 3.

phrase, he could have produced an appealing second phrase through dynamic gradations and ritard. Instead, through developing variation, he has created a musical phrase of great variety through an uncommon economy of means.

The "Emerson" movement from Ives's *Concord Sonata* also uses developing variation extensively. By the third page (second edition, 1947), Ives has introduced and preliminarily explored nearly all of the important thematic and motivic material of the entire sonata. Though his presentation of these ideas does not contain the organic seamlessness often present in Schoenberg (as in Op. 11), he handles much of his musical material through a technique of developing variation analogous to Schoenberg's. For example, on this third page Ives begins an extended interplay between two themes important specifically to the "Emerson" movement (ex. 5.2): a foreshadowing of a theme developed later in the movement (a), and a declamatory, prose-like statement marked by dotted rhythms (b). Both were presented in the opening moments of the movement but are now combined and developed. These themes are stated first as basic cells and then are followed by variations. Accompanied by dominant-tonic movement in the bass, first in C and then in B♭, and by chord clusters above, these melodies are developed simultaneously at the phrase level through the next twenty beats (ex. 5.3). The varied statements use transposition, alteration of rhythmic values, syncopated entrances, elision, register changes, fragmentation, and melodic elaboration to modify the two themes. All these techniques are applied to the *Grundgestalt* (a and b in ex. 5.3) presented in the opening of this section. The passage is organically conceived, as is typical of developing variation. The polyphony presents an interplay between two voices whose character and content are dependent upon elaboration of two original motives.

Another manifestation of this technique at a much larger structural level can be found in what J. Peter Burkholder terms "cumulative form,"

EXAMPLE 5.3. Ives, *Concord Sonata*, second edition (1947), "Emerson," p. 3.

which Ives uses in over twenty movements.[59] According to Burkholder, this is a thematic form in which the theme, most commonly an existing tune, appears in its full form only at the end of the movement. The theme often has an accompaniment and an obbligato countermelody that is paraphrased from the same or another tune. The final statement is preceded by "fragments and paraphrases of both the theme and the countermelody, often including a statement of the complete countermelody and harmonization without the theme."[60] These fragments, observes Evan Rothstein, develop gradually into a recognizable whole.[61] The cumulative effect, argues Burkholder, enables Ives to use folk tunes, marches, hymns, and other melodies that otherwise would not be easily adaptable to extended development of the type normally found in art music. The resulting form is one that moves from "complexity to clarification."[62]

Within cumulative form, Ives reaffirms a traditional technique, but he does so by reversing its fundamental process. Schoenberg's basic premise of developing variation stipulates that principal themes grow out of a basic idea, whereas with Ives they grow into it, culminating in an unambiguous, resolute presentation of the original melody. Though they may be the reverse of each other, both processes are clearly related. As Rothstein points out, it is Ives's use of the motive as structurally significant and his "concern for and particular approach to achieving unity and structural integrity . . . which links Ives to a larger musical tradition," a tradition in which developing variation is a basic premise.[63]

Ives did not develop this new form in a vacuum. As Burkholder points out, cumulative form, like sonata form, requires the presentation, development, and resolution of a musical idea.[64] It varies, develops, fragments, recombines, and transposes primary and secondary themes. However, instead of a traditional approach in which one digresses from ideas presented in an exposition and moves toward a resolution, Ives constructs the material in a way that leads to a culminating statement, creating one large structural crescendo. By doing so, Ives has taken something from his tradition, modified it, and preserved those parts which he finds useful. Though he does not apply as much rigor to his methods as Schoenberg did, he nevertheless does show a commitment to an Austro-Germanic tradition of music based on developing themes and motives.

The need that the two composers share, the inner compulsion alluded to earlier in this essay, is the need to express a subconscious image as accurately as possible without the confinements of tradition, technical limitations, or aesthetic tastes. Schoenberg and Ives independently renounced the musical establishment by exploring new compositional techniques that were outgrowths of their shared musical tradition. They addressed the need to find an appropriate mode of expression while holding on to certain inherited principles. Ives would have sympathized with Schoenberg's distaste for "artists who want to 'go back to a period,' who try to obey the laws of an obsolete aesthetic or of a novel one, who enjoy themselves in eclecticism or in the imitation of a style, [who] alienate themselves from nature."[65]

In pursuing this need, Schoenberg and Ives followed unyielding paths. As Middleton has suggested, each wrote music that was sometimes unidiomatic while remaining true to their desire to translate as closely as possible the idea from its subconscious roots.[66] Ives questioned whether a song must be sung,[67] whereas Schoenberg wrote a song, "Herzgewächse," Op. 20 (1911), whose demanding range makes it barely singable. In the second movement of the *Concord Sonata* ("Hawthorne"), Ives finds a pianist's ten fingers inadequate to recreate his idea, so he instructs the pianist to use a board fourteen and three-quarters inches long to play clusters. In these examples, Schoenberg and Ives expected the performers to compensate for the demands of the musical idea, not vice versa.

Many contemporaries of Ives and Schoenberg taxed the limits of instruments and performers as well. One thinks of the bassoon solo that opens Stravinsky's *Rite of Spring* (1913) or of Ravel's conscious effort to compose a piano work of transcendent virtuosity in *Gaspard de la nuit* (1908). However, there is a difference between writing music that is challenging technically and that which is difficult because it is unidiomatic. With the latter, challenge stems from the disregard for the physical limitations of the instrument; instead the composer recreates an inspiration as closely as possible.

Such an approach caused both composers trouble. Peter Yates recounts his being with Schoenberg when the composer received his Violin Concerto, Op. 36 (1936), back from Jascha Heifetz. The famous violinist commented that the piece was unplayable. According to Yates, Schoenberg said "Heifetz cannot play it, nobody can play it," speaking "as if he were proud of having written a piece of absolute impracticality."[68] Ives had received similar complaints as well. In the margin of a manuscript page of his Third Violin Sonata, Ives wrote: "This Sonata #3 is not much good. It was finished just after a famous German Virtuoso violinist . . . [Franz] M[ilcke] . . . by name, was here in Redding to play Oct 1914 the 1st Sonata. . . . no resemblance to music he said (politely). . . . So many similar complaints about & before that time . . . that I began to think there must be something wrong with me to like this & get so much fun *[out]* of it, etc. so I tried to *[make]* a nice piece for the nice ladies.—Har 'tis—N[o] G[ood]."[69] Perhaps it is no surprise that Ives admired Beethoven in part for his lack of idiomatic writing.[70]

In satisfying their expressive needs before addressing physical limitations, both composers made conscious choices. They did not write for virtuosi but for the sake of expressing the intuitive idea that lay at the roots of their inspiration.[71] Both expected listeners as well as performers to work hard to understand extreme dissonances and complex textures. Whether it was Schoenberg's critics or Ives's "aunts," both composers expected their audiences to be attentive and to think; they did not want to be limited by listeners' imaginations. In this regard, contrary to Middleton, they did write for the same audience, making the same demands on their audiences as did many of their contemporaries.[72]

Around 1909, when Schoenberg was struggling with a new language free of tonal constraints, he explored intensely the nature of his expressive need. In an undated letter to Busoni in which he discusses his recently completed set of piano pieces (Op. 11, 1909), he reflects:

> It will maybe take a long time yet before I can write the
> music I feel urged to, of which I have had an inkling for
> several years but which, for the time being, I cannot
> express . . .
> I strive for: complete freedom from all forms
> from all symbols
> of cohesion and
> of logic.
> > Thus:
> away with "motivic working out[.]"
> Away with harmony as
> cement or brick of an edifice.
> Harmony is *expression*
> and nothing else.
> > Then:
> Away with Pathos!
> Away with protracted ten-ton scores, from erected or
> constructed towers, rock and other massive claptrap.
> My music must be
> *brief.*
> Concise! In two words: not built, but *expressed!*
> And the results I wish for:
> no stylized and sterile protractedness.
> People are not like that:
> it is *impossible* to have only *one* sensation at a time.
> One has *thousands* simultaneously. And these thousands can
> be added together no better than an apple and a pear can be
> added together. They go their own ways.
> And this variety, this multifariousness, this *illogicality* which
> our senses demonstrate, the illogicality presented by their
> interactions, set forth by some mounting rush of blood, by
> some reaction of the senses or of the nervous system, this I
> should like to have in my music.
> It must express our sensations in the way our sensations
> really are, bringing us in contact with our *subconscious*, no
> cocoon made up of sensation and "applied logic."[73]

In the second and third decades of the twentieth century, Schoenberg strove to find an ideal manner of expression. He tried concise forms, as in his *Sechs Klavierstücke*, Op. 19 (1911); he continued in a vein similar to Op. 11 in *Erwartung*, Op. 17 (1909); and he explored a new expressivity with *Sprechstimme*. The appeals in his letter to the subconscious, the identification of simultaneous sensations, the multifariousness, the apparent illogicality, and an ideal expression of variety are strikingly similar to the style of music Ives was writing around 1910 and which is best exemplified in such works as the *Concord Sonata* and the Fourth Symphony.[74] It strengthens even further the contention that Ives and Schoenberg were exploring similar theses during a time of significant change in music history. Perhaps this was part of the "problem of how to preserve one's self-esteem" that Ives solved and Schoenberg so admired. It suggests that Ives may have been physically isolated from the contemporary musical debate, but aesthetically he was in the thick of it.

The final link between Schoenberg and Ives lies in their mutual appeal to an eternal spirit of constant, ongoing change as a justification of their music. As with dualism, the two composers were not singularly allured by this thought; the significance lies in their shared, simultaneous use of it as a basic tenet of their respective styles. Schoenberg's friend Kandinsky depicts this ongoing change well in *Über das Geistige in der Kunst (Concerning the Spiritual in Art)* with a description of a floating triangle, representing the life of the spirit, in which the small, upper portion represents the innovative and the lower half the status quo. In Kandinsky's representation the triangle ascends through time, the upper part filling the lower. What was once considered innovative becomes the accepted mode of expression; the "prophets" of a bygone era become understood and appreciated by future generations as their innovations are replaced by new discoveries.[75] Emerson, whose beliefs Ives revered, represented this ongoing situation through a circle which, "from a ring imperceptibly small, rushes on all sides outward to new and larger circles, and that without end." In this transient state, every "ultimate fact" becomes only the "first of a new series."[76] This process is one of continuous "becoming."

Both Schoenberg and Ives accepted this fluid state through their shared belief in the transience of musical expression. In practice, both did not seek *the* solution, but *a* solution, despite Schoenberg's occasional insistence in his prose to the contrary. Ives expressed this through the transcendental state of "ever-becoming," whereas Schoenberg professed it through a style that was not constrained by a compositional technique that he himself devised (composing with twelve tones). Neither was enslaved by preestablished, preconceived systems; they always permitted other forms of expression that responded to particular musical ideas.

Schoenberg, for example, composed works between 1930 and 1950 that were either tonal, atonal, or twelve-tone; he disavowed the principle of a single method of composition. The diverse styles that constitute Ives's musical idiom adhere to the same ideal. Both composers acknowledged that the only constant in existence—in all art—is change. In the "Epilogue" to *Essays Before a Sonata*, Ives speaks at length about the "law of perpetual change . . . ever going on in ourselves, in nature, in all life."[77] Schoenberg's trust in the ability of intuition to lead him into new realms, such as into his development of twelve-tone composition, resonates with Ives's statement.[78]

The belief in constant change, described by Ives and Schoenberg in nineteenth-century terms as a constant, ongoing progress that provides the basis for a better, improving musical world, supplied both with sustenance to continue. Indeed, it is through historical precedence that both addressed the changing tastes of generations and the eventual appreciation of misunderstood masters from the past. Schoenberg declares that "[t]he laws [of beauty] native to the genius . . . are the laws of future generations."[79] Ives suggests that future generations might sing in quarter tones, using a standard system with which he, and his father before him, had merely experimented.[80] Both composers believed that future generations were destined to understand them.

Ives and Schoenberg found tonal grammar inadequate for expressing most, though not all, of their ideas. They searched for the ideal musical language, championing an aesthetic that accepted absolutes as temporary solutions. Their works and their words reveal this struggle between stability and fluidity, structure and freedom, all of which were challenges faced anew by composers at the turn of the century. Many writings on Ives have focused on his Yankee individualism, depicting him as a lone pioneer on the musical frontier of the New World. Though the uniqueness of his music and the innovation that he pursued in near isolation cannot be ignored, we also cannot forget that he was reared in a tradition, and that he dealt with issues that concerned his turn-of-the-century colleagues as well. Like Schoenberg, Ives was a person of his times.

:6:

Ives and Berg: "Normative" Procedures and Post-Tonal Alternatives

PHILIP LAMBERT

Prior to Schoenberg's invention of the twelve-tone method, composers of atonal music were compelled to examine the need for an established and systematically defined set of pitch relations. In the words of George Perle, the pitch language that atonal composers were leaving behind was one of "normative" procedures—principles and relations that operate in the same basic form in various musical contexts. Composers were asking whether new norms were necessary and whether satisfactory musical coherence could arise from "reflexive" procedures, that is, principles and relations that operate solely within the context of an individual composition.[1] The variety of responses to these questions during the years that saw the development and adoption of the twelve-tone method is testimony to the difficulty of redefining what is "normative" and to the considerable freedom these reflexive procedures afforded. For Schoenberg and his circle, a basic need emerged for a new normative procedure; the twelve-tone method provided their solution.

Leonard Bernstein characterized Ives's *Unanswered Question* as a musical portrayal of the post-tonal quandary, interpreting one sense of the "question" as "Whither music in our century?"[2] Indeed, this is a question that Ives asks from several philosophical perspectives and that inspires diverse musical responses. The latter range from full-blown adoptions of the normative tonal system that his contemporaries were trying to abandon, to earnest attempts at developing normative procedures that could replace the tonal ones, to works based on reflexive procedures that would seem to deny any basic need for pre-compositional norms. As Robert P. Morgan points out, Ives was acutely aware of the ramifications of these various choices and of the importance of keeping options available.[3] In Ives's words, "Why tonality as such should be thrown out for good, I can't see. Why it should be always present, I can't see. It depends, it seems to me, a good deal—as clothes depend on the thermometer—on what one is trying to do, and on the state of mind, the time of day or other accidents of life."[4]

It is the pursuit of new normative procedures, within this diversity of musical responses, that offers a most revealing glimpse into Ives's approach to the problem. His ideas are spelled out in a distinctive series of sketches and exercises, comprising a separate and smaller category within his oeuvre, that, according to the composer, "show how one's mind works."[5] These explorations of normative structure concentrate on procedures that have the potential to serve as new norms for composition, ranging from numerical patterns, which might determine rhythmic relationships or intervallic distances, to logically conceived schemes for musical form.[6] J. Peter Burkholder observes that Ives rejected the view that the tonal system was more natural or desirable than any other logical system that one might develop; apparently, any newly conceived alternatives could readily step in as replacements.[7]

The music of Schoenberg and Webern during the atonal, pre-twelve-tone period is concerned largely with internal processes of self-reference and reflexivity that would eventually be systematized in the twelve-tone method. Although Berg, of course, adopted the same approach in some of his music from this period, it is also Berg, among the composers of the Second Viennese School, who most strongly shares Ives's interest in exploring patterns, systems, and processes that might substitute for the normative procedures of tonal music.[8] Douglas Jarman characterizes these elements of Berg's work as "procedures which promote a feeling of directed movement and of harmonic continuity."[9] Perle similarly emphasizes the normative aspects of such materials.[10] Later, when Berg embraced the twelve-tone method, it was his continuing interest in these types of strategies that helped give his twelve-tone music its unique character.

A comparison of Ives's and Berg's approaches to post-tonal composition must extend deeper than this similarity of interest in new potentially normative procedures to consider the many resemblances between the procedures themselves—the actual compositional solutions to the basic challenges.[11] Though Ives's composing life contrasts sharply with Berg's or with that of many European contemporaries because of the fundamental differences in lifestyle and divergences between European and American cultures, there are enough relevant points of similarity to make such musical comparisons seem only natural. Both composers were products of musical educations structured along standard Germanic lines and were thoroughly familiar with Western musical traditions.[12] The materials and procedures of these traditions that atonal composers wished to renounce were at the same time the primary sources for new normative ideas. Any alternatives to tonality would start with the earlier principles and redefine their contexts, recasting them in new roles and with new meanings.

The noteworthy differences between Berg and Ives are those between a professional composer—a musician who makes his living by writing music—and a composer who does not depend on his craft as a source of livelihood. A work by Berg, for example, is carefully crafted and refined into a final, artistically viable form that may be presentable to the public as a "work of art." But some works of Ives are not intended for this purpose. Burkholder makes a valuable distinction between "concert" works composed for purposes of public presentation and "experimental" works written as a means of private exploration.[13] Many of Ives's "experimental" works are not at all refined or artistically complete; they may not have been subjected to revision and reflective scrutiny, and they may have malleable forms. The contrasts between the music of Ives and Berg are most acute when one views aspects of large-scale structure: Berg's work is by nature concerned with structural cohesion on several levels, whereas Ives's experimentation may or may not encompass large-scale concerns. Yet the distinction between Berg's art and Ives's experimentation does not hold true in every respect. It is possible to observe a spirit of exploration and experimentation, of traveling in uncharted waters, in much of the European atonal repertoire. Even while maintaining high artistic standards, composers searching for alternative principles of organization often employed untested, or at least non-standardized, compositional procedures. And Ives eventually encouraged the publication and dissemination of many of his experimental efforts, placing them before the public alongside works that he claimed to have endowed with higher artistic substance.

A survey of new normative procedures in music of Ives and Berg is best prefaced by an overview of materials and techniques that were not new to atonal music or unique to these composers but that illustrate similarities in their basic approaches to composition. The simplest tools of normative reference are those borrowed from tonality, as in Berg's early works especially and throughout Ives's music. A common borrowing, for example, is a bass line moving by fifths to provide a skeleton on which various chord types may be placed. Any references to tonality occur primarily because of this bass and not necessarily in the projected chords, which appear to "distort" the tonal implications. In Berg's song "Dem Schmerz sein Recht," Op. 2, No. 1 (1909–10), one of the last of his pre-atonal works, a D tonal center that has prevailed throughout mm.

1–10 gives way to the succession of fifth-related bass notes C♯ (m. 11), F♯ (m. 11), B (m. 12), and E (m. 12) circled in example 6.1. An anticipated continuation to A and a return to D are interrupted by a separate fifths sequence involving the bass notes E♭ (m. 13), G♯ (m. 13), and C♯ (m. 14), and by a chromatic descent from the C♯ in m. 14 to the G stated in mm. 16 and 17. The note A, the long-awaited continuation of the previous fifths sequence, arrives in m. 18, and then a chromatic line ascends within m. 18 to reestablish D in m. 19. (This is followed by a stabilization on G, continuing the fifths sequence one note further, in mm. 20–22.)

These bass notes support chord types in Berg's accompaniment that work to deny inherent tonal implications. The arpeggiated chord in m. 11, for example, presents five notes of a whole-tone collection, the A in the voice adding the sixth note to complete the collection. With the change of bass in the second half of m. 11, the piano states notes that are absent from the preceding chord; that is, the four new notes (F♯, E, B♭, D) constitute a subset of the complementary whole-tone collection. This shift from one whole-tone collection to the other creates a sense of forward harmonic movement, a technique favored by composers of the period, including Debussy and Scriabin as well as Berg and Ives. The sonorities in m. 12, which occur over the next two notes in the bass sequence, are half-diminished seventh-chords with some embellishing tones. As the passage becomes more extensively chromaticized in the ensuing measures, tonal references withdraw further into the shadows, though ultimately the song concludes as it began, on a D-minor triad.

Ives's references to normative harmonic progressions include analogous harmonic distortions. The excerpt from the *Concord Sonata* (published 1920) in example 6.2 divides into four parts articulated by texture changes. Part 1 extends from the interplay of triads in system 1 through the climactic pronouncement of the motive from Beethoven's Fifth Symphony and the chord labeled "B" in system 2. Part 2 is the more diverse, somewhat contrapuntal texture extending up to chord C in system 3. Part 3 is comprised of the motivic chord repetitions leading up to the key change in system 4. Part 4 begins at the end of system 4, with a texture of melody with accompaniment that continues for some time thereafter. A bass progression in fifths emerges from emphasized notes in each part, as circled in example 6.2: C in part 1; F at the beginning and end of part 2, supporting dominant harmonies with respect to the B♭-major tonality of this part; then B♭ in part 3, and finally E♭ in part 4.

Whereas Berg's distortions result from an avoidance of the kinds of chords that might be expected within a progression by fifths, Ives's distortions are comprised of familiar chords with added chromatic notes, forming chord types that appear frequently in his harmonic vocabulary.[14] The typical chord includes a triad and at least one additional note a half-

EXAMPLE 6.1. Berg, "Dem Schmerz sein Recht," Op. 2, No. 1, mm. 10–20.

Alban Berg, Songs for voice and piano, Op. 2.
© 1928 by Robert Lienau, Berlin.

step removed from one of the tones of the triad; in example 6.2, such sonorities are labeled as chords A (C-minor triad plus F♯), B (F-major triad plus C♯), and D (B♭-major triad plus G♭). This kind of chromatic distortion is pervasive in part 3 of the excerpt, as high-register triads float above distorting tones in the middle register. Here and in other works, the chromatic pitches are often registrally and rhythmically separated from the triad, producing a kind of echo effect; Ives describes the dis-

EXAMPLE 6.2. Ives, *Concord Sonata*, "The Alcotts," pp. 54–55.

torting tones in chords A and B as "a kind of overtone echoes over the 'Orchard House' elms."[15]

The distortion of familiar practices is also evident in a basic approach to musical style shared by Ives and Berg. For both composers, style is a flexible compositional element, as subject to variation and development as is a motive or a theme. In this respect, both composers reveal more of a spiritual kinship with Mahler than they do a strong connection with their closer contemporaries Schoenberg and Webern.[16] In Ives's music, stylistic change usually results in stark contrasts between divergent idioms and ideas.[17] This is the case, for instance, when sounds borrowed from common-practice tonality are juxtaposed with dissonant, non-tonal ones; the four movements of the Fourth Symphony, to cite one of many examples, present sounds from various points in the tonal-atonal continuum, from functional tonality (third movement) to non-functional tonal centricity (fourth movement) to general avoidance of tonal vestiges (second movement). Uses of tonality in Berg's music are more likely to include "impurities" that may bring the music slightly closer to atonality, though without masking the contrasting effect. Jarman finds that Berg was particularly attracted to tonality as a counterbalance to twelve-tone writing, mentioning especially Berg's use of Wedekind's "Lautenlied" in act 3 of *Lulu* and the various appearances of Bach's chorale setting in the Violin Concerto.[18]

Heterogeneity results not just from specific tonal allusions but also from uses of idiomatic features of a certain style. The existing style thereby provides a normative compositional framework, as the music is composed not to adapt older ideas into different styles but to reflect and comment on the nature of those ideas. The "Ragtime" in Stravinsky's *L'histoire du soldat*, for example, is not a work of ragtime but a reflection on the rhythms and gestures of that style. Ives's stylistic evocations include ragtime (as in the First Piano Sonata) as well as parlor songs and religious music. In *Wozzeck*, Berg evokes ragtime (in act 3, scene 3: the music for on-stage piano), in addition to styles that are more indigenous to his milieu such as the "Hunting Song" (act 1, scene 2) and "Ländler" (act 2, scene 4).[19]

Ives's most frequent target is the march. In such works as *Country Band March, Overture and March 1776, The Fourth of July, Putnam's Camp* from *Three Places in New England,* and the second movement of the Fourth Symphony, he offers extensive commentary on the march conventions that were familiar to him largely through his early association with his father's activities as a leader of community bands.[20] The march provides Ives not only a familiar stylistic model but also an embodiment of the events and images from American life that are being recalled. Among Berg's forays into march writing are the third of the Three Pieces for Orchestra, Op. 6, and the Military March in *Wozzeck* (act 1, scene 3). Perle calls the former "an ideal, if unintentional" reflection on the beginnings of the First World War, whereas the march in *Wozzeck* heralds an ominous dramatic event: the initial entry of the Drum Major into the plot.[21] In the marches of both composers the standard rhythms, melodic figures, and styles are variously distorted, fragmented, and combined in unorthodox ways. Perle's description of Berg's march from Op. 6 could apply equally to many of Ives's creations: "Fragmentary rhythmic and melodic figures typical of an orthodox military march repeatedly coalesce into polyphonic episodes of incredible density that surge to frenzied climaxes, then fall apart. It is not a march, but music *about* a march, or rather about *the* march."[22]

There are also instances where a convention of form or style is used not for commentary and distortion but as a legitimate source of continuity and cohesion, refashioned into a new pitch language. Such is the case with the techniques and formal conventions of counterpoint, reflecting a heightened interest by Berg and Ives in strictly organized compositional plans, or structural models. For Ives, the techniques of counterpoint reached back to his earliest musical training and his first experiences with the kinds of planning and calculation that pervade his experimentation; it was therefore natural to reuse and exploit these devices as his ideas about musical structure advanced.[23] Counterpoint played a similarly prominent role in the music of Berg and other Europeans. Of course, as Perle points out, the art of counterpoint was much simplified in a non-tonal language, in the absence of traditional restrictions on simultaneity and progression.[24]

Exploitations of structural models based on canonic techniques frequently appear in brief passages of works with diverse textures. For example, Berg concludes the orchestral song "Sahst du nach dem Gewitterregen" Op. 4, No. 2 with a canon between voice and cello (mm. 8–11). He also uses canon in one presentation of the chorale melody in the Violin Concerto (second movement, mm. 184–90). Ives, similarly, interjects a canonic central section (mm. 16–20) in the predominantly homophonic *Psalm 67*. Both composers also use canonic techniques over larger spans. Berg's double canon in the third movement of the *Lyric Suite* (mm. 30–38) calls to mind the double canon in Ives's *Psalm 54* (mm. 14–36).[25] Ives's most expansive canonic treatments are in the finale of the Trio (between violin and cello, mm. 87–125) and in the center of the second movement of the Second String Quartet (all instruments, mm. 42–73).

Structural models based on fugue are similarly prevalent. Berg realizes fugal models twice in *Wozzeck* (act 2, scene 2; act 3, scene 1), and Ives's fugal treatments begin with early experiments in "four-key fugues" and extend to his mature writing. The fugal techniques of both composers are similarly focused on multiple subjects and extensive episodic development. The fugal section of act 2, scene 2 of *Wozzeck*, for example, resembles the beginning of a large triple fugue, with separate expositions for each of the three subjects and episodes in which the subjects are developed. Ives's most extensive fugal treatment is *Tone Roads No. 1*, which begins with an exposition of two subjects and continues with development of basic motives and, later, a presentation of a variant form of the second subject.[26] In both works, subjects are presented at various transposition levels and transformed by mirror inversion. Both works also contain methodical manipulations of rhythm: in the Berg, a rhythmic acceleration of the second subject (mm. 302–6), in the Ives a use of rhythmic patterns that do not coincide with concurrent pitch patterns (mm. 13–22), recalling the isorhythmic practice of fourteenth- and early fifteenth-century music.

The concept of *structural model* has broad importance in music of Ives and Berg. Whether referring to the conventional strictures of contrapuntal devices or to the abstract prescriptions of a contrived plan, the idea became crucial to their post-tonal thinking. Large-scale models, for example, may dictate an overall plan based on logical orderings of sections or devices, or on a schematic grouping of related structures; *Wozzeck*, for example, implements both conventional prototypes and contrived designs.[27] The model of theme and variations provides a common tradition-inspired source of overall cohesion. The variations in the first movement of Berg's Chamber Concerto are arranged according to the manner in which the main theme is transformed: the first variation reiterates the pitch ordering of the theme, and this is followed by a pitch retrograde in variation 2, inversion in variation 3, retrograde inversion in variation 4, and a restatement of the original pitches in the final variation.[28] Ives's most expansive adaptation of a variation form is *In Re Con Moto Et Al*, where the subject of variation is a palindromic series of prime numbers: 2–3–5–7–11–7–5–3–2. The series is variously expressed by patterns of meter changes, phrase lengths, and rhythmic groupings; sectional beginnings are demarcated by distinctive chord structures.[29]

Another common basis of large-scale form is a model based on symmetrical ordering: the second half of a two-part design restates ideas from the first half in reverse order. When the reordering is applied to entire sections of music, the result can be an arch form, as in Ives's *Calcium Light Night* and other works.[30] Berg's arch forms are basic ABA structures, although the ABA arch in his song Op. 2, No. 1 is enriched by symmetrical relationships between melodic details, as Robert P. Morgan has observed.[31] More common with both composers, however, is a realization of the symmetrical model based not on a reordering of sections but on a reversal of orderings of pitches—a note-to-note palindrome. Morgan describes passages from the *Lyric Suite*, *Lulu*, and *Der Wein* where palindromic procedures are rigidly applied.[32] The techniques in these works parallel those of Ives's brief scherzo *All the Way Around and Back*, where a pitch palindrome depicts the journey of a base-runner in a baseball game from first to third base and back during a foul ball, and the song "Soliloquy," whose piano accompaniment is completely palindromic (excluding the introduction).[33]

The ideal of normative structure enjoys easy realization in these symmetrical models, as it does in the tonal and contrapuntal structural models. Given their history and extensive prior usage, these models provide familiar, normative frameworks within which novel ideas may be explored. More crucial to the development of a "new" music, however, is the adoption of normative principles that do not derive their status as such primarily from historical precedent. The resulting models may start with a familiar musical principle but may then expand its importance, in ways that obscure other conventional features while promoting any potential for a new kind of normalcy. A model may also derive non-conventional normative ideas solely from numerical patterns or spatial configurations, realized in melodic, harmonic, or rhythmic dimensions.

Structural models based on *interval cycles* represent Ives's and Berg's most extensive pursuits of new normative procedures.[34] An interval cycle is a repetition of a certain interval to generate a series of notes that is "cyclic" in that it returns to its starting note. For example, a cycle of half steps generates a chromatic scale before returning to its starting note; a cycle of whole steps similarly generates a whole-tone scale. For convenience in labeling interval cycles, we may refer to intervals by the number of half steps they contain.[35] The number of different notes in a cycle before it returns to its starting point varies from two for an interval-6 cycle (that is, a cycle of intervals of six half steps) to three for cycles of intervals 4 or 8, four for cycles of intervals 3 or 9, six for cycles of intervals 2 or 10, and twelve for cycles of intervals 1, 5, 7, or 11.

Cycles are at least latent and at times overt in tonal music. They become useful resources in post-tonal music when their roles and contexts are redefined. A typical objective in using the cycles is the creation of a new pitch language analogous to that provided by a diatonic scale— a collection of notes that can be presented in any scalar, reordered, or fragmented form. The ability of a cycle to achieve this goal varies, with usages generally falling into two categories. In one category are the cycles that generate all twelve notes: intervals 1, 5, 7, and 11 (the half step, perfect fourth, perfect fifth, and major seventh). A distinctive compositional language drawn from one of these cycles in its complete form is an impossibility, since no combination of notes would be excluded from membership in such a language. Any grouping of notes would be possible, and a given grouping could not be unequivocally traced to a particular cycle. Composers interested in using such cycles have typically used only a portion of the cycle while retaining the original ordering.[36] This usage thereby negates original "cyclic" features. The second category of cycles is comprised of those that generate fewer than twelve notes. These can, in principle, define a distinctive language allowing any combination of adjacent and non-adjacent scale tones. The possibilities are again limited, however, since cycles of two, three, or four notes are too small to be of extensive practical use. Only the "whole-tone" (interval-2 or -10) cycle, with six members, is of sufficient size to provide a distinctive and sufficiently rich harmonic vocabulary.

A technique common to the whole-tone writing of Ives and Berg is centered on an interplay between the two complementary whole-tone collections. The notes in these collections are C–D–E–F♯–G♯–A♯ and C♯–D♯–F–G–A–B, also known as the "even" and "odd" collections, respectively.[37] The vocal line of Ives's song "The Cage" (1906) provides a simple example of the interplay. As indicated above the vocal line in example 6.3, a five-part division of the melody reveals an alternating whole-tone derivational pattern starting with notes from the even collection in phrase 1, switching to odd in phrase 2, returning to even in phrase 3, odd in phrase 4 (except for the E), and even in phrase 5. This five-part division is supported by the phrasing of the text except where the setting of phrase 2 extends past the semicolon to end the phrase, appropriately, on the word "stopped." Only the middle phrase presents a complete whole-tone collection; phrases 1, 2, and 5 state five-note whole-tone subsets, and phrase 4 has the five-note subset plus the E.

An analogous even-odd interplay occurs in Berg's early song "Nacht" (1905–8). Within the accompaniment in the first five measures, the alternation begins with a saturation of notes from the even collection in mm. 1–3, then switches to the odd collection in m. 4, returns to even in the first half of m. 5, and concludes with odd in the second half of m. 5 (ex. 6.4). The even collection is first articulated in an arpeggiation that brings out the two augmented triads it contains: in m. 1, the augmented triad E–G♯–B♯ (plus an F♯ "passing tone") in the left hand alternates with the augmented triad F♯–B♭–D in the right hand. Then, in m. 2, these two triads are stated together: E–G♯–B♯ (right hand) is paired with F♯ and A♯ from the other triad (left hand), followed by an exchange, so that F♯–A♯–D (right hand) is paired with E–G♯–B♯ (left hand). These pairings are then repeated in eighth notes throughout the measure. Measure 3 repeats m. 1, and m. 4 repeats m. 2 a half step higher, resulting in the other (odd) whole-tone collection. The passage concludes in m. 5 with a final use of triad pairings in the first half of the measure (from the even collection) and the beginnings of a new texture taken from the odd collection in the second half of the measure.[38]

Ives uses augmented triads and alternating whole-tone collections similarly in his song "Mists" (1910) (ex. 6.5). Measure 2 of the song begins with notes from the odd collection, in augmented-triad pairings quite like Berg's, and m. 3 begins as an upward half-step transposition of the previous measure—thus, a statement of triad pairings from the even collection—reverting to the odd collection on the fourth beat. This process is repeated in mm. 4 and 5, with a slight rhythmic change in the

EXAMPLE 6.3. Ives, "The Cage."

latter. In both "Nacht" and "Mists," the notes of the vocal lines are members of the underlying collections; Berg's melody generally reflects the whole-tone character of the accompaniment, whereas Ives's actually appears remarkably diatonic, though this feature is obscured in the context of the accompaniment.[39]

Usages of the twelve-note cycles (intervals 1, 5, 7, and 11) by early post-tonal composers include many examples of chromatic voice leading and complete unfoldings of the chromatic scale. In Berg's early song excerpted in example 6.1, chromatic movement pervades the bass in the interruption of the fifths sequence (mm. 13–17), and appears intermittently

EXAMPLE 6.4. Berg, "Nacht," mm. 1–5.

in the upper voices. The conclusion of the passage in mm. 18–19, where the earlier bass fifths sequence is resumed, connects the final A and D in the bass with a chromatic ascent that is mirrored by a chromatic descent in the upper piano and vocal lines.[40] Similar unfoldings can be found in Ives, though his interests often sway toward full chromatic completion, as first occurs in early experiments with octave displacements of chromatic scale tones.[41] Among mature works, complete unfoldings appear in *Study No. 5*, which employs octave displacements, and *Study No. 20*, where a single registral shift forges a connection between beginning and ending notes four octaves apart.[42] The latter passage calls to mind a bass chromatic unfolding at the end of the exposition of Berg's Piano Sonata Op. 1 (mm. 49–54).

EXAMPLE 6.5. Ives, "Mists," mm. 2–5.

The interval-5 and -7 cycles are familiar as generators of quartal and quintal harmony. Archibald points out the prominence of chords in fourths at climactic moments in Berg's Op. 1.[43] The most overt use of quartal structures in *Wozzeck* occurs during Marie's "Cradle Song" in act 1, scene 3 (mm. 378–79). Among Ives's usages, the accompaniment to the song "The Cage" (ex. 6.3) is the most extensive. The quartal chords labeled A through F and the chord labeled G in the piano introduction establish a pattern that is transposed and projected throughout the rest of the piece. First, chords A–G are transposed up a perfect fourth to derive the first seven chords accompanying the voice (numbered 1–7 in ex. 6.3). Thus the interval of transposition connecting the introduction with chords 1–7 is the same as the basic interval comprising most of the individual chords that are being transposed. Then, in the center of the song, chords A, B, C, and E from the introduction are transposed up a minor third (plus an octave) to produce chords 8, 10, 13, and 18; chord 15 is a minor-third transposition of chord D, but from top to bottom. The final three chords (20–22) return to the original perfect-fourth transposition level. The chords not accounted for in these transformations include half-step transpositions from chord 8 to chord 9 and from chord 10 to chords 11 and 12 and the quintal chords numbered 16 and 17, echoing the structure of chord 15. Only chord 19 relates to the cyclic (whole-tone) source for the vocal line; its seven notes in the treble staff, plus the low A, present the complete odd whole-tone collection, while D–F♯–C in the bass staff presents half of the even collection.

A cyclic model often forms the basis for a pattern of mirrored voice-leading, a *wedge*. In this spatially defined model, two concurrent cycles gradually come together or grow apart; the wedge contracts or expands. Perle, who describes the technique as "voice leading through symmetrical movement," cites its ability to "provide the effect of 'normal' harmonic continuity" in atonal music.[44] Jarman notes that wedge patterns represent "one of the primary devices for obtaining a sense of directed movement in Berg's early music."[45] A contracting wedge is apparent, for example, at the conclusion of the fifths sequence in mm. 18 and 19 of example 6.1: the chromatic descent D–D♭–C–B–A♯ in the voice (doubled in the upper line of the piano) is mirrored by A–A♯–B–C–C♯–D in the bass. Other instances of wedges in the music of Berg include the accompaniment to the song "Warm die Lüfte," Op. 2, No. 4 (mm. 12–15) and the opening of the second movement of the String Quartet Op. 3, described by Robert Bruce Archibald as a "*tour de force* of wedges."[46]

The wedge model was a consistent preoccupation of Ives.[47] His early sketches include wedges of triad sequences and the oft-cited evocation of a football formation in *A Yale-Princeton Football Game*.[48] In the choral *Psalm 24*, successive verses exhibit wedges based on gradually larger intervals, so that the expanding wedge idea within each verse is also projected in the growth of intervallic content from verse to verse.[49] Ives extended the concept to encompass a "cluster" wedge made by saturating the space between the principal wedge voices; often, as in *Psalm 90* (mm. 60–65), the same interval is used both in the outer melodic voices and in the notes filling in the space between them.[50] Ives's most sophisticated applications of the wedge idea appear in a much-used chord series in which successive chords are based on interval cycles of gradually changing size. In the song "On the Antipodes," the chord series appears at the beginning, middle, and end, and influences most of the structure of the accompaniment in passages where the actual series is absent.[51]

Another wedge variation realized by both Ives and Berg distributes the notes of the diverging or converging lines within a single melodic line, as a *compound melody*. The prominent theme from "Seele, wie bist du schöner," the first of Berg's orchestral songs Op. 4 (1912) is a realization of the model shown below the melody in example 6.6a: a chromatic divergence between an upper voice C–D♭–D–E♭–E, highlighted with upward stems, and a lower voice C–B–B♭–A–A♭–G–F♯–F–E, shown by downward stems. The first and last notes are parts of both voices, creating an overall distribution of five upper notes filling in a major third and nine lower notes filling in a minor sixth. Ives chose the same five-plus-nine partitioning (filling in the same melodic intervals) in a compound wedge from his song "Soliloquy" (1907); in example 6.6b the upper wedge voice is F–G♭–G–G♯–A, the lower F–E–D♯–D–D♭–C–B–B♭–A.[52]

In the same family as musical wedges created by lines moving in opposite directions by the same interval are wedges created by lines moving in the same direction but by different intervals. The wedge effect results from the gradually changing distances between the two lines, even though the lines themselves do not literally mirror each other. The result

EXAMPLE 6.6a. Berg, Op. 4, No. 1, viola, mm. 10–15.

EXAMPLE 6.6b. Ives, "Soliloquy," voice, mm. 2–4.

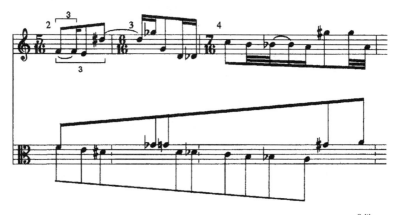

is a simultaneous projection, or *stacking*, of different cycles. Perle has publicized Berg's prototype—or "master array"—for stackings of cycles, which is formed by simultaneously presenting all eleven interval cycles; the prototype finds application in, among other works, act 2 of *Wozzeck*.[53] In Ives's music there are occasional experiments with the same basic idea and one extensive application in the song "Like a Sick Eagle" (ca. 1913). The primary model in the song stacks a whole-tone cycle with a seven-note segment of a half-step cycle (ex. 6.7a). This results in the formation of intervals 4 through 10 as vertical dyads between corresponding notes (these dyads are numbered 1–7 in ex. 6.7a). Much of the song's vocal line joins with the right-hand piano part to project the dyads continually, usually moving adjacently within the model. In the second system of the score, for example (ex. 6.7b), the voice and piano right hand begin with dyad 1,

EXAMPLE 6.7a. Ives, "Like a Sick Eagle," basic model.

whole-tone:	F#	G#	A#	C	D	E	F#
chromatic:	D	D#	E	F	F#	G	Ab

interval:	4	5	6	7	8	9	10
dyad #	1	2	3	4	5	6	7

EXAMPLE 6.7b. Ives, "Like a Sick Eagle," second system of score.

which completes a previous statement of the entire model, move through dyads 4, 3, and 2, and then realize the complete model (bracketed) before starting another descent with dyads 6, 5, and 4 at the end of the system.[54]

Berg uses a stacking of identical cycles as a model for his song "Der Glühende," Op. 2, No. 2 (1909–10) but then varies the model to resemble a stacking of different cycles. The model for the song is based on successive chromatic transpositions of a four-note chord (ex. 6.8a). The model could also be explained as a stacking of descending chromatic lines. With respect to content, chord 7 and any further chords would repeat the contents of earlier ones: chord 7 has the same content as chord 1 (the upper and lower dyads change places), a chord "8" would be identical in content to chord 2, and so on.

Measures 1–9 contain three realizations of some or all of the model (ex. 6.8b). The realizations are faithful to the contents of chords in the model, but they often redistribute the notes to emphasize intervals other than the half-step relations unfolded in the model. First, chords 1–6 are presented in the first three measures, including the non-chord tones that are circled in example 6.8b. There are some brief chromatic lines in the upper voices, but the most prominent intervallic line is the series of perfect

EXAMPLE 6.8a. Berg, "Der Glühende," Op. 2, No. 2, mm. 1–9, basic model.

```
          G#  G   F#  F   E   D#  D
          E   Eb  D   Db  C   B   Bb
          D   C#  C   B   Bb  A   G#
          Bb  A   Ab  G   Gb  F   E
chord #   1   2   3   4   5   6   7   (=1)
```

EXAMPLE 6.8b. Berg, "Der Glühende," Op. 2, No. 2, mm. 1–9.

fourths and fifths in the bass spanning chords 1 through 7; this bass line is comprised of alternate notes from the second and fourth rows of the model. The second realization of the model, in m. 4 through the first beat of m. 7, presents the model in reverse order and is elaborated with more extensive rhythmic activity and added notes (circled). Measures 4, 5, and 6 unfold a sequence (with some non-sequential notes) rising by whole steps from measure to measure. Thus, the pitch structure shifts upward by two places in the model from one measure to the next, again obscuring the model's basic chromaticism. Finally, a third statement of the model (never completed) begins in mm. 7–9, employing still more elaboration techniques. Each of mm. 7 and 8 unfolds a kind of exchange between the two major thirds from within the same chord; these dyads are boxed and connected by lines in example 6.8b (only the notes that directly reflect the model are highlighted). The exchanges have a prolonging effect analogous to prolongations through voice exchange in tonal music.[55]

EXAMPLE 6.9a. Ives, *Study No. 20*, chord from m. 94.

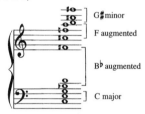

EXAMPLE 6.9b. Ives, "On the Antipodes," upper vocal line, mm. 28–34.

Another category of models encompasses the methods a composer uses for organizing statements of all twelve tones, the *chromatic set.* Whereas models based on interval stackings or wedge patterns may provide spatial designs or multi-voice relationships, models for presenting the chromatic set simply determine a particular ordering of notes that might be realized as a chord or melody, in a variety of musical contexts. In works of Ives and Berg, including music from both before and after Berg's adoption of the twelve-tone method, vertical and horizontal statements of the chromatic set appear within variously organized works, not only those in which a version of the chromatic set plays a central role. The chromatic sets formed by compound wedges (illustrated in ex. 6.6) exemplify the interest of Berg and Ives in using particular models for these types of structures. In addition, Ives's model carries through to other aspects of the same song, which include other melodic relationships as well as a wedge of chords gradually decreasing, then increasing, in size at the center of the accompaniment, which is entirely palindromic.[56] Another area of common ground is the use of cyclic intervallic repetition to construct a chromatic set, explored by Ives in many works but especially in music based on the gradated chord series seen in "On the Antipodes."[57] Among Berg's cyclically organized statements of the chromatic set are the complete stacking of fourths in the orchestral piece Op. 6, No. 2 (mm. 60–67) and the juxtaposition of non-intersecting interval-3 cycles to present all twelve notes in act 3, scene 4 of *Wozzeck* (m. 364).

Example 6.9 illustrates subdivisions of the chromatic set into non-overlapping three-note subsets. In several works, Ives partitions the chromatic set into triads. For example, a chord from *Study No. 20* (ca. 1907–8) is formed by stacking C-major, B♭-augmented, F-augmented, and G♯-

Philip Lambert

EXAMPLE 6.9c. Berg, Op. 4, No. 3, chord from mm. 1 and 25.

F# diminished

Eb major

minor triads (ex. 6.9a). A melodic line from the end of Ives's "On the Antipodes" (1915–23) is constructed not of triads but of the three-note subsets labeled w, x, y, and z in example 6.9b; the latter are equivalent via various combinations of transposition, inversion, and reordering. Specifically, subset z (B♭–D♭–A) is a transposition of w (G♯–B–G), a reordered y (F♯–D–F) is a transposition of x (E–C–E♭), and w and z are equivalent to x and y through inversion.[58] A similar organization of the chromatic set occurs in Berg's music, taken from the beginning and end of the orchestral song "Über die Grenzen des All," Op. 4, No. 3 (ex. 6.9c). The chord is constructed of E♭-major and F♯-diminished triads in the center; trichords at the bottom and top are related by transposition (E–F–B at the top is a transposition up a minor third of C♯–D–A♭, that is, the bottom trichord C♯–A♭–D reordered). The upper trichord (E–F–B) restates the notes of an important chordal motive from earlier in the work ("Seele, wie bist du schöner," Op. 4, No. 1, piano, mm. 1–5; harmonium, mm. 28–38).

When statements of the chromatic set appear not as isolated harmonic events but as objects of transformation, Ives and Berg explore methods that extend beyond those which Schoenberg adopted for his twelve-tone method (transposition, inversion, and retrograde). Their non-Schoenbergian techniques are based on reordering rather than on systematic operations; their basic method entails a subdivision of the chromatic set into smaller segments and then a redistribution of these segments to create a new ordering. The new entity clearly is related musically to the original, but not via transposition, inversion, or retrograde.[59] Of course, Berg's treatment of the chromatic set usually involves rows derived through his adaptation of the twelve-tone method, whereas Ives is concerned simply with thematic development.

The purpose of these segmental reorderings is usually to preserve certain groups of notes while shifting others, all the while continuing to present all twelve tones. The technique is observed by Jarman and Perle, for example, in two rows from the first movement of the Chamber Concerto (1923–25) (ex. 6.10).[60] Segment X in example 6.10a reappears in its origi-

EXAMPLE 6.10a. Berg, *Chamber Concerto*, first movement, first row (English horn, trumpet, horn: mm. 1–5).

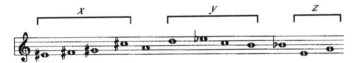

EXAMPLE 6.10b. Berg, *Chamber Concerto*, first movement, third row (bassoon: mm. 4–5).

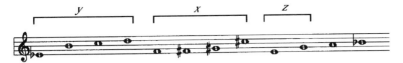

nal ordering in the center of example 6.10b; segment Y travels from the center of example 6.10a to the beginning of example 6.10b, with internal ordering changes; and segment Z moves forward by a few places from example 6.10a to example 6.10b. The latter then concludes with the two notes not included in the tripartite segmentation of example 6.10a; these are the notes A and B♭, representing the composer's monogram.[61]

Ives's *Study No. 5* for piano (ca. 1907–8) is replete with segmental relationships of this type. The work opens with the dense contrapuntal texture shown in example 6.11a, which is transcribed in a chart that displays several statements of the chromatic set and segmental redistributions (ex. 6.11b). All the notes of voice 1 plus the first six notes of voice 2 complete the chromatic set, holding G (underlined in ex. 6.11b) in common. This ordering is then divided into segments (labeled P, Q, R, S in the example) and redistributed in the lower voices. Segments P and Q of voice 1 reappear in reverse order in voice 4, now with the redundant G present in both segments, and segments R and S in voice 2 reappear in reverse order in voice 3, with the redundant G removed. Thus, each hand states a version of the chromatic set that is segmentally related to one stated by the other hand. Furthermore, as a result of the segmental rearrangements, versions of the chromatic set are formed by the four segments appearing in all voices in rough vertical alignment, first (top to bottom) PRSQ and then QSRP.

As *Study No. 5* progresses, Ives continues the manipulation of segments of the chromatic set. The first important theme is derived from

EXAMPLE Example 6.11a. Ives, *Study No. 5*, beats 1–5.

EXAMPLE 6.11b. Ives, *Study No. 5*, segmental relationships in beats 1–5.

voice

```
                    P              Q
1            D   D♯  F   G   G♯  E   A

                    R            S
2            F♯  G   C   D♭  B   B♭

              S         R
3            B   B♭  G♭  C   D♭

                    Q             P
4            G   G♯  E   A   D   E♭  G   F
```

the version of the chromatic set first seen in the right hand at the beginning of the piece. Example 6.11c shows the segmentation that gives rise to the theme: segment V is the first two notes of voice 1; segment X is the first two notes of voice 2, excluding the redundant G; segment W includes only notes in close registral proximity in the center of voice 1, thus excluding the G♯ that is paired with the more proximate D♭ from voice 1 to form segment Y; and segment Z is the last two notes of voice 2 plus the last one of voice 1. The low-register theme that begins three beats later is formed from these segments in the order Z, W, X, Y, and V (ex. 6.11d). This derivation process continues in subsequent measures, so that many of the most important musical ideas in *Study No. 5* can be linked within a chain of segmental relationships.

Another technique of relating and transforming statements of the

EXAMPLE 6.11c. Ives, *Study No. 5*, source segmentation of right hand, beats 1–5.

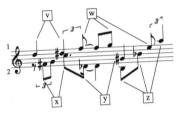

EXAMPLE 6.11d. Ives, *Study No. 5*, first main theme (lowest voice, beats 8–17).

chromatic set in music of Ives and Berg is a repositioning of isolated notes. Berg does this to create a new row in the *Lyric Suite*; as Perle observes, "the fourth and tenth notes of [the primary row] are interchanged to produce the series on which the outer sections of the third movement are based."[62] Ives employs a similar procedure in *Psalm 25*, deriving a series of orderings of the chromatic set that become more different from the initial one as the passage evolves even while maintaining close relationships between consecutive orderings. Other applications of these methods can be seen in Ives's *Study No. 5*, *Study No. 6*, and *Robert Browning Overture*.[63]

Finally, Ives displays some interest in ways of organizing the chromatic set that are more logical or systematic and that form many parallels with methods used by Berg to derive different rows in his twelve-tone music.[64] For example, in one of the "explosion" sections of *The Fourth of July*, Ives says that he "worked out combinations of tones and rhythms very carefully by kind of prescriptions, in the way a chemical compound which makes explosions would be made."[65] Example 6.12 shows selected parts from one measure of an explosion section. The pitch aspect of the "compound" appears to be based on the segmentation of the chromatic set into four trichords as illustrated in the trombone and first violin parts: segments W (G#–D#–A), X (F#–C#–G), Y (E–B–F), and Z (C–A#–D).[66] W is

EXAMPLE 6.12. Ives, *The Fourth of July*, selected parts from m. 119 (concert pitch).

transposed down a whole step to produce X, and X is transposed down a whole step to produce Y.

The three other voices of example 6.12 are systematically related to the four-part segmentation (ex. 6.13). The first twelve notes of the flute part are derived by translating each of W, X, Y, and Z, from the trombone and first violin (bottom to top) into a melodic segment. Berg similarly derives the four trichords known as the "Picture Chords" from a four-part segmentation of the primary row in *Lulu*.[67] Ives's trumpet unfolds the same trichords as the flute but reverses the internal orderings: what was G♯–D♯–A (W) in the flute becomes A–E♭–G♯ in the trumpet, F♯–C♯–G (X) becomes G–C♯–F♯, and so on.[68] In the oboe, each flute trichord is rotated by moving the first note to the end and the second and third notes back toward the beginning: the flute's G♯–D♯–A (W) becomes D♯–A–G♯ in the oboe, F♯–C♯–G (X) becomes C♯–G–F♯, and so forth. The parts not illustrated employ different derivations, including other rotations (clarinet) and extractions of two notes from the trichords combined with various dispersals of the other notes (cornet). Although Berg does not seem to have employed precisely these methods of transformation in order to derive different rows, Ives's interest in systematic relationships between statements of the chromatic set finds many parallels in Berg's methods of deriving rows through cyclic and schematic operations.[69]

EXAMPLE 6.13. Ives, *The Fourth of July*, segments in m. 119.

	W	X	Y	Z
A. flute	G# D# A	F# C# G	E B F	C A# D
B. trumpet	A Eb G#	G C# F#	F B E	D A# C
C. oboe	D# A G#	C# G F#	B F E	A# D C

The approaches to composition with the chromatic set in music of Ives and of Berg can be contrasted with some of their other points of common ground; the techniques of manipulating the chromatic set do not consistently value a normative compositional source. Although an ordering of the chromatic set can serve as a kind of structural model, the sense in which such a model is normative will vary.[70] Berg's interest in cyclic transformations of rows may be traced to normative concerns, but he also forms rows, including some discussed above, whose structural meaning is wholly contextual. In Ives's case, normative and reflexive approaches coexist in a body of work in which no single method or ideology would be expected to prevail. Ultimately, the most pronounced differences between the two composers are apparent in the eventual destinations of their compositional developments, Berg having achieved an apparently satisfying degree of organization in his adaptation of the twelve-tone method, Ives having explored strict and free constructive tools with equal intensity before abandoning composition altogether for the last twenty-odd years of his life.

Whether normative or not, the techniques and materials of non-tonal composition show the importance of method and of systematic constraints. Stravinsky describes an "infinitude of possibilities" and an "abyss of freedom" in music without tonality that can be daunting without the imposition of "limitations" and a "narrow frame" for any compositional undertaking. He writes, "My freedom will be so much the greater and more meaningful the more narrowly I limit my field of action and the more I surround myself with obstacles. Whatever diminishes constraint, diminishes strength. The more constraints one imposes, the more one frees one's self of the chains that shackle the spirit."[71] Perle speaks of a "chaos" that can result from complete freedom, "where the greatest sense of formal abstraction exists side by side with the most chaotic formlessness."[72] Whereas Berg seems to have resolved the issue for himself with his adoption of twelve-tone constraints, Ives's various experiments with systematic methods take their place alongside much freely inspired work to portray a composer without such a singular resolution. Certainly, it is true that Ives sought no single method, that he was not temperamentally or philosophically inclined in the same direction as his Viennese contemporaries. At the same time, however, the decline and cessation in his productivity may be partly attributable to a dissatisfaction with the post-tonal solutions he had explored; the "question" remained unanswered and, for him, unanswerable. Perhaps this was a disenchantment parallel to a philosophical dilemma that has also been blamed for the decline in his compositional activity. Burkholder suggests that the *Essays Before a Sonata* established lofty goals that Ives felt he could not achieve, that "his artistic aims exceeded his grasp."[73]

Not only the technical tools but also the aesthetic goals and philosophical orientations shared by Ives with Berg, as well as with Debussy, Mahler, and Schoenberg, among other contemporaries, are revealing indicators of a common musical ancestry. Likewise are glances further back at the ancestors themselves—from the late romantics back to Beethoven— strong evidence of the history and culture from which Ives evolved. Scholarship that draws attention to these currents and connections has begun to establish a tradition of its own, a process of historical revision placing Ives in the mainstream of European musical history.[74] But this new historical perspective will not only acknowledge Ives's connections with his musical past; it will also clarify his relationship with his musical present and future. In particular, it will help answer some of the questions raised by Maynard Solomon about Ives's status as innovator and modernist. Citing ambiguous and contradictory evidence from Ives's music and writings, Solomon suggests that the chronology has been falsified and mythologized to give Ives illegitimate precedence over his contemporaries and undeserved stature as a prophet of later post-tonal composition.[75] But once we have demonstrated that Ives was not isolated, we have supported his image as innovator. We have shown that he possessed the tools and background necessary to break from traditional molds and was open to the influence of contemporaneous currents of modernism. When composers of similar musical ancestry, such as Ives and Berg, are viewed side by side, it seems only logical that the musical training, compositional philosophies, and questions about the future of music shared by many western composers of the time would yield similar sorts of musical innovation.

The traditional chronology of Ives's work gives him historical precedence in exploring new techniques and materials that appear shortly thereafter in music of Berg and other Europeans. Ives is not portrayed as an imitator of his European contemporaries, nor, certainly, are his successors assumed to be imitating him, and these circumstances are not difficult to accept. The answers to a revisionist's questions lie in the substance of Ives's questions and in his musical responses to issues and challenges faced by many at the dawn of the post-tonal era.

:7:

Ives and Stravinsky:
Two Angles on "the German Stem"

ANDREW BUCHMAN

Although Charles Ives and Igor Stravinsky began their lives on op-posite sides of the margins of Europe, they had many methods and in-terests in common. Their earliest symphonies reveal training in the nineteenth-century European tradition. Formative experiences with ver-nacular music helped each to establish a personal identity. Using melodic paraphrases in polyrhythmic layerings and harmonic distortions of tonal structures, each developed a unique but convergent set of procedures for dealing with borrowed musical sources, both classical and vernacular. Each found inspiration in some of the same musical styles, including Beethoven's symphonies and piano sonatas, the music of Tchaikovsky, and ragtime.[1]

Both Ives and Stravinsky used Beethoven as a mirror for their own aesthetic agendas, seeing misconceptions in the criticisms of others that echoed their own discontents with critics' comments about their works. The subtext of Stravinsky's defense in his *Autobiography* of Beethoven's instrumentation implies a desire to be taken seriously as a constructor of musical objects rather than as a brilliant orchestrator dependent on oth-ers' musical ideas for inspiration.[2] Similarly, Ives, who also defended Bee-thoven's instrumentation, sought a historical justification for his use of "the sounds that Beethoven didn't have," seeking in Beethoven both inspiration and someone to transcend, making the *Concord Sonata* a cri-tique of Beethoven as well as a tribute.[3]

Both men showed a remarkable resistance to completing definitive versions of their best-known works, the *Rite of Spring* (1913) and the *Concord Sonata*. Multiple versions of both works exist despite the many years each composer took to prepare a definitive version and despite, in Stravinsky's case, compelling financial reasons for doing so. The performance histories of the two works reveal continuing ambivalence on the part of both composers about finalizing them.[4]

Both Ives and Stravinsky helped craft their reputations in published memoirs and explanations of their music. As he grew older, Stravinsky consistently deemphasized the collaborative and programmatic origins of the *Rite* and even denied that it should exist beyond its increasingly established place as a work of "absolute" (or at least unstaged) orchestral music. Choreographer Millicent Hodson's speculative 1987 reconstruction of the ballet for the Joffrey Company led to a new awareness of Stravinsky as a ballet composer working within dramatic limits, as opposed to the modernist visionary he preferred us to see. Similarly, Ives's public pronouncements emphasizing his estrangement from the musical world of his time may accurately reflect the rejections his music received but may be disingenuous about the degree of his own disengagement from the music and musical ideas of others.

The similar experiences, choices, and strategies of the two composers led to very different musical legacies and widely divergent private and public careers. Except in their student works, it is difficult to find a moment by Ives that sounds like one by Stravinsky, or vice versa, and there probably was no direct influence of one on the other. Ives left no theater piece comparable to *L'histoire du soldat* or *Oedipus Rex*, no ballets or operas (although he apparently planned one of the latter). Stravinsky wrote no solo piano works comparable in scope to the First or Second (*Concord*) Sonata and no group of art songs approaching the quantity of the *114 Songs*, no organ works, and no experimental pieces using microtones or unobtainable forces.

The problems that composers faced at the turn of the century, particularly peripheral composers—and this is what Stravinsky and Ives most importantly have in common—centered around the problem of achieving an individual voice within a received tradition. The most obvious technical response to their respective traditions shared by Ives and Stravinsky was the use of melodic paraphrases in polyrhythmic layerings. Both used essentially similar techniques of paraphrasing: deconstructing melodies into small units, adding or subtracting notes and rests to create irregular rhythms, and lowering or raising selected pitches to create unexpected angularities. Although Ives's alterations are sometimes more readily recognizable (especially to American ears) than those of Stravinsky, scholars working after the latter's death and the publication of the sketches of the *Rite* have made the composer's use of borrowed melodic paraphrases in the work widely known.[5]

Ives also liked to write music "all made of tunes." One example is

EXAMPLE 7.1. Ives, *Three Places in New England,* second movement (*Putnam's Camp*), mm. 34–35, with "Yankee Doodle," mm. 1–2.

From *Three Places in New England.*
© 1935 and 1976 by Mercury Music Corporation.
Reprinted by Permission.

Ives's use of "Yankee Doodle" in *Putnam's Camp,* the second movement of *Three Places in New England,* which was Ives's first orchestral work to be performed (and reviewed) in Europe, in 1931. The tune passes from trumpet to flute, where it is raised by a whole step and given a leap down of a diminished fifth rather than a perfect one, all by the end of the first phrase (ex. 7.1).[6] Both composers earned modernist accolades for their rhythmic invention. In his *Memos,* Ives refutes at length correspondences claimed by critics between *Putnam's Camp* and the *Rite.*[7] In certain passages, overlaid ostinatos of different lengths recall similarly polymetric moments in the *Rite,* such as the transition between the "Ritual of the Two Rival Tribes" and the "Procession of the Oldest and Wisest One."[8] In each case, several ostinatos that vary in length are layered one over another, creating the sense of a shifting musical landscape. It is plausible to consider these to be instances of convergent evolution. Nevertheless, although the music of Ives and Stravinsky is similar in technical "manner," it diverges in "substance."

For Ives, this difference seems crucial. His denial of influence is preceded by a critique of Stravinsky's use of ostinatos. Ives writes: "It wasn't until about 1919 or '20 that I first heard any of Stravinsky's music. At that time I did hear a part of *Firebird* [perhaps the repetitive 'Berceuse' and 'Finale'] and I thought it was morbid and monotonous. (The idea of a phrase, usually a small one, was good enough and interesting in itself, but he kept it going over and over, and [it] got tiresome."[9] Stravinsky was in good company; in his *Essays Before a Sonata,* Ives criticized Tchaikovsky, as well, as repetitive.[10] Of course, when it suited him, Ives could repeat an ostinato over and over with the best of them, as in the song "General William Booth Enters Into Heaven" or the second and fourth movements of the Fourth Symphony. Ives did trim down the repetitive ostinatos in the orchestral version of *The Housatonic at Stockbridge,* the third movement of *Three Places in New England.* But the point here is not to catch Ives in an inconsistency but to glean from his words an insight into how he viewed Stravinsky's music and his own. Elliott Carter commented in 1972 that "underneath these criticisms [of Stravinsky] . . .

there is a clear note of respect for what Ives calls the 'manner,' and an evident awareness of what was going on. He was far from being the recluse that some have pictured."[11]

Ives's and Stravinsky's common solutions to the problem of extending the harmonic vocabulary of the nineteenth century are highlighted in the practice dubbed bitonality. What has often been called bitonality in Stravinsky, most famously the "Petrushka chord"—a C-major triad in root position played against an F♯-major triad in first inversion—is simultaneously an artifact of Stravinsky's unique synthesis of diatonic and octatonic harmonies and a tonal expansion of the work's key intervallic device, the tritone.[12] Stravinsky was also adept at writing counterpoint with multiple melodies in different meters within coherent diatonic contexts. The concurrent tunes of the Ballerina and the Moor in *Petrushka* (reh. F nos. 71–74) use the same diatonic pitch collection but different tonal centers and meters to achieve an effect of sonic schizophrenia. For Ives, too, bitonality was a pleasant rebellion against functional tonal conventions, but one unimaginable without the tonal tradition: "If you can play a tune in one key, why can't a feller . . . play one in two keys?"[13] J. Peter Burkholder elucidates the interpenetrating pitch collections, analogous to Stravinsky's octatonic-diatonic ones, underlying passages that Ives characterized as bitonal, as in Ives's setting of *Psalm 67*.[14] *Central Park in the Dark*, an orchestral work by Ives comparable to the *Rite* in its use of intervallically organized aggregates of pitches subdivided into unusual chords, includes "whole-tone chords and chords built of fifths, fourths, and fourths mixed with tritones."[15]

The habit of both men of improvising at the piano might have had something to do with their common fondness for bitonality. The practice of jamming conflicting harmonies together can also be considered a new species of chord substitution, a logical extension of such classical practices as Beethoven's frequent substitution of the submediant for the dominant in his sonata forms.[16] But the essential aspect of both men's harmonic invention was the mingling of tonal structures with nontonal intervallic and pitch structures. *Les cinq doigts*, a set of eight very easy pieces from 1921, includes fine miniature examples of Stravinsky's "strong misreadings" of tonality into pandiatonic and octatonic interpenetrations.[17] The first piece is an elegant study in pandiatonicism, what William E. Benjamin calls "tonality without fifths." The sixth piece uses a common octatonic-diatonic "link," to use van den Toorn's useful term: the bluesy major-minor triad, with the major third in the right hand, the minor in the left. Richard Taruskin places the "exact moment" of Stravinsky's "reintroduction into his music of the dominant function" in no. 3 of *Les cinq doigts*, which he identifies as an arrangement of the Russian folksong "Kamárinskaya," previously used by Glinka.[18] These little studies are perhaps the closest Stravinsky came to the many small experimental pieces in which Ives explored all manner of technical devices.[19]

How could Ives and Stravinsky have followed such similar creative strategies, given their differences in geographic, political, and cultural origins? Family and schooling were key commonalities. Both men had fathers who were practicing musicians, and both studied with influential music educators who forced them to reconcile their life experiences and developing aesthetics with a musical pedagogy defined around European models.

Ives learned vernacular music from his father. Styles of music characteristic of George Ives's public repertoire included vernacular marches and gospel hymns, sentimental parlor songs, and arrangements of classical music for band.[20] Marches were grist for the young composer's mill, beginning at the age of twelve with his *Schoolboy March* and continuing the next summer in his first song, the "Slow March."[21] Stuart Feder finds the kernels of stylistic features characteristic of the mature Ives in this piece and explains the significance of Ives's use of a musical quotation from Handel redolent with personal associations.[22] The "Dead March" from the oratorio *Saul* was a must at any military funeral during the Civil War, "the most musical war in world history," a conflict in which Ives the father served (at seventeen) as the youngest bandmaster in the Union Army.[23]

Ives's early ascent to professional work as a church organist (at the age of fourteen) helped solidify the thorough grounding in harmony and performance that his father had inherited from his European immigrant teacher Charles Foepple (Carl Foeppl). The younger Ives worked on virtuoso repertoire by Bach and others before entering Yale. The gospel hymn *Jerusalem the Golden* and patriotic song "America" served as the basis for juvenilia in more or less conventional variation forms. George and Charles Ives shared a home world of musical experimentation. Hence, for Ives, childhood was a time of exciting musical collaboration with a dynamic adult model who regularly crossed the lines between art and vernacular music.

The young Stravinsky and his more distant father appear to have had less in common. Not atypically, the father who was thwarted in life was far more solicitous of his son's gifts than the father with a larger sphere of influence. Stravinsky dismissed his childhood as a time of years of loneliness and ill health, missing the city of St. Petersburg more than his family. Feodor Ignatievich Stravinsky was a leading bass at the Imperial Opera House in St. Petersburg. In his *Autobiography*, Stravinsky recalls an early childhood glimpse of Tchaikovsky in the flesh, thus connecting himself symbolically to a strong precursor.[24] In addition to spending many afternoons and evenings at the opera, he received formal musical training beginning at the age of nine, including lessons in piano, harmony, and counterpoint.[25]

Unlike that of Ives, the young Stravinsky's bond to vernacular traditions was forged not within the family but without. Folk music was early acknowledged as a profound influence; in his writings he emphasizes the sonic impressions received during summers spent in the countryside.[26] In addition, the Russian literary and musical culture within which the young Stravinsky was trained followed a nationalistic trend. Members of the "Mighty Handful" had paved the way for the acceptance of art music that incorporated folk music, something Ives perhaps feared that his teacher Horatio Parker would not sanction despite Dvořák's recent example.[27]

Stravinsky's engagement with the popular music of the emerging mass culture of Europe is less easy to trace. He remembered his earliest experiments at the keyboard as attempts to reproduce the sounds of a fife, tuba, and drum band at a marine barracks near his family's flat.[28] Certainly, popular music could be found among the amusements of St. Petersburg; another source might have been the family's servants, especially his nurse from East Prussia. Young Stravinsky evidently experimented with vernacular musics when his teachers were out of the room. Rimsky-Korsakov's granddaughter remembers him playing *Long Live the Tsar*, a march, in waltz time for a reward of twenty kopecks.[29]

There is no doubt that their respective childhoods provided both future composers with exposure to a wide diversity of music, which enabled each to develop an appreciation of more than one musical language. More significantly, each was attracted to many styles and genres of music and documented these attractions in autobiographical writings. Stravinsky and Ives's formal schooling with prominent academic figures, the composers Nicolai Rimsky-Korsakov and Horatio Parker, respectively, resulted for both in a splitting of an interest that had been assimilative and whole, a channeling of creativity into segregated literary, vernacular, and personal musical spheres.

In 1894 Ives was accepted into the Yale class of 1898, two months before his father died at the age of forty-nine. "From his first days in New Haven, Charlie aspired to the elite. The vernacular music of this period tracks the process," writes Feder, citing Ives's score of "Pass the Can Along," a drinking song.[30] On the same piece of manuscript paper, Ives sketched an organ prelude—later to become a movement of his Second Symphony—based on a musical remembrance of his father composed out of the gospel hymn *Missionary Chant*, among other sources. A note by Ives, jammed into the score's margin, angrily denounces Parker's criticism of the organ prelude—on the same grounds as his criticism of the First Symphony, tonal instability—followed by nine exclamation points. By the time Ives left Yale, he had learned to cross between different musical worlds as organist and church composer, fraternity composer of "stunts" or "take-offs," and serious student of Western art music composition. Ives began composing deeply felt art compositions that attempted to achieve an inner integration of the values and attitudes that could not be expressed outwardly if he were to succeed socially at Yale and thus justify his family's expectations and sacrifices. Feder notes that "Charlie was already establishing and practicing a pattern of creative privacy in the context of multiple lives."[31]

Young Stravinsky achieved a similar accommodation between his family's ambitions and his own by splitting his musical studies off from college entirely. Stravinsky's parents refused to allow him to pursue a musical career and insisted on his going to St. Petersburg University and studying law; evidently his performance there over four years was analogous to Ives's gentleman's D+ average at Yale. Stravinsky obtained access to a mentor analogous to the august Parker by approaching Rimsky-Korsakov, the director of the Imperial Conservatory of Music, when the two crossed paths while traveling in Germany in 1902.[32] Rimsky-Korsakov accepted him as a private student. Like Parker, Rimsky-Korsakov combined the virtues of an active and well-respected composer's creative approach to musical pedagogy with a solid mastery of the forms and techniques of the "German stem." Like Parker, Rimsky-Korsakov encouraged his students to use pre-existing "museum pieces" as models.[33] He also greeted the young Stravinsky's efforts with a dubiousness that might well have created as much retrospective bitterness as Parker's dismissals did for Ives, had not Stravinsky's subsequent success dispelled any lingering insecurities.

Stravinsky's and Ives's student works were based on nineteenth-century models. In his first songs—three settings of Pushkin poems—Stravinsky used works by Wagner, Tchaikovsky, and Debussy as models; Dvořák held special appeal for Ives.[34] Ives began his First Symphony during his freshman year, the year in which he became a student of Parker. Stravinsky's first published piece, a Symphony in E♭ written under Rimsky-Korsakov's supervision, was dedicated to his teacher. Listening to Ives and Stravinsky's first symphonies successively, one is struck by the similarities in orchestration, pitch language, and late Romantic symphonic style. These are well-crafted student imitations, particularly in the melodies, the mostly seamless transitions, and the rarely awkward harmonizations and orchestrations.

The use of historical models was an essential aspect of the genesis of each composition. Stravinsky incorporates a Russian folk song into the scherzo movement of his symphony; it is closer to the manner of Tchaikovsky (or, for that matter, Beethoven) than to his mature manner of remaking through paraphrase, although the tune is very similar to the first theme of the "Dance of the Nursemaids" in *Petrushka*. Ives did not risk even a tastefully harmonized overt vernacular quotation in his scherzo. Instead he used the scherzo from Beethoven's Ninth Symphony as a model; Geoffrey Block notes that Beethoven was Ives's most frequently used model.[35] A prefiguration of Stravinsky's mature manner is the inclusion of a self-quotation: a theme from the young composer's childhood improvisations in the fourth movement. Stravinsky would recast this tune again in *Three Little Songs (Recollections of My Childhood)* in 1913.[36] The urge to remake the past could thus be channeled into a personal declaration of musical and personal growth while remaining true to one's childhood.

Burkholder deduces a synthesis of a melody from Schubert's "Unfinished" Symphony with the vernacular hymns *Shining Shore* and *Beulah Land* in the beginning, middle, and end, respectively, of the first theme in the first movement of Ives's First Symphony—a density of interrelationships characteristic of the mature Ives.[37] Another characteristic feature is Ives's tonal restlessness in the exposition of the first movement, which might have struck Parker as a student's misunderstanding of the necessity of projecting tonal stability in a sonata-allegro movement.[38] Yet, it was by following his restless ear that Ives became a truly original symphonist while retaining connections to both his vernacular roots and the "German stem" through quotation and parody and through formal strategies such as cumulative form.[39]

Serge Diaghilev was in the audience at the premiere of Stravinsky's *Fireworks*, an orchestral composition completed two years after the Symphony in E♭. No such angel appeared to the young Ives during his early attempts to present his music to the world. The young Stravinsky began his professional career under the firm artistic direction of the impresario of the Ballets Russes. Diaghilev was a supremely practical mentor, with a much deeper stake in the young composer's success than either the latter's emotionally absent father or the academic paragon Rimsky-Korsakov. Although Stravinsky's later writings obscure the fact, his early successes were programmatic assignments, collaborative works of dance drama with musical accompaniment. But they were also significant creative assignments whose stylistic latitude was perhaps broader than that of contemporary concert music. Ballets in the repertoire included many pastiches; the first works by Stravinsky performed in Paris were his orchestrations of two pieces by Chopin for Diaghilev's new production of *Les sylphides*, featured in the 1909 Ballets Russes season.[40]

If Ives had had a similar opportunity, would he have taken it? He never had the chance to do so, unless we count his early collaborations with fraternity brothers (some published commercially). Aside from sonic experiments disguised as undergraduate "stunts" and "take-offs," Ives never had an opportunity to combine vernacular and art music into commercially feasible vehicles of extended length comparable to Stravinsky's ballets. Nevertheless, he and Stravinsky both mined common veins of vernacular and classical music in the course of constructing "strong misreadings." Two complementary genres of comparable works are pieces incorporating American ragtime influences and works inspired by the Russian "strong precursor" Tchaikovsky.

Stravinsky composed the ambitious *Piano-Rag-Music* (1919) for the rising virtuoso Artur Rubinstein, who refused to play it in public, finding it too percussive.[41] Eric Salzman writes: "Stravinsky was not the first 'serious' composer to use ragtime—Ives had introduced it into many of his works a decade before—but he was probably the first to transplant it into European music and thus begin to define a rebellious post-war spirit of the '20s."[42] Stravinsky's earlier essays in the style include a ragtime dance in *L'histoire du soldat* (1918) and the *Rag-Time* (1918) for eleven instruments. These works can be considered the start of a longer series that used elements of vernacular music overtly; Stravinsky returned to the series when he moved to the United States in 1939, writing the *Tango* (1940), the *Circus Polka* (1942) for Barnum and Bailey's elephants, and *Ebony Concerto* (1945) for Woody Herman's swing band.

Ives's uses of ragtime were also extensive. James B. Sinclair lists twelve specific (albeit often closely related) works using passages or quotations from the *Four Ragtime Dances*, including the First Piano Sonata.[43] Burkholder notes the coincidence of Ives's switching from organ and piano with his rising interest in ragtime. Something similar can be said of Stravinsky, who was turning from the expansive (and expensive) orchestral pallette of his pre-war works to smaller forces, including works for his own use as a pianist.[44] Ives was familiar with ragtime from his college days and perhaps as early as his visit to the 1893 Columbian Exposition in Chicago with his uncle Lyman Brewster. Stravinsky apparently started collecting phonograph records of ragtime as early as 1914.[45] Characteristic these reuses of ragtime shared was a deconstruction of the marching, duple meter. The scintillating syncopations at the heart of ragtime became a conceptual starting point for all sorts of polyrhythmic play. Ives described section IVa of the second scherzo of the First Piano Sonata as "a study in 'Rag' for 5's 3's and 2's together, changing accents, etc."—but this piece is perhaps the most Stravinsky-like, least rag-like Ives rag.[46] Stravinsky's *Piano-Rag-Music* switches meters six times in the first nine measures and includes divisions of beats into sevens and fives.

According to Burkholder, Ives forged ragtime into "concert pieces that are 'about' vernacular styles and vernacular performance," approaching "the character of fiction, operating on more than one level."[47] The same may be said of Stravinsky's *Piano-Rag-Music*, which, like Ives's First Piano Sonata, speaks in many styles but in a unique voice. Ives's uses of ragtime result in some of his most heavily disguised quotations. Sometimes his versions of ragtime, like Stravinsky's, are thoroughly dressed up in modernistic rhythms and harmonies. But although no specific ragtime models have yet been identified for Stravinsky's works in the idiom, Joseph E. Howard's "Hello! Ma Baby" (1899) is paraphrased in Ives's *Study No. 23* for piano, and Harry von Tilzer's 1904 hit "Alexander" figures prominently in *Study No. 20*.[48]

For both composers, ragtime was a popular harbinger of a trend in modern music with which each strongly identified: the development of rhythmic complexities seldom explored by nineteenth-century European composers. But it is probably fair to say that for Stravinsky ragtime was more an absorbing novelty rather than the deeply resonant, nostalgic style it was for the New Englander. Ives used ragtime in concert pieces, even ragging hymns, most notably in the First Piano Sonata and *The Rockstrewn Hills* of the Second Orchestral Set.[49] For a comparable density of remakings in Stravinsky we must search for a model closer to his boyhood. The ballet *The Fairy's Kiss* (1928) offers marked correspondences in genesis and substance to Ives's procedures in working with musical materials that possessed spiritual and patriotic resonances.

For Stravinsky, the music of Tchaikovsky, not ragtime, marked out a terrain of childhood memories. Like the hymns and marches of Ives's youth, every bar evoked a culture of a time and place lost not only to Stravinsky but to an entire generation of Russians at home and abroad. Richard Taruskin has described *The Fairy's Kiss* as a consciously "counterrevolutionary" artwork, conceived in opposition to socialist-realist works that proclaimed their authentic Russianness.[50]

Lawrence Morton notes that Stravinsky uses his Tchaikovsky quotes as motivic material.[51] Here we approach a vital affinity between Ives and Stravinsky in the domain of large-scale form: their common use of manipulated quotations to create unities over long musical time spans. Gordon Cyr has written perceptively that Ives shared Stravinsky's (and Schoenberg's) "concern for the interval as a prime factor in pitch-organization."[52] Dennis Marshall decodes Ives's selection of several hymn tunes having the same cadential melody (re–do–mi–re–do) as motivic materials for the First Piano Sonata. The correspondence between the "fate knocking at the door" motif from Beethoven's Fifth Symphony and the hymns *Martyn* and *Missionary Chant* is another example of Ives's using source tunes with as much care as other composers might lavish on the creation of complementary symphonic themes.[53] Taruskin and van den Toorn both note the centrality of the (0 2 3 5) tetrachord (e.g., D–E–F–G) in possible folk song sources for the *Rite*. Similar processes of tune selection and adjustment for architectural purposes are also evident.[54]

In *The Fairy's Kiss*, interpenetrating quotations from over a dozen short compositions by Tchaikovsky are used in a web that approaches Ivesian density (although within neoclassical restraints of harmony and texture). According to Morton, "One senses Tchaikovsky's presence even when one cannot point out precisely what makes the presence felt." The tunes are transformed into unique shapes. "Instead of . . . Tchaikovsky's inevitable squares, they are Stravinsky's rhomboids, scalenes, trapeziums. . . . Tchaikovsky's faults—his banalities and vulgarities and routine procedures—are composed *out* of the music, and Stravinsky's virtues are composed *into* it." *The Fairy's Kiss* "is thus an act of criticism," comparable to Ives's treatment of Beethoven in the *Concord Sonata*.[55] There is more than an element of repetition in *The Fairy's Kiss*, most obviously in the fortissimo tutti accents and jaunty folk-like quality of the "Village Fête." Stravinsky is evoking not only the world of Tchaikovsky but his own past success in *Petrushka*. Some of Ives's works have a similar density of historical and self-quotation, as in the reuse of his *Country Band March* and *Overture and March "1776"* in *Putnam's Camp*, the middle movement of *Three Places in New England*.

Ives's uses of works by Tchaikovsky were more humorous than a Russian sensibility might allow. In this sense, Tchaikovsky's music complements ragtime as a reflection of the cultural differences between Stravinsky and Ives. In the latter's song "The Side-Show," the five-beats-to-the-measure theme of the second movement of Tchaikovsky's *Pathétique* Symphony is reworked into a musical depiction of the unsteady horse powering a carnival merry-go-round. For the Anglo-American, the work that evokes pathos for Russians everywhere evoked another resonance that made the tune perfect for a fraternity show at Yale and still seemed worth arranging as a song in 1921. As Burkholder notes, Ives uses the resemblance between the waltz theme in $\frac{5}{4}$-time and Pat Rooney's immensely popular comic song of 1883, "Is That You, Mr. Riley?," to create a musical joke, a quodlibet combining American vernacular and European art music.[56]

In their explorations of ragtime and Tchaikovsky, Stravinsky and Ives worked with limited genres. In their sonata-form pieces, they wrestled with "the paradigmatic form of tonal music."[57] Although a thorough study of all their symphonies and sonatas is beyond the scope of this chapter, it is possible to define a smaller frame of reference by comparing the final cadences of their first mature solo piano sonatas. In Stravinsky's case, his first was also his last. For both men, the strong sonata precursor of choice was Beethoven.

In his study of Schoenberg, the composer until recently regarded as

EXAMPLE 7.2a. Ives, First Piano Sonata, first movement, final cadence.

EXAMPLE 7.2b. Ives, First Piano Sonata, second movement, final cadence.

Stravinsky's polar opposite, Charles Rosen contrasts Stravinsky's treatment of sonata form: "Stravinsky alone, treating tonality as if it were an archaic and foreign language, created a genuine and viable neoclassical style *en grand seigneur*: he used nonchromatic tonal relations ruthlessly, disrupting both their harmonic and rhythmic aspects, and made no attempt to create effects of nostalgia or respectability; the opening of his piano sonata, for example, interchanges tonic and dominant (harmonizing a note of the tonic triad with a dominant chord, and vice versa) until their functions are almost obliterated and the tonal hierarchy disappears."[58] An exact cognate to the ruthless harmonic practice discussed by Rosen can be found in Ives's First Piano Sonata, in which each of the five movements ends in a mix of two triads (exx. 7.2a–e). The harmonic context at the end of the first movement combines E- and A-major triads (ex. 7.2a). The first section of the second movement ends on D major plus A minor (V and ii of G major); the movement ends in A major but on D (IV), with E♯ and B as neighbors (ex. 7.2b). The third movement

EXAMPLE 7.2c. Ives, First Piano Sonata, third movement, final cadence.

EXAMPLE 7.2d. Ives, First Piano Sonata, fourth movement, final cadence.

EXAMPLE 7.2e. Ives, First Piano Sonata, fifth movement, final cadence.

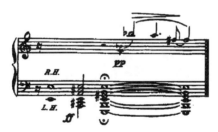

ends on the tonic E major with a fifth-chord above it (ex. 7.2c). The
fourth movement ends in a genuine tonic-dominant mix most suggestive
of Stravinsky's procedures (ex. 7.2d). The final sound of the piece is the
flatted root and natural seventh and fifth of the dominant hovering high
and pianissimo over the dense low cloud of a fortissimo tonic chord (ex.
7.2e). The result is a developed critique of a central ritual of functional
tonality, the final cadence.

EXAMPLE 7.3a. Stravinsky, Piano Sonata, first movement, final cadence.

EXAMPLE 7.3b. Stravinsky, Piano Sonata, second movement, final cadence.

Rosen referred to the steady tumble of "Beethoven frisé" in mm. 13–31 of the first movement of Stravinsky's Piano Sonata (1924).[59] The endings of this work's three movements (exx. 7.3a–c) are also complex tangles of references. This is due in part to a detail in Stravinsky's negation of tonic and dominant, which Rosen notes: almost all of Stravinsky's dominants are incomplete. In mm. 156–57 (ex. 7.3a), Stravinsky jams together two such chords, comprising together an octatonic collection, in the penultimate position normally accorded the dominant in tonal music. In m. 158, the left hand arrives prematurely at the tonic pitch C, buried by four dissonant pitches, F, A♭, D, and B. In m. 159, only A♭ and B♮ are explicitly retained from the quasi-dominant (V$^{9♭}$) collection, while the other voices stagger unevenly through stepwise diatonic progressions towards the tonic. Significantly, nowhere in the coda does Stravinsky proffer a complete dominant. Instead, he creates an emphatic cadence using only his own synthetic octatonic-dominant harmonies and one final courtly C-major triad in root position (m. 160). Ives's *Three-Page Sonata* ends in much the same way.

The final cadence of Stravinsky's second movement uses a much

EXAMPLE 7.3c. Stravinsky, Piano Sonata, third movement, final cadence.

more conventional incomplete dominant (viiᵍ̸) to set up another staggered final tonic chord, in a flurry of ornaments in which the bass rushes to its tonal goal a fraction of a beat before the upper voices (ex. 7.3b). The third movement ends with a reference back to the first and a similarly emphatic but deracinated quasi–dominant-to-tonic cadence (ex. 7.3c). In the antepenultimate measure, the leading tone (D♯) hangs prominently in the soprano but is forced to coexist with a contradictory G♯ below, which staggers home much too early. Beneath, Stravinsky weaves in a bit of the first movement's opening gesture, a startling octatonic staccato, ending on a murky bass F. Only the archaic Phrygian mode employs such a cadence, with the half step above the tonic emphasized immediately before the final sonority; the piece ends with a fall to low E. Alternatively, this cadence can be interpreted as an augmented-sixth chord (F, A, D♯,) with E added, anticipating the resolution.

As these closes demonstrate in microcosm, octatonic pitch relations are ultimately subsumed by diatonic, quasi-tonal pitch relations, but the resolution is neither easy nor conclusive, even at the largest structural span (from beginning to end). The first movement is in C, the second movement in A♭, and the finale in E—deliberately irreconcilable keys. Despite Stravinsky's deliberate deracination of tonality, the web of associations which the term "sonata" arouses remains useful. It is part of Stravinsky's manner to provide ambiguities between figure and ground within his model of sobriety. Tonal allusions to Beethoven tempt us. The opening tune of the first movement, despite the purposefully inappropriate accompaniment that Rosen noted (mm. 13–31), ascends to the supertonic and the mediant, as does that of Beethoven's First Symphony. The ritornello structure—the opening bars return at mathematically precise intervals, every forty measures in this 160-measure movement—suggests the baroque or classical concerto as a formal model. A subtler formal aspect is Stravinsky's substitution of contrasting pitch sets in place of the contrasting themes used in some classical sonatas. Two types of harmonic material are introduced on the first page, one primarily octatonic (mm. 1–12), the other primarily diatonic (mm. 13–31). In the central eighty measures of the piece, these pitch worlds are then pitted against one another à la Beethoven in a series of witty, ritualistic confrontations. For Stravinsky, as for Ives, Beethoven's sonatas and symphonies became touchstones for remakings of the piano sonata tradition.

Block notes Stravinsky's use of the oracular "fate" motif from Beethoven's Fifth to set Jocasta's words "Oracles always lie" in *Oedipus Rex*, the semi-staged melodrama of 1927.[60] This urbane, ironic counterpoint between manner and meaning is typical of Stravinsky's neoclassic music and a far cry from the identifiable quotes in *Petrushka* or Ives's use and reuse of Beethovenian motives in the *Concord Sonata*. Again, significantly similar outlooks, training, techniques, and styles led to uniquely different musical solutions by the two composers. Each reworked elements of existing music in order to create works that reflect back on the European art tradition and are in some way *about* the experience of music.

In their careers as composers, Stravinsky was a bit like Aesop's peripatetic hare, Ives like the stoic tortoise. Stravinsky rose rapidly to fame between 1909 and 1913, and remained famous all his long life. Sparked by his self-published scores and essays from the early 1920s onward, Ives's reputation grew slowly but steadily, fueled not by popular success but by critical appreciation. When Ives's music first came to the attention of European audiences in the 1930s, his work (along with that of other American composers) was held up to what might be called the *Rite* standard by contemporary critics, who generally focused on modernist issues of innovation and priority.[61] For Ives, the crucial territory to defend was *Putnam's Camp*, about which he wrote, "I've been told (and shown notices of critics etc., saying) that . . . *Putnam's Camp* . . . had been strongly influenced by the *Sacre du Printemps* . . . I've never heard or seen the score of the *Sacre du Printemps*. The places in this movement which some say come from Stravinsky were written before Stravinsky wrote the *Sacre* (or at least before it was first played), and came direct from the habit of piano-drum playing."[62]

Feder discerns here the increasingly important role that Ives's father George played throughout Charles's life as musical precursor.[63] Ives almost certainly would not have heard the *Rite* in its orchestral version until the 1920s—but he could have read a score.[64] The genesis of *Three Places in New England* continues to be a focus for academic investigations of Ives's chronology, just as the *Rite of Spring* has provided a focus for studies of Stravinsky's compositional techniques, including melodic quotation and parody.[65] For now, the questions surrounding Stravinsky's influence on Ives (or vice versa) must remain unresolved; Ives's experiments of the 1890s and early 1900s, before Stravinsky had achieved prominence, would give him pride of place as an innovator in any case, as Stravinsky (in much later life) acknowledged while implicitly casting himself as the more skillful engineer of musical objects.

Ives's angry protestations that Stravinsky had no influence on him, his pecks at the "morbid and monotonous" *Firebird*, and the repetitive improvised parody of the *Rite* that Elliott Carter recounts are perhaps understandable.[66] During the 1930s and 40s, Ives saw younger composers, many of whose careers he had partially bankrolled, leaping ahead of him by "imitating the courtly muses of Europe," which were being conveyed from Nadia Boulanger's hands to Aaron Copland and Carter, but not to Carl Ruggles or himself. Through the efforts of performers and critics, word of Ives's inventions of the years before 1913 spread steadily. Now it was the stubborn Ives who started looking like the authentic hare of modern music, at the finish line before Stravinsky, before Schoenberg, before anyone.

Ives's feigned hostility towards the European tradition may have helped spark the wary tone of Stravinsky's assessments of Ives in the conversation books of the 1960s. Stravinsky praised a few pieces lavishly, but he also repeated the judgment he says he had made in the 1940s: "badly uneven in quality, however, as well as ill-proportioned and lacking strength of style; the best pieces—the *Tone Roads*, for example—were always the shortest."[67] However, Stravinsky then volunteers that Ives's status as " 'The Great Anticipator' " is reason enough to consider his objections "unimportant." Stravinsky generously ceded any claims to innovation while carefully retaining technical and aesthetic priority for his own works.

The defensible modernist grounds from which each chose to criticize the other illuminate aspects of each man's complex inner and outer negotiations between personal "substance" and public "manner." Each adopted parts of the prevailing modernist art-music aesthetic as a bulwark against marginalization while inwardly reserving the Romantic artist's prerogative of self-expression. Each criticized the other by adopting the language of what each saw as the cultural mainstream. To borrow Richard Crawford's useful formulation, each man sought to be both "authentically" and "accessibly" modern.[68] For Ives, using popular music as source material was no sin, nor was the use of tonality with wrong notes. But too much repetition was outside the pale of musical good taste. For Stravinsky, there was nothing wrong with playing two tunes at once, but uniform excellence, formal elegance, and stylistic signature were also important.

Stravinsky and Ives had a great deal in common in their use of other music—of both past and present—as grist for their compositional mills.

Each suffered critical assaults on his reputation as a result, and felt compelled to respond on behalf of his music and his career. But on the whole, Stravinsky suffered a good deal less, due to a combination of factors. His Russian tunes were not well known in Western Europe, especially as compared to Stephen Foster's or John Philip Sousa's. Stravinsky was also an adept disguiser of sources. His brilliance as an arranger and orchestrator, his rhythmic alterations to source tunes, the inherently irregular rhythms of many Russian folk songs, and his pandiatonic and octatonic harmonic vocabularies helped him to create settings that sounded a good deal less familiar than the tonal settings of better-known melodies by Ives. Although the neoclassical works forced difficult confrontations with modernist ideology in the domain of manner, Stravinsky still kept the modernist faith by maintaining his distance from romantic excess. From the Octet to *The Rake's Progress*, Stravinsky remained disengaged from unabashed emotionalism: neoclassic, yes; neoromantic, no.[69] This did not protect him from continuing critical assaults based on the quasi-Romantic tendency of his music to ravish the ear, despite its quasi-formalistic astringency—and there were lapses to account for, such as the surging finale of *The Fairy's Kiss*.

Ives possessed neither an impeccably formalist method nor a consistent focus on explorations of the psychology of extreme emotional states and intuitions as bulwarks for his expressionism (as did Schoenberg). In 1933, Ives's early champion Henry Cowell eloquently put the best possible face on Ives's eclectic output as "a wonderfully universal, rounded-out whole, not technical, but deliciously and fascinatingly human and charming, and with an emotional but not a sentimental basis." He went on to counter a number of already-standard criticisms of Ives's music, including the observation that "It is complained that his texture is too thick. That is, of course, because the style, now, is to have thin music."[70] It is perhaps due as much to its lucid, relatively thin or at least distinctly layered textures—so different from those of the *Concord Sonata* and, indeed, the bulk of Ives's output—as to its vivid program and music that *The Unanswered Question* became one of the first Ives works to enter the orchestral repertory.

Until recently, it was accepted critical practice to think of Stravinsky and Schoenberg as polar opposites on the continuum of twentieth-century art music. Now a new, more complex and historical picture is emerging: parallel early stylistic periods of lush late Romanticism, atonal explorations (with differing adoptions of a method, one proclaimed, the other veiled), neoclassic reinterpretations of received models, and finally, late works combining serial methods and eclectic sources, including tonality. As debates framed by rival personalities and ideologies recede, new critical priorities give rise to new paradigmatic metaphors.[71]

Whereas Leonard Meyer and Charles Hamm, writing in the 1960s, found that most music of the first half of the twentieth-century could be understood as a continuation of nineteenth-century theory and practice, literary critics Harold Bloom and Walter Jackson Bate in the 1970s developed theories centering on influence.[72] More recently, J. Peter Burkholder has explored the implications of a culture based on designated "museum pieces," and Joseph Straus has applied Bloom's theory to music by Stravinsky and others.[73] Approaches drawn from other disciplines are adding new tools to critical musical discourse. As their century draws to a close, Ives and Stravinsky look more and more like two of "late, late Romanticism's" strongest "strong misreaders"—fully engaged in related issues of appropriation and synthesis and leaving comparable artistic legacies of works that are full of references to other music yet uniquely their own.[74]

Despite the distance between the two men, Stravinsky's final published comment on Ives in 1969 pointed towards just such a reconciliation as the present collection of essays has attempted: "The time has come to turn criticism around and rather than continue to emphasize his isolation, consider his share in the ideas of the century."[75] The delicate balance that both men achieved between pluralistic personal aesthetics and modernistic cultural necessities is a testament to the way humans go about being innovative in preserving the past even as Rome, or, in this case, the unitary edifice of Germanic musical culture crumbles. To turn from an architectural metaphor to a perhaps more sustainable botanical one, the shoots growing at an "angle" may survive, even as the old growth is felled all around them.

Notes

Introduction: "A Continuing Spirit"

1. Bernard Herrmann, quoted in "New York Artists Reshape America Over the Week End," *New York Herald Tribune*, 10 July 1932, 14; Leonard Bernstein, quoted on the jacket of his recording with the New York Philharmonic of Charles Ives, Symphony No. 2 (New York: Columbia KL 5489, 1960).

2. Donald Jay Grout and Claude V. Palisca, *A History of Western Music*, 4th ed. (New York: W. W. Norton, 1988), 786; Gerald Abraham, *The Concise Oxford History of Music* (London: Oxford University Press, 1979), 824.

3. Letter of 7 April 1964 to Michael O. Zahn, published as one of "Two Statements on Ives," in John Cage, *A Year from Monday: New Lectures and Writings* (Middletown, Conn.: Wesleyan University Press, 1967), 38.

4. Vivian Perlis, *Charles Ives Remembered: An Oral History* (New Haven: Yale University Press, 1974), 87–88. Editorial insertion by Perlis.

5. Charles Ives, *Essays Before a Sonata, The Majority, and Other Writings*, ed. Howard Boatwright (New York: W. W. Norton, 1970), 85; see also pp. 36, 73–74, 82–86, and 88 for praise for Beethoven.

6. Ibid., 30, 51, and 47.

7. Charles E. Ives, *Memos*, ed. John Kirkpatrick (New York: W. W. Norton, 1972), 135; see also the similar comments on pp. 30, 43–44, and 100. The combination of praise for Beethoven's greatness with condemnation of his music as "too cooped up" (p. 100) indicates the strong sense of competition Ives felt with his predecessor.

8. John Jeffrey Gibbens, "Debussy's Impact on Ives: An Assessment" (D.M.A. diss., University of Illinois at Urbana-Champaign, 1985) traces the dissemination of Debussy's music in American musical circles, identifies when Ives probably came to know it, and demonstrates the influence of Debussy on several

Ives works. Gibbens interprets Ives as adopting some of Debussy's typical procedures and textures while rejecting much of his aesthetic. David Michael Hertz, *Angels of Reality: Emersonian Unfoldings in Wright, Stevens, and Ives* (Carbondale and Edwardsville: Southern Illinois University Press, 1993), 97–113, also explores the influence of Debussy on Ives, showing several parallel passages in their music and arguing that both composers had similar goals of evoking reality in music.

9. Ives, *Essays*, 51.

10. Robert P. Morgan, "Rewriting Music History: Second Thoughts on Ives and Varèse," *Musical Newsletter* 3/1 (January 1973): 3–12 and 3/2 (April 1973): 15–23, 28 (quoting from 3/1: 5).

Chapter 1: Ives and the European Tradition

1. Eric Salzman, *Twentieth-Century Music: An Introduction*, 3d ed. (Englewood Cliffs, N.J.: Prentice Hall, 1988), 134.

2. For a fuller discussion of the problems modern composers faced and the strategies they pursued in competing with the masterworks of the past, see J. Peter Burkholder, "Museum Pieces: The Historicist Mainstream in Music of the Last Hundred Years," *Journal of Musicology* 2 (1983): 115–34, and idem, "The Twentieth Century and the Orchestra as Museum," in *The Orchestra: Origins and Transformations*, ed. Joan Peyser (New York: Charles Scribner's Sons, 1986), 408–33.

3. Chester Ives, interview of 7 May 1969, in Vivian Perlis, *Charles Ives Remembered: An Oral History* (New Haven: Yale University Press, 1974), 87–88.

4. See, for instance, Kagel's *Ludwig van* (1969), a collage of music by Beethoven with the various parts realigned and in other ways distorted to create a travesty of the original.

5. The standard view of Ives's relationship with Parker originates in Ives's reminiscences in his *Memos*, ed. John Kirkpatrick (New York: W. W. Norton, 1972), 39, 48–49, 51, 52, 86, 115–16, 183–84, and 257–58, and in the account based on these passages in the first biography of Ives: Henry Cowell and Sidney Cowell, *Charles Ives and His Music* (New York: Oxford University Press, 1955; 2d ed., 1969), 31–34, 42, and 67. For a more positive view of Parker, see William K. Kearns, *Horatio Parker, 1863–1919: His Life, Music, and Ideas*, Composers of North America, 6 (Metuchen, N.J.: Scarecrow Press, 1990), where Parker's resistance to his teachers is described on pp. 6, 9, and 239–40. For parallels between Ives and Parker, see Nicholas E. Tawa's essay in the present volume.

6. See Parker's comments in his introduction to *Music and Public Entertainment*, ed. Horatio Parker, vol. 9 in *Vocations*, ed. William DeWitt Hyde (Boston: Hall and Locke, 1911; reprint, New York: AMS Press, 1980), xiii–xxii: "It seems safe to advise young people not to try to be composers unless they must . . . if their craving for utterance is real and strong, and if it can be satisfied in no other way" (p. xiv). "Excepting a few men who devote themselves chiefly to light opera or dance music, the writer knows not one composer in America who can possibly live by the exercise of his chosen vocation. One who aspires to compose must therefore be prepared to content himself with little beyond his

work. The exaltation which attends the continued pursuit of beauty should be his. The communion and fellowship of the great masters of music should comfort and encourage him, but he must seek his rewards in spiritual and not in material things" (p. xvi).

For Schoenberg, see *Style and Idea: Selected Writings of Arnold Schoenberg*, ed. Leonard Stein, with translations by Leo Black (London: Faber & Faber, 1975), especially "New Music, Outmoded Music, Style and Idea" (p. 124: "art can only be created for its own sake") and "Criteria for the Evaluation of Music" (p. 135: "every creator creates only to free himself from the high pressures of the urge to create. . . . Ambition or the desire for money stimulates creation only in the lower ranks of artists"). On the links between Ives and Schoenberg, see Keith Ward's essay in the present volume; on parallels between Ives and Berg, see that of Philip Lambert.

7. See the discussion of exoticism and folklorism in Carl Dahlhaus, *Nineteenth-Century Music*, trans. J. Bradford Robinson (Berkeley and Los Angeles: University of California Press, 1989), 302–6. Dahlhaus points out that the exotic and folkloric references of nineteenth-century composers rely on deviations from the common practice of European art music and often depend on the same small number of musical devices, no matter which locale or type of music is being evoked. Nationalist references by modern composers such as Berg, Bartók, and Ives are usually much more particular, though they still depend for their effect on contrast with a non-nationalist context.

8. Charles Ives, *Essays Before a Sonata, The Majority, and Other Writings*, ed. Howard Boatwright (New York: W. W. Norton, 1970), 81.

9. There are too many such studies to list here. Together with several colleagues, I am currently at work on an annotated bibliography on musical borrowing, which already includes over three hundred items on nineteenth- and twentieth-century composers. See my article "The Uses of Existing Music: Musical Borrowing as a Field," *Music Library Association Notes* 50 (1994): 851–70, and Andreas Giger, "A Bibliography on Musical Borrowing," *Notes* 50 (1994): 871–74.

10. This is demonstrated in J. Peter Burkholder, "The Critique of Tonality in the Early Experimental Music of Charles Ives," *Music Theory Spectrum* 12 (1990): 203–23.

11. Ives, *Memos*, 47.

12. On the relationship of traditional models of counterpoint to Ives's experiments and later development, see J. Philip Lambert, "Ives and Counterpoint," *American Music* 9 (1991): 119–48.

13. This paradigm is explored in J. Peter Burkholder, "The Evolution of Charles Ives's Music: Aesthetics, Quotation, Technique" (Ph.D. diss., University of Chicago, 1983), 461–694.

14. For a full account of the development of Ives's uses of existing music, see my *All Made of Tunes: Charles Ives and the Uses of Musical Borrowing* (New Haven: Yale University Press, 1995).

15. Manuscript page f3019/y6068, Ives Collection, John Herrick Jackson Music Library, Yale University, New Haven, Conn. (The first number indicates

the frame number in the master microfilm of Ives's music manuscripts, and the second is the number assigned to the negatives of Ives's manuscripts made between 1927 and 1960.) Because the sole manuscript is in George Ives's hand, the work cannot be dated precisely; John Kirkpatrick, *A Temporary Mimeographed Catalogue of the Music Manuscripts and Related Materials of Charles Edward Ives 1874–1954* (New Haven: Library of the Yale School of Music, 1960; reprint, 1973), 62, guesses "?1887."

16. Clayton Henderson, *The Charles Ives Tunebook*, Bibliographies in American Music, 14 (Warren, Mich.: Harmonie Park Press, 1990), 172, shows the opening accompanimental vamp as the material quoted from *Lucia* but does not mention the melodic resemblances. Laurence D. Wallach, "The New England Education of Charles Ives" (Ph.D. diss., Columbia University, 1973), 120, refers to the Polonaise as "an arrangement" of the Donizetti, which is clearly not the case.

17. For additional examples of early works based on models, see J. Peter Burkholder, " 'Quotation' and Emulation: Charles Ives's Uses of His Models," *Musical Quarterly* 71 (1985): 1–26, particularly pp. 5–10; and *All Made of Tunes*, chap. 2.

18. See Wallach, "New England Education," 146–59.

19. For a complete list, see Kirkpatrick, *Catalogue*, 240. Ives dated his *Minnelied* to 1892 and a few other songs to the mid-1890s, but at least the German settings seem to date from Ives's last year at Yale through ca. 1902, according to Gayle Sherwood (personal communication, 26 May 1994) based on the dating techniques described in her article "Questions and Veracities: Reassessing the Chronology of Ives's Choral Works," *Musical Quarterly* 78 (1994): 429–47. The French songs seem to post-date Yale.

20. I borrow the terminology of emulation, homage, and competition from Howard Mayer Brown, "Emulation, Competition, and Homage: Imitation and Theories of Imitation in the Renaissance," *Journal of the American Musicological Society* 35 (1982): 1–48. Ives states in *Memos*, 51, 87, 149, and 155 that he wrote the symphony in college and dates it 1896–98. In memos on the scores, printed in Kirkpatrick, *Catalogue*, 1–3, he indicated that the work was begun in 1897 (an 1895 date of completion for the first movement is certainly too early), that movements 2 and 4 were accepted as part of his thesis for Parker's course in June 1898, and that the full score was copied in 1903. Gayle Sherwood (personal communication, 23 May 1994) dates the handwriting on the surviving manuscripts slightly later: the sketch and score-sketch for the first movement ca. 1898 and all other work on the symphony between 1898 and 1902.

21. On the resemblance between these two melodies in scoring, mood, and largely pentatonic sound, see David Eiseman, "Charles Ives and the European Symphonic Tradition: A Historical Reappraisal" (Ph.D. diss., University of Illinois at Urbana-Champaign, 1972), 246–47. Paul Echols, "The Music for Orchestra," *Music Educators Journal* 61/2 (October 1974): 32–33, mentions the resemblance of the two passages.

22. For instance, Ives records in *Memos*, 123, that Edgar Stowell, a violinist in the New York Symphony, tried out Ives's First Violin Sonata with Ives at the

piano, "but Stowell said it was too difficult and stopped. He said there were too many ideas too close together." After they played through a sonata by Daniel Gregory Mason, "Stowell said Mason's was better than mine because it was Geigermusik, but he did say that one page of mine had more ideas than Mason's whole sonata. Whether he meant this as advice in restraint and prudence I don't know." Later, Ives mentions hearing Stravinsky's *Firebird* and thinking that "it was morbid and monotonous. (The idea of a phrase, usually a small one, was good enough and interesting in itself, but he kept it going over and over, and [it] got tiresome.)" Ibid., p. 138; editorial brackets and parentheses by Kirkpatrick.

23. For a close analysis of borrowings in the Second Symphony, see J. Peter Burkholder, " 'Quotation' and Paraphrase in Ives's Second Symphony," *19th-Century Music* 11 (1987): 3–25. In his manuscripts, Ives dates the work 1900–1902 and the revision 1909. Gayle Sherwood (personal communication, 23 May 1994) dates the sketches ca. 1902–7 and the full score ca. 1907.

24. For a discussion of "musical prose" and "developing variation" as they apply to Brahms, see Arnold Schoenberg, "Brahms the Progressive," in *Style and Idea*, 398–441.

25. Ives dated the Third Symphony 1911 in his earlier work-lists, 1904 in his later ones (see *Memos*, 150 and 160), and noted on a copy that it was "finished summers Elk Lake 1910–1911" (Kirkpatrick, *Catalogue*, 7). According to Gayle Sherwood (personal communication, 26 May 1994), the outer movements are sketched on a type of music paper that was first available in 1907, in a hand dating from soon after 1907, perhaps ca. 1908–9. The middle movement sketches are in a hand of ca. 1907, and the full score is in a slightly later hand.

26. See the discussion of cumulative form (also called "cumulative setting" when the theme used is a borrowed tune) in Burkholder, "The Evolution of Charles Ives's Music," 385–407, and in *All Made of Tunes*, chap. 5.

27. Program note for the Third Violin Sonata, in *Memos*, 69, note 1. The history of cumulative form has yet to be written, but there are clear precedents for Ives's procedures in nineteenth-century music and parallels among his contemporaries. Maynard Solomon, "The Ninth Symphony: A Search for Order," in *Beethoven Essays* (Cambridge, Mass.: Harvard University Press, 1988), 3–32, shows that the "Ode to Joy" theme is prefigured by a number of melodic ideas of similar shape in all movements and thus functions as "the culmination of a series of melodies aspiring to achieve an ultimate, lapidary form" (p. 14); Schumann's song "Die beiden Grenadiere" (1840) culminates with a quotation from "La Marseillaise" that is increasingly hinted at over the course of the song; Smetana's *Tábor* (1878), the fifth movement of *Má vlast*, is based on a Hussite tune that is gradually assembled from its parts during both sections of the piece; symphonies by Tchaikovsky, Mahler, and Sibelius include themes that are first stated in part and achieve definitive form only after a process of growth; and the slow movement of Sibelius's Fourth Symphony (1911) is a full-fledged cumulative form on an original theme. See Burkholder, *All Made of Tunes*, chap. 6, on the development of this form in Ives's music.

28. For analyses of *The Fourth of July*, see Arthur Maisel, "*The Fourth of*

July by Charles Ives: Mixed Harmonic Criteria in a Twentieth-Century Classic," *Theory and Practice* 6/1 (August 1981): 3–32, and Mark D. Nelson, "Beyond Mimesis: Transcendentalism and Processes of Analogy in Charles Ives' The Fourth of July," *Perspectives of New Music* 22 (1984): 353–84. Ives dated the work between 1911 and 1913 (see *Memos*, 83, 104, 150, and 160, and Kirkpatrick, *Catalogue*, 11–12). But Gayle Sherwood (personal communication, 31 May 1994) dates the extant sketches ca. 1914, no earlier than 1913; the score-sketch ca. 1914–19, closer to 1919; the full score ca. 1919–23; and later revisions ca. 1923–29.

29. See, for example, the analyses cited in the previous note and the sketch study by Wayne Shirley, " 'The Second of July': A Charles Ives Draft Considered as an Independent Work," in *A Celebration of American Music: Words and Music in Honor of H. Wiley Hitchcock*, ed. Richard Crawford, R. Allen Lott, and Carol J. Oja (Ann Arbor: University of Michigan Press, 1990), 391–404.

Chapter 2: The "Sounds That Beethoven Didn't Have"

1. Manuscript pages f7459–7464/n1947–52 in the Ives Collection, John Herrick Jackson Music Library, Yale University, New Haven, Conn. John Kirkpatrick dates this arrangement 1889 or 1890 in *A Temporary Mimeographed Catalogue of the Music Manuscripts and Related Materials of Charles Edward Ives 1874–1954* (New Haven: Library of the Yale School of Music, 1960; reprint, 1973), 222. Gayle Sherwood (personal communication of 19 May 1994 to J. Peter Burkholder) dates the handwriting of this arrangement ca. 1898, using a more reliable method for dating Ives's music described in her article "Questions and Veracities: Reassessing the Chronology of Ives's Choral Works," *Musical Quarterly* 78 (1994): 429–47. Burkholder, *All Made of Tunes: Charles Ives and the Uses of Musical Borrowing* (New Haven: Yale University Press, 1995), 436, n. 12, points out that Ives took a class in instrumentation from Parker during his last two years at Yale and may have made this transcription for one of those classes.

2. Burkholder, *All Made of Tunes*, 47.

3. The quotation is from Charles Ives, *Essays Before a Sonata, The Majority, and Other Writings*, ed. Howard Boatwright (New York: W. W. Norton, 1970), 88; and Charles E. Ives, *Memos*, ed. John Kirkpatrick (New York: W. W. Norton, 1972), 30, 43–44, and 100. That Ives was similarly conflicted about surpassing the musical accomplishments of his genealogical father may be inferred from his apparent exaggeration of George Ives's musical influence. Most of Ives's remarks on his father's legacy are dispersed throughout *Memos*. The degree to which Ives was musically indebted to his father has been explored at length by Stuart Feder and challenged by Maynard Solomon. See Maynard Solomon, "Charles Ives: Some Questions of Veracity," *Journal of the American Musicological Society* 40 (1987): 443–470, and Stuart Feder, *Charles Ives: "My Father's Song": A Psychoanalytic Biography* (New Haven: Yale University Press, 1992), 351–57.

4. *Memos*, 43–44.

5. J. Peter Burkholder, " 'Quotation' and Paraphrase in Ives's Second Symphony," *19th-Century Music* 11 (1987): 3–25.

6. Some have drawn a tenuous connection between Beethoven's Fifth

Symphony motive and the *Missionary Chant* reference in the third movement. See J. Peter Burkholder, " 'Quotation' and Paraphrase," 22, n. 22.

7. The relationship between the scherzos of Ives's First Symphony and Beethoven's Ninth is discussed in greater detail in Burkholder, *All Made of Tunes.*

8. Ives also uses the Fifth Symphony motive prominently in the second movement of his own Fourth Symphony (much of which is derived from "Hawthorne"), in several other works related to the *Concord Sonata*—the unfinished *Emerson Overture/Concerto, Study No. 9, Four Transcriptions from "Emerson,"* and *The Celestial Railroad*—and more tangentially and speculatively in "Dreams" (*114 Songs,* no. 85) and the *Three-Page Sonata* for piano.

9. On the first performances of Beethoven's Fifth Symphony in New York, see Howard Shanet, *Philharmonic: A History of New York's Orchestra* (Garden City, N.Y.: Doubleday, 1975), 5, 72–73, 88–91, and 142–45. For one prominent person's response to early performances of the work, see George Templeton Strong, *Strong on Music: The New York Music Scene in the Days of George Templeton Strong, 1836–1875,* vol. 1, *Resonances 1836–1850,* ed. Vera Brodsky Lawrence (New York and Oxford: Oxford University Press, 1988), 111 and 244.

10. John Sullivan Dwight, "Music in Boston During the Last Winter," *The Harbinger* 1/1 (August 1845): 154–57; Margaret Fuller, "Goethe," *The Dial* 2/ 1 (July 1841): 1; see also *The Writings of Margaret Fuller,* ed. Mason Wade (Clifton, N.J.: Augustus M. Kelley, 1973), 242–72. Dwight heard the first movement of Beethoven's Fifth Symphony as nothing less than "*the great life-struggle* ... the whole movement seems to represent the genius of man in conflict with necessity—man pleasing and wrestling with the iron limitations which rise up against him, charging with his half-fledged immortal wings against the bars of the Actual." He concludes his review with a reference to Bettina von Arnim's widely circulated remarks on Beethoven's creative process, which, "if he [Beethoven] did not say it in words, he certainly did repeatedly in his music." Emerson and Fuller first came across von Arnim's reminiscences of Beethoven in *The Gentleman's Magazine* (October 1838), 393–97. See Emerson's *Journals,* vol. 7 (1838–42), ed. A. W. Plumstead Harrison and Harrison Hayford (Cambridge, Mass.: Harvard University Press, 1975), 158. Certainly von Arnim gave the Transcendentalists what they wanted to hear about Beethoven.

11. *Essays,* 86 (emphasis in original).

12. In the "Prologue," Ives's brief and inconclusive personal debate on the nature of program music, Ives uses Beethoven to deride Tolstoy: "From his [Tolstoy's] definition of art, we may learn little more than that a kick in the back is a work of art, and Beethoven's *Ninth Symphony* is not" (*Essays,* p. 5).

13. *Essays,* 72.

14. Daniel Gregory Mason, *Contemporary Composers* (New York: MacMillan, 1918), 41, and separate chapters on d'Indy and Elgar. Mason singles out Rachmaninoff as a third carrier of the "great tradition" but does not honor him with a separate chapter—no doubt to the relief of Ives, who on a pencil sketch page for his *Study No. 20* referred to the Russian somewhat disrespectfully as "Rachnotmanenough." See John Kirkpatrick's edition of *Study No. 20* (Bryn Mawr,

Pa.: Merion Music, 1981), 17, notes for mm. 69–70. Frank R. Rossiter discusses what Ives absorbed from Mason's assessment of twentieth-century composers in "The 'Genteel Tradition' in American Music," *Journal of American Culture* 4 (1981): 107–15. For Ives's reading list at Asheville, see J. Peter Burkholder, *Charles Ives: The Ideas Behind the Music* (New Haven: Yale University Press, 1985), 111. Nicholas Tawa cites additional evidence of Ives's admiration for Mason's writings in his essay in this volume.

15. *Essays*, 73.

16. Ibid. 73–74.

17. Ibid. 74. Keith Ward discusses the distinctions between Ives's "substance" and "manner" in relation to Schoenberg's "style" and "idea" in his essay in this volume.

18. *Essays*, 82–83.

19. Alexander Wheelock Thayer, *Ludwig van Beethovens Leben*, 3 vols. (Berlin: Schneider, 1866; Weber, 1872–79). For the first English edition (based on Thayer's notes up to 1816), see Henry Edward Krehbiel, 3 vols. (New York: Beethoven Association, 1921). For a revised, edited, and updated version of Thayer, see *Thayer's Life of Beethoven*, rev. and ed. Elliot Forbes, 2 vols. (Princeton: Princeton University Press, 1964; rev. ed., 1967).

20. For example, Schindler, referring to the almost psychotic behavior that Beethoven exhibited in the prolonged custody battle for his nephew, writes that "through these new conflicts, the moral man Beethoven first gains occasion to show himself in all his energy, and even momentarily to outweigh the creative genius." Anton Felix Schindler, *The Life of Beethoven*, ed. Ignace Moscheles, (Boston: Oliver Ditson, n.d. [1841]), 67.

21. Margaret Fuller, *Papers on Literature and Art* (London: Wiley and Putnam, 1846), 2: 96. For a balanced discussion of Beethoven's relationships with his nephew and sister-in-law, see Maynard Solomon, *Beethoven* (New York: Schirmer Books, 1977), 231–55.

22. *Essays*, 84–85.

23. Ibid., 36. The phrase "fate knocking at the door" appears in the 1860 edition of Schindler, in language echoed by Ives: "no work bears out more fully than Beethoven's C minor symphony the maxim that every true work of art is a realization of the divine . . . The composer himself provided the key to these depths when one day, in this author's presence, he pointed to the beginning of the first movement and expressed in these words the fundamental idea of his work: 'Thus Fate knocks at the door!' " Quoted from Schindler, *Beethoven as I Knew Him*, ed. Donald W. MacArdle (New York: W. W. Norton, 1966), 147. In his *Harbinger* essay Dwight also refers to Schindler's recollection: "Beethoven, explaining the *time* of those first three [*sic*] notes one day to a friend, said: *"So knocks Fate at the door."*

24. Henry Cowell and Sidney Cowell, *Charles Ives and His Music*, 2d ed. (New York: Oxford University Press, 1969), 191–92.

25. All references to the *Concord Sonata* cite page and system numbers from the second edition (New York: Associated Music Publishers, 1947).

26. In the earliest extant sketches of "The Alcotts" and "Thoreau" (Ives

Collection, f3252/n2856 and f3993/n3176), the Fifth Symphony motive was not yet incorporated within the "human faith melody." In all other crucial respects (besides key) these early "human faith melody" sketches correspond to the published version of the sonata.

27. Henry Cowell and Sidney Cowell, 190–201. Somewhat surprisingly, the "human faith melody," which occupies the lyrical center of the *Concord Sonata*, was ignored by Henry Cowell, who wrote the analytical portions of the biography.

28. *Missionary Chant* shows up in the *Concord Sonata* most prominently at the beginning of "The Alcotts" (p. 53) and just before the first statement of the "human faith melody" two pages later (see the beginning of the first system in ex. 2.8a). The first eight notes of the top line on p. 53 are those of Beethoven's Fifth Symphony, with one exception (a repeated B♭ instead of three Cs). When the figure returns later in the system, the D is repeated a fourth time and the melody becomes *Missionary Chant*, unaltered, for eight notes.

29. Oliver Strunk affirms the likelihood that Zeuner (1795–1857) was familiar with Beethoven when he assesses the composer of *Missionary Chant* as "one of the first thoroughly grounded musicians to settle in the United States," "Zeuner," *Dictionary of American Biography* (New York: Charles Scribner's Sons, 1936) 20: 651–52.

30. Previously noted by Fred Fisher, *Ives' Concord Sonata* (Denton, Tex.: C/G Productions, 1981), 32.

31. In *Essays*, Ives mentions by name only Beethoven's Fifth Symphony. A second reference, to the chorus of Stephen Foster's "Massa's in de Cold Ground" (1852) in "Thoreau," can be found in his performing note that follows the music of the second edition. "Sometimes, as on pages 62–65–68, an old Elm Tree may feel like humming a phrase from 'Down in the Corn Field,' but usually very slowly." Ives also mentions that Beth Alcott played Scotch songs and hymns, but he does not specify which ones (*Essays*, 47). Clayton W. Henderson, *The Charles Ives Tunebook* (Michigan: Harmonie Park Press, 1990), 205, and Kirkpatrick's handwritten emendations to his *Catalogue*, 89–90, add to the list of borrowings in "Hawthorne" and "The Alcotts" not mentioned by Ives.

32. Allen Gimbel, "Elgar's Prize Song: Quotation and Allusion in the Second Symphony," *19th-Century Music* 12 (1989): 233.

33. In addition, in the Ives Collection at Yale University is a score of the funeral march from Beethoven's Piano Sonata in A♭, Op. 26, included in *Fourteen Celebrated Marches* (Ives Collection, Box 60, folder 7). Among the scores owned by Ives and discovered after his death in his home at West Redding, Conn., are vol. 1 of the Beethoven piano sonatas, ed. Hans von Bülow and Sigmund Lebert (New York, G. Schirmer, 1894), and the Piano Sonata Op. 14, No. 1. Ives's collection of music is described in Vivian Perlis, ed., *Charles Ives Papers*, Yale University Library Archival Collection Mss, 14 (New Haven: Yale University Press, 1983), 187–95.

34. The New Haven Symphony programs are listed in David Eiseman, "Charles Ives and the European Symphonic Tradition: A Historical Reappraisal," Ph.D. diss., University of Illinois, 1972, 266–69. For a comprehensive

list of New York Philharmonic programs from 1842 to 1917, see Henry Edward Krehbiel, James Gibbons Huneker, and John Erskine, *Early Histories of the New York Philharmonic* (New York: Da Capo Press, 1970), 1: 95–163 and 2: 49–130.

35. William S. Newman, "Some 19th-Century Consequences of Beethoven's 'Hammerklavier' Sonata, Op. 106," *Piano Quarterly* 67 (1969): 12–18 and 68 (1969): 12–17.

36. Dwight writes: "Then came the Brook Farm experiment, and it is equally a curious fact that music, and of the best kind, the Beethoven Sonatas, the masses of Mozart and Haydn, got at, indeed, in a very humble, home made, and imperfect way, was one of the chief interests of those halcyon days." John Sullivan Dwight, "Music as a Means of Culture," *Atlantic Monthly* 26 (1870): 322.

37. Harold Bloom, *The Anxiety of Influence: A Theory of Poetry* (New York: Oxford University Press, 1973). See Joseph N. Straus, *Remaking the Past: Musical Modernism and the Influence of the Tonal Tradition* (Cambridge, Mass.: Harvard University Press, 1990) for an application of Bloom's theories to the music of Stravinsky, Schoenberg, Webern, Berg, and Bartók. For a discussion of how Ives used Emerson to overcome influences, see David Michael Hertz, *Angels of Reality: Emersonian Unfoldings in Wright, Stevens, and Ives* (Carbondale and Edwardsville: Southern Illinois University Press, 1993), 93–113.

38. *Essays*, 88–89.

39. *Memos*, 30. On the misogyny in Ives's *Memos*, see Judith Tick, "Charles Ives and Gender Ideology," in *Musicology and Difference: Gender and Sexuality in Music Scholarship*, ed. Ruth A. Solie (Berkeley: University of California Press, 1993), 83–106, and Catherine Parsons Smith, " 'A Distinguishing Virility': Feminism and Modernism in American Art Music," in *Cecilia Reclaimed: Feminist Perspectives on Gender and Music*, ed. Susan C. Cook and Judy S. Tsou (Urbana and Chicago: University of Illinois Press, 1994), 90–106, especially pp. 94–96.

40. *Memos*, 100.

41. Ibid., 135.

42. Ibid., 43–44. Kirkpatrick adds to Ives's "memo" that the all-Beethoven concert included three sonatas (Op. 2, No. 2; Op. 57; and Op. 110), the Thirty-two Variations in C Minor, and the Rondo in G, Op. 51, No. 2. In his sketches for *Study No. 20*—in the same sentence in which Ives disparages Rachmaninoff (see note 14)—Ives refers to Gabrilowitsch as "Ossy Gab" and considers the great pianist another of the "star lady bird pleasers" and "Rollo boys."

43. Ives adopts the last four notes of the opening phrase of "Columbia" (which elides with phrase B of *Martyn*) to conclude the "human faith melody" (ex. 2.8a). See also Dennis Marshall, "Charles Ives's Quotations: Manner or Substance?" *Perspectives of New Music* 6 (1968): 45–56, reprinted in *Perspectives on American Composers*, ed: Benjamin Boretz and Edward T. Cone (New York: W. W. Norton, 1971), 13–24; and Gordon Cyr, "Intervallic Structural Elements in Ives' Fourth Symphony," *Perspectives of New Music* 9–10 (1971): 291–303. In addition to his Beethoven and *Martyn* borrowings (and the "Columbia" close in "Hawthorne" and "The Alcotts"), Ives, in his "human faith melody," also borrows from himself. Melodic notes 4–6 (see ex. 2.3, 2.8a, and 2.8b) incorporate a

motive that Ives will display more prominently on many occasions in his sonata (e.g., p. 14, system 2, last three notes of m. 1), and notes 10–14 of the "human faith melody" invert the distinctive pentatonic lyrical theme that introduces the central section of "Emerson" (pp. 8–11).

44. Vivian Perlis, *Charles Ives Remembered: An Oral History* (New York: W. W. Norton), 87–88. Chester Ives's recollection is discussed in J. Peter Burkholder's introduction to the present volume.

Chapter 3: Ives and the New England School

1. J. Peter Burkholder, *Charles Ives, the Ideas Behind the Music* (New Haven: Yale University Press, 1985), 96; Nicholas E. Tawa, *The Coming of Age of American Art Music* (Westport, Conn.: Greenwood Press, 1991), 58.

2. Victor Yellin, *Chadwick, Yankee Composer* (Washington, D.C.: Smithsonian Institution, 1990), 15.

3. George W. Chadwick, *Horatio Parker* (New Haven: Yale University Press, 1921), 5–6.

4. Yellin, *Chadwick*, 223, n. 1.

5. The beliefs and music of these three composers are explored in detail in Nicholas E. Tawa, *Mainstream Music of Early Twentieth Century America* (Westport, Conn.: Greenwood Press, 1992).

6. William K. Kearns, *Horatio Parker, 1863–1919* (Metuchen, N.J.: Scarecrow Press, 1990), 8, 236, and 243; Macdonald Moore, *Yankee Blues* (Bloomington, Ind.: Indiana University Press, 1985), 22 and 54–55.

7. Burkholder, *Charles Ives*, 39.

8. Rosalie S. Perry, *Charles Ives and the American Mind* (Kent, Ohio: Kent State University Press, 1974), 8.

9. See Kearns, *Horatio Parker*, 49–51, 195, and 236, and Burkholder, *Charles Ives*, 61–62.

10. Isabel Parker Semler, in collaboration with Pierson Underwood, *Horatio Parker* (New York: Putnam's Sons, 1942), 74–75, and 164–65.

11. Charles Ives, *Essays Before a Sonata, The Majority, and Other Writings*, ed. Howard Boatwright (New York: W. W. Norton, 1970), 39 and 73.

12. Letter to John Tasker Howard, reprinted in Charles E. Ives, *Memos*, ed. John Kirkpatrick (New York: W. W. Norton, 1972), 238–39.

13. Chadwick, *Horatio Parker*, 12.

14. Kearns, *Horatio Parker*, 235; Semler, *Horatio Parker*, 96; interview with John Kirkpatrick, in *Charles Ives Remembered: An Oral History* (New Haven: Yale University Press, 1974), 225; Kirkpatrick, in album notes to the recording MHS 824501.

15. Ives, *Memos*, pp. 181–83; Kearns, *Horatio Parker*, p. 29.

16. Henry Bellamann, "Charles Ives: The Man and His Music," *Musical Quarterly* 19 (1933): 47.

17. Ives, *Memos*, 49.

18. Something similar may have lain behind the criticisms of Virgil Thomson, who remarked in a letter of 20 January 1970, "I realize that Ives is a very interesting composer but his carelessness and volubility are sometimes hard to

take." Tim Page and Vanessa Weeks Page, eds., *Selected Letters of Virgil Thomson* (New York: Summit Books, 1988), 329.

19. Ives, *Memos*, 47.

20. Burkholder, *Charles Ives*, 64.

21. Kearns, *Horatio Parker*, 9.

22. Ives, *Memos*, 51.

23. Frank R. Rossiter, *Charles Ives and His America* (New York: Liveright, 1975), p. 57; Ives, *Memos*, pp. 51–52.

24. Ives, *Memos*, 183–84. The editorial emendations are by John Kirkpatrick.

25. George Whitefield Chadwick, *Harmony* (Boston: Wood, 1897), 259.

26. Vivian Perlis, ed., *Charles Ives Papers*, Yale University Library Archival Collection Mss, 14 (New Haven: Yale University Press, 1983), 187–88 and 193–94.

27. Ives, *Essays*, 94–95. See also, Burkholder, *Charles Ives*, 111; Moore, *Yankee Blues*, 54; and Geoffrey Block's essay in this volume.

28. On the attitudes of Mason and other contemporary American composers toward musical nationalism, see Tawa, *Mainstream Music*, 103–36.

29. Perlis, *Charles Ives Remembered*, 45; Rossiter, *Charles Ives and His America*, 29; Ives, *Memos*, 49, n. 4.

30. David Eiseman, "Charles Ives and the European Symphonic Tradition": A Historical Reappraisal (Ph.D. diss., University of Illinois, 1972), 110–113, 116, and 266–69; Ives, *Memos*, 49 n. 4.

31. For example, the march "The Mulligan Guard," with words by Edward Harrigan and music by David Braham, was featured in several of the Harrigan and Hart "Mulligan" stage burlesques, achieving great popularity in the late seventies and the eighties.

32. Perry, *Charles Ives and the American Mind*, 11–12.

33. Kearns, *Horatio Parker*, 241–43.

34. Rossiter, *Charles Ives and His America*, 16.

35. Daniel Gregory Mason, *Music in My Time and Other Reminiscences* (New York: Macmillan, 1938), 35–36.

36. For further verification of Ives's romantic inclination toward the past, see Michael J. Alexander, *The Evolving Keyboard Style of Charles Ives* (New York: Garland, 1989), 49; Virgil Thomson, *Music Reviewed, 1940–1954* (New York: Vintage, 244–45, which reprints a review written 13 March 1948; Henry Cowell and Sidney Cowell, *Charles Ives and His Music*, 2d ed. (New York: Oxford University Press, 1969; reprint, New York: Da Capo, 1983), 71; Neely Bruce, quoted in *An Ives Celebration: Papers and Panels of the Ives Centennial Festival-Conference*, ed. H. Wiley Hitchcock and Vivian Perlis (Urbana: University of Illinois Press, 1977), 38–39; and J. Peter Burkholder's essay in the present collection.

37. John Kirkpatrick, s.v. "Ives, Charles (Edward)," in *The New Grove Dictionary of American Music*, edited by H. Wiley Hitchcock and Stanley Sadie (London: Macmillan, 1986). When referring to the formal genres cultivated by Ives and their connection with the European-American mainstream, Kirkpatrick had in mind the conclusions reached by J. Peter Burkholder, "The Evolution of

Charles Ives's Music: Aesthetics, Quotation, Technique" (Ph.D. diss., University of Chicago, 1983).

38. H. Wiley Hitchcock, *Ives: A Survey of the Music* (London: Oxford University Press, 1977), 34.

39. See also Victor Yellin's comparative discussion of *The Celestial Country* and *Hora novissima*, in *Musical Quarterly* 60 (1974): 500–508.

40. The subject of this and the next paragraph has been discussed by Yellin and by J. Peter Burkholder, in the *Musical Quarterly* 71 (1985), 15.

41. Ives, *Memos*, 62–63.

42. See Maynard Solomon, "Charles Ives: Some Questions of Veracity," *Journal of the American Musicological Society* 40 (1987): 443–69, and the response in Stuart Feder, *Charles Ives: "My Father's Song": A Psychoanalytic Biography* (New Haven and London: Yale University Press, 1992), 351–57.

43. Burkholder, *Charles Ives*, p. 81.

44. Kirkpatrick, "Ives, Charles (Edward)."

45. Henry Bellamann, "Charles Ives," 49. See also J. Peter Burkholder's discussion of "cumulative form" in chap. 1.

46. Semler, *Horatio Parker*, 73–74.

47. Ibid., 75.

48. Wendell Clarke Kumlien, "The Sacred Choral Music of Charles Ives" (D.M.A. thesis, University of Washington, 1969), 36; Hitchcock, *Ives*, 28; Bruce, in *An Ives Celebration*, 37.

50. At letter B, of "Jubilee," one of the four *Symphonic Sketches* (New York: Kalmus, n.d.).

Chapter 4: Ives and Mahler

1. Cf. Theodor W. Adorno, *Mahler* (Frankfurt: Suhrkamp, 1960), 30ff.

2. See Donald Mitchell, *Gustav Mahler: The Wunderhorn Years* (Boulder, Col.: Westview Press, 1976), 73ff.; also Ernest Jones, *Sigmund Freud* (New York: Basic Books, 1955), 2: 79–80.

3. Charles E. Ives, *Memos*, ed. John Kirkpatrick (New York: W. W. Norton, 1972), 71.

4. The classic statement is Victor Shklovsky's "Art as Technique" (1917), reprinted in English in *Russian Formalist Criticism: Four Essays*, trans. and ed. Lee T. Lemon and Marion J. Reis (Lincoln: University of Nebraska Press, 1965), 3–24.

5. The relationship of Mahler's symphonies to his earlier songs, as well as his use of material borrowed from other sources, is discussed in Monika Tibbe, *Lieder und Liedelemente in instrumentalen Symphoniesätzen Gustav Mahlers* (Munich: E. Katzbichler, 1972).

6. Henry Cowell and Sidney Cowell, *Charles Ives and His Music*, 2d ed. (New York: Oxford University Press, 1969), 144–45.

7. Natalie Bauer-Lechner, *Erinnerungen an Gustav Mahler* (Leipzig: E. P. Tal, 1923), 147. This passage has been quoted and discussed in several recent books: Adorno, *Mahler*, 147ff.; *Flawed Words and Stubborn Sounds: A Conversation with Elliott Carter*, by Allen Edwards (New York: W. W. Norton, 1971), 102fn.;

and Mitchell, *The Wunderhorn Years*, 339ff., from which the above translation is taken. Both Carter and Mitchell also touch upon, though briefly, similarities between Ives and Mahler. Mitchell feels that "one must not let the parallel, such as it is, carry one away" and attempts to draw a basic distinction between the two composers' attitudes toward their material:

> It might have been, one guesses, that Mahler would have been intrigued by the acoustic experience from life that gave rise to, say, Ives's *Putnam's Camp* (the second of his *Three Places in New England*), but one does not need to guess at all that, had Mahler actually written a piece out of that experience, it would have been purely musical considerations that would have governed its composition: the original acoustic event would, so to speak, have been musicalized, would have played a far less prominent role than the one alloted it by Ives [p. 170].

Although there is no question that Ives and Mahler transform what they have borrowed in very different ways, Mitchell's suggestion that Mahler's approach is governed more by "purely musical considerations," whereas Ives's is more "realistic" or "photographic," seems to me to miss the point completely. Ives's materials (in *Putnam's Camp*, for example) are every bit as "musically" transformed—as "musicalized" (and thus as "unrealistic")—as are Mahler's. Mitchell, I suspect, has chosen the wrong word. Perhaps what he means is that Mahler's approach to his material is more traditional, not more musical.

8. See my discussion of Ives in this connection in "Rewriting Music History: Second Thoughts on Ives and Varèse," *Musical Newsletter* 3 (1973): 3–12.

9. Hugo von Hofmannsthal, *Gesammelte Werke: Prosa IV*, ed. Herbert Steiner (Frankfurt: S. Fischer, 1966), 489–90.

10. For a wide-ranging collection of essays on fragmentation as a historical phenomenon in the arts, see *Das Unvollendete als künstlerische Form*, ed. J. A. Schmoll a.k.a. Eisenwerth (Bern and Munich: Francke, 1959).

11. Ives, *Memos*, 121. For evidence that Mahler might have performed the symphony in Munich in 1910, see David Wooldridge, *From the Steeples and Mountains: A Study of Charles Ives* (New York: Knopf, 1974), 150–51.

Chapter 5: Ives, Schoenberg, and the Musical Ideal

1. Henry Cowell and Sidney Cowell, *Charles Ives and His Music*, 2d ed. (New York: Oxford University Press, 1969), 114n. John Kirkpatrick added the following note, dated 20 February 1976, to Gertrud Schoenberg's accompanying letter: "In October 1975, Peter Yates told John Kirkpatrick that Mrs. Schoenberg told him that this slip of paper in Schoenberg's hand was 'from the 1944 box.' " See Gertrud Schoenberg to Charles Ives, 17 November 1953, in Vivian Perlis, ed., *Charles Ives Papers*, Yale University Library Archival Collection Mss, 14 (New Haven: Yale University Press, 1983), 89. Peter Yates also suggests the year 1944, in "Charles Ives: An American Composer," *Parnassus: Poetry in Review* 3/2 (Spring–Summer 1975): 323. For a facsimile of Schoenberg's note, see H. Wiley Hitchcock, "Schoenberg on Ives," *Institute for Studies in American Music*

Newsletter 10/2 (May 1981): 5. I would like to thank H. Wiley Hitchcock for bringing to my attention his article as well as the Cowells' misreading of Schoenberg's note ("self-esteem" transcribed as "self and to learn").

2. One is reminded of Schoenberg's resentment toward Richard Strauss when the older composer turned against him. See H. H. Stuckenschmidt, *Arnold Schoenberg: His Life, World and Work*, translated by John Calder (London: John Calder, 1977), 71–73.

3. Peter Yates, *Twentieth Century Music* (New York: Random House, 1967), 262.

4. This account of the meeting has been pieced together from the following sources: Stuckenschmidt, *Arnold Schoenberg*, 440; Yates, "Charles Ives: An American Composer," 323; Peter Yates, "Charles Ives: The Transcendental American Venture," *Arts and Architecture* 58 (1961): 8; and a telephone conversation between this writer and John Kirkpatrick on 21 July 1983. Yates's recollections are based upon conversations he had had personally with Schoenberg, as are Kirkpatrick's with Ives. See "Charles Ives: An American Composer," 323.

5. I am grateful to Jerry McBride of Middlebury College for conveying this information through personal correspondence from the Arnold Schoenberg Institute.

6. Yates, *Twentieth Century Music*, 261. They reportedly heard it in 1933. However, because *The Unanswered Question* was apparently premiered in 1946, Yates may be mistaken.

7. *Evenings on the Roof Fourth Report: The History of a Self-Made Musical Organization in Los Angeles* (Los Angeles: Roof Publications, 1946), 1–6.

8. Stuckenschmidt, *Arnold Schoenberg*, 440. Some of Schoenberg's pupils attended these concerts. In 1941 Frances Yates, Peter Yates's wife, wrote Ives that "movie music writers who are pupils of Schoenberg" received her performance of "Hawthorne" (*Concord Sonata*, second movement) enthusiastically. They may have shared their excitement with their teacher. See Frances Yates to Charles Ives, 28 June 1941, in *Charles Ives Papers*, 108.

9. Allen Forte, "Ives and Atonality," in *An Ives Celebration: Papers and Panels of the Ives Centennial Festival-Conference*, ed. H. Wiley Hitchcock and Vivian Perlis (Urbana: University of Illinois Press, 1977), 159, and Yates, "Charles Ives: The Transcendental American Venture," 8.

10. Reprinted in Charles E. Ives, *Memos*, ed. John Kirkpatrick (New York: W. W. Norton, 1974), 27. Ives was referring to a review by *New York Times* correspondent Henry Prunières of a concert in Paris during the 1931 concert season in which his *Three Places in New England* was performed. Prunières remarks that Ives "knows his Schoenberg, yet gives the impression that he has not always assimilated the lessons of the Viennese master as well as he might have." Later, Prunières confirms his Euro-centered perception of art music when he identifies the "embryonic stage" of an American school "in which the influences of Europe are all too easily discernible." See his article, "American Compositions in Paris," *New York Times*, 12 July 1931; excerpts in *Memos*, 15.

11. Elliott Carter, "Documents of a Friendship with Ives," *Tempo* 117/2 (June 1976): 3.

12. Elliott Carter, "Expressionism and American Music," *Perspectives of New Music* 4/1 (Fall–Winter 1965): 3n.

13. See John Jeffrey Gibbens, "Debussy's Impact on Ives: An Assessment" (D.M.A. diss., University of Illinois at Urbana-Champaign, 1985); Charles Ives, *Essays Before a Sonata, The Majority, and Other Writings*, ed. Howard Boatwright (New York: W. W. Norton, 1970), 81–82.

14. For Prunières, see note 10. According to Carter, music by Schoenberg and his circle did not draw significant interest from even the "ultramodern" American composers in the 1920s ("Expressionism and American Music," 2–4). Thus, the prospect of Ives's having heard Schoenberg's music during the decade when Ives met some of America's progressive composers becomes even more unlikely.

15. Yates suggests this scenario as a possibility in "Charles Ives: An American Composer," 323.

16. Cowell had even asked Ives for advice on whether to publish Schoenberg's piano piece; thus, Ives actually knew before publication that the piece was forthcoming. See Rita H. Mead, "The Amazing Mr. Cowell," *American Music* 1/4 (Winter 1983): 81.

17. See *Charles Ives Papers* 185–95. In a telephone conversation with this writer on 21 July 1983, John Kirkpatrick said he had no recollection of ever seeing any scores of Schoenberg's music at Ives's house in West Redding.

18. See Larry Starr, *A Union of Diversities: Style in the Music of Charles Ives* (New York: Schirmer Books, 1992), 8–17.

19. Although he does not refer specifically to Ives and Schoenberg, Robert Morgan's identification of the difference between new compositional content with traditional form and new form for traditional musical content seems an apt way of distinguishing Schoenberg's and Ives's approaches to musical syntax. See his "Rewriting Music History: Second Thoughts on Ives and Varèse," *Musical Newsletter* 3/1 (1973): 9.

20. For a discussion of Ives's unwillingness to abandon tonality, see Robert P. Morgan's essay in this volume.

21. Richard Middleton, "Ives and Schoenberg: An English View," *Saturday Review/World*, 21 September 1974, 40. Middleton overlooks, on the one hand, Schoenberg's cognizance of the complacent artistic tastes of the public and his bitterness toward the masses for rejecting his art, and Ives's naivete regarding the intelligence of the commoner, on the other.

Since Ives decided against "starving on his dissonances," he did not suffer financially as Schoenberg did. If he had not been so isolated and had attempted to lead the life of a modern artist, Ives's belief in the mutual transcendental aspirations of humankind might have been seriously challenged, though probably not abandoned. Concerning his eventual disillusionment, see his song "Nov. 2, 1920," in *114 Songs*, written after the Democrats lost the presidential election that year.

22. Charles Rosen, *Arnold Schoenberg* (Princeton: Princeton University Press, 1975), ix and 71. One senses Schoenberg's need to rally behind Germanic music in a letter to E. Fromigeat, dated 22 July 1919, in which he alludes to the

intellectual hangover from war propaganda against all things German that continued in some intellectual circles in France following the end of the First World War. See Arnold Schoenberg, *Schoenberg's Letters*, ed. Erwin Stein, trans. Leo Black (New York: St. Martin's Press, 1964), 66–67.

23. Eric Salzman suggests that this timeless character is created by Ives's recreation of America's "musical melting pot." See his "Charles Ives, American," *Commentary* 46/2 (August 1968): 38. See also Howard Isham, "The Musical Thinking of Charles Ives," *Journal of Aesthetics and Art Criticism* 31 (1973): 395–404, and Hans G. Helms, "Charles Edward Ives: Ideal American or Social Critic?," *Current Musicology* 19 (1973): 37–44. Isham refers to Ives's "style of musical thinking which forms the aesthetic foundation for new directions in the contemporary musical scene" (p. 395). Helms maintains that "Schoenberg's elitist and esoteric music does not intrigue our consciousness, whereas Ives's musical, philosophical, and political writings, as a continuous whole, fascinate a growing minority among professional and lay musicians, among fellow composers, performers, and audiences" (p. 38).

24. Middleton, "Ives and Schoenberg," 41. Though Schoenberg may have disliked the bourgeoisie, he was complacent about the social hierarchy in which he lived, which included the preservation of the Habsburg monarchy in pre-War Austria. See Jane Kallir, *Arnold Schoenberg's Vienna* (New York: Rizzoli, 1984), 72–74.

25. For a compelling discussion of Ives's thorough training in compositional skills, see J. Philip Lambert, "Ives and Counterpoint," *American Music* 9 (1991): 119–48.

26. Nachum Schoffman attempts to demonstrate Ives's understanding and assimilation of serialism of not only pitches, but also rhythms and other musical elements. See his "Serialism in the Works of Charles Ives," *Tempo*, 138/21 (September 1981): 21–32.

27. J. Philip Lambert, "Aggregate Structures in Music of Charles Ives," *Journal of Music Theory* 34 (1990): 31–38, 50.

28. Lambert, "Ives and Counterpoint," 140–44. See also H. Wiley Hitchcock's discussion of "On the Antipodes" and the *Three-Page Sonata*, in *Ives: A Survey of the Music* (London: Oxford University Press, 1977), 20, 46.

29. Ives, *Memos*, 164.

30. Ibid. Ives is chiding a simplistic application of all twelve chromatic pitches. In this context, Schoenberg probably would have agreed with him.

31. Geoffrey Block, *Charles Ives: A Bio-Bibliography* (New York: Greenwood Press, 1988).

32. Fred Fisher, "Ives and Schoenberg: The Impulse to Greatness," *Connecticut Review* 8/2 (April 1975): 82–88; Middleton, "Ives and Schoenberg," 39–41. See also Keith Ward, "Musical Idealism: A Study of the Aesthetics of Arnold Schoenberg and Charles Ives" (D.M. diss., Northwestern University, 1985).

33. Concerning George Ives's training, see Lambert, "Ives and Counterpoint," 121–22, and notes 10–12 (pp. 144–45). For a description of and commentary on George Ives's teaching of music theory, see David Eiseman, "George Ives as Theorist: Some Unpublished Documents," *Perspectives of New Music* 14/

1 (Fall–Winter 1975): 139–47, and Carol K. Baron, "George Ives's Essay in Music Theory: An Introduction and Annotated Edition," *American Music* 10 (1992): 239–88. On Parker's studies, see William K. Kearns, *Horatio Parker, 1863–1919: His Life, Music and Ideas* (Metuchen, N.J.: Scarecrow Press, 1990), 9.

34. Middleton, "Ives and Schoenberg."

35. For a brief discussion of dualism, see J. Peter Burkholder, *Charles Ives: The Ideas Behind the Music* (New Haven: Yale University Press, 1985), 8–11. For revealing discussions within the canon of American Studies of Ives and dualism, see Betty Chmaj, "Sonata for American Studies: Perspectives on Charles Ives," *Prospects* 4 (1979): 9–12, and "The Journey and the Mirror: Emerson and the American Arts," *Prospects* 10 (1985): 355–58, 369–70, and 391–400. Chmaj suggests that a comparison of Ives and Schoenberg may help explain Ives's appeal to our time ("Sonata," 44).

36. Ives, *Essays*, 75.

37. Ives, paraphrased from a quotation in Cowell and Cowell, *Charles Ives and His Music*, 143.

38. Ives, *Essays*, 63.

39. See the discussion of these issues in Geoffrey Block's essay in this volume.

40. Middleton, "Ives and Schoenberg," 39.

41. Schoenberg, "New Music, Outmoded Music, Style and Idea" (1946), in *Style and Idea: Selected Writings of Arnold Schoenberg*, ed. Leonard Stein, with translations by Leo Black (Berkeley and Los Angeles, University of California Press, 1975), 121 (emphasis added).

42. Ibid., 133f.

43. Allan Janik and Stephen Toulmin, *Wittgenstein's Vienna* (New York: Simon and Schuster, 1973), 110.

44. Schoenberg, letter to Wassily Kandinsky, 24 January 1911, in *Arnold Schoenberg–Wassily Kandinsky: Briefe, Bilder und Dokumente einer Außergewöhnlichen Begegnung*, ed. Jalena Hahl-Koch (Salzburg: Residenz, 1980), 21; my translation.

45. Ives, *Essays*, 81.

46. Schoenberg, "New Music, Outmoded Music, Style and Idea," in *Style and Idea*, 123.

47. Kandinsky's manifesto, *Über das Geistige in der Kunst* (Munich: Piper, 1912), clearly shows that he and Schoenberg were exploring similar realms. For more on this aspect of Kandinsky's thought, see his *Concerning the Spiritual in Art*, tr. Michael Sadleir and retranslated by Francis Golffins, Michael Harrison, and Ferdinand Ostertag. (New York: Wittenborn, Schultz, 1947).

48. "New Music, Outmoded Music, Style and Idea," in *Style and Idea*, 123.

49. In *Essays* (p. 81) he writes: "if local color, national color, any color, is a true pigment of the universal color, it is a divine quality, it is a part of substance in art—not of manner."

50. Schoenberg, "How One Becomes Lonely" (1937), in *Style and Idea*, 152.

51. Ives, *Essays*, 92.

52. Henry Cowell gives the phrase "music of the Idea," as a quotation, perhaps from Ives, in describing Ives's *Universe Symphony*. See Cowell and Cowell, *Charles Ives and His Music*, 203.

53. Schoenberg, cited in Egon Wellesz, *Arnold Schoenberg*, trans. W. H. Kerridge (New York: Da Capo Press, 1969), 53.

54. Schoenberg, *Harmonielehre* (Vienna: Universal, 1922), 392–93, quoted and translated in Wellesz, *Arnold Schoenberg*, 53–54. See also Ives's discussion of beauty in *Essays*, 76–77. For another comparison of the composers' similar depictions of beauty, see Carter, "Expressionism and American Music," 7.

55. The fact that Ives and Schoenberg were eclectic thinkers, not systematic philosophers, makes the drawing of clear lines of influence problematic. Concerning Schoenberg, John Covach uses Dahlhaus's ideas of the roots of the composer's aesthetic to explain further Schoenberg's "aesthetic theology" ("The Sources of Schoenberg's 'Aesthetic Theology,'" unpublished paper read at the November 1991 meeting of the American Musicological Society, Chicago, Ill.). Covach describes Schoenberg's debt to Kant, Schopenhauer, Swedenborg, Goethe, and Rudolf Steiner (and ultimately Plato). For Ives, an understanding of this heritage comes most likely from Ralph Waldo Emerson's writings, particularly from essays dealing with aspects of transcendentalism and from his collection *Representative Men* (1876; reprint, Boston: Houghton Mifflin, 1930), in which Emerson writes about Plato ("or, the Philosopher"), Swedenborg ("or, the Mystic"), and Goethe ("or, the Writer"). For more on the New England Transcendentalist movement's debt to eighteenth- and nineteenth-century German philosophers and men of letters, see Octavius Brooks Frothingham, *Transcendentalism in New England: A History* (New York: Putnam's, 1876; reprint, Philadelphia: University of Pennsylvania Press, 1972).

56. Schoenberg, "Bach," in *Style and Idea*, 397. For further discussion of Schoenberg and developing variation, as well as a retrospective application of the theory, see Walter Frisch, *Brahms and the Principle of Developing Variation* (Berkeley: University of California Press, 1984), and idem, *The Early Works of Arnold Schoenberg, 1893–1908* (Berkeley: University of California Press, 1993).

57. See Arnold Schoenberg, *Fundamentals of Musical Composition*, ed. Gerald Strang (New York: St. Martin's Press, 1967). For a summary of Schoenberg's concept of *Grundgestalt*, see Joseph Rufer's remarks on Schoenberg's teaching, quoted in David Epstein, *Beyond Orpheus: Studies in Musical Structure* (Cambridge: MIT Press, 1979), 18.

58. Dieter Gostomsky, "Tonalität-Atonalität: Zur Harmonik von Schoenbergs Klavierstück, Opus 11, Nummer 1," *Zeitschrift für Musiktheorie* 7 (1976): 55, analyzes the accompanying chords as derivations of this basic cell. For analyses that use set theory as the basis for identifying fundamental structures in this piece, see Allen Forte, "The Magical Kaleidoscope: Schoenberg's First Atonal Masterwork, Opus 11, Number 1," *Journal of the Arnold Schoenberg Institute* 5/2 (November 1981): 127–68, and Gary Wittlich, "Interval Set Structure in Schoenberg's Opus 11, Number 1," *Perspectives of New Music* 13/1 (Fall/Winter 1974): 41–56.

59. See Burkholder's analysis of the finale of the Third Symphony, chap.

1. For a more thorough examination of this form, which Burkholder also calls "cumulative setting," see his *All Made of Tunes: Charles Ives and the Uses of Musical Borrowing* (New Haven: Yale University Press, 1995), 137-266.

60. As Burkholder observes in chap. 1.

61. Evan Rothstein, "What Its Signs of Promise Are: Ives, the Tradition of 'Developing Variation,' and the Problem of 'Folkloristic' music in Ives's First Violin Sonata, Third Movement" (unpublished typescript).

62. Burkholder, *All Made of Tunes*, 146.

63. Ibid.

64. See chap. 1.

65. Schoenberg, "Criteria for the Evaluation of Music" (1946), in *Style and Idea*, 134.

66. Middleton, "Ives and Schoenberg," 40.

67. Ives, "Postface," in *114 Songs*.

68. Yates, "Charles Ives: The Transcendental American Venture," 8.

69. Reproduced in John Kirkpatrick, *A Temporary Mimeographed Catalogue of the Music Manuscripts and Related Materials of Charles Edward Ives* (New Haven: Library of the Yale School of Music, 1960), 79. Italicized emendations are Kirkpatrick's.

70. See Ives, *Essays*, 84–86, and the essay by Geoffrey Block in this volume.

71. Ives was particularly outspoken against virtuosi. See, e.g., his comparison of Joachim, Paganini, and Jan Kubelik in *Essays*, 85.

72. On the change in musical reception and rhetoric that contributed to the development of the modern-day concept of concert-hall masterworks, see J. Peter Burkholder, "Museum Pieces: The Historicist Mainstream in Music of the Last Hundred Years," *Journal of Musicology* 2 (1983): 115–34, and Burkholder, "Musical Time and Continuity as a Reflection of the Historical Situation of Modern Composers," *Journal of Musicology* 9 (1991): 412–29. Burkholder describes the changing demands composers placed upon listeners at the turn of the century. In the latter article, he suggests that nineteenth-and twentieth-century composers, unlike their counterparts from the eighteenth century, expected listeners to study their music and to listen to repeated performances in order to understand a composition.

73. Schoenberg, undated letter, quoted and tr. in Anthony Beaumont, "Busoni and Schoenberg," *Piano Quarterly* 28/108 (Winter 1979–80): 37f., from Jutta Theurich, "Briefwechsel zwischen Arnold Schoenberg und Ferruccio Busoni, 1903–1919 (1927)," *Beiträge zur Musikwissenschaft* 19 (1977): 163–211. All italics are Schoenberg's.

74. For a description of Ives's music in similar terms, see Cowell and Cowell, *Charles Ives and His Music*, 144–51.

75. Kandinsky, *Concerning the Spiritual in Art*, 27–29.

76. Ralph Waldo Emerson, "Circles," in *Selected Writings of Ralph Waldo Emerson*, ed. Brooks Atkinson (New York: Random House, 1940), 281.

77. Ives, *Essays Before a Sonata*, 71–73.

78. See the interview with Felix Greissle in Joan Allen Smith, *Schoenberg and His Circle: A Viennese Portrait* (New York: Schirmer Books, 1986), 198. Greis-

sle recounts the meeting that Schoenberg called with his students and friends in February 1923 to explain his development of twelve-tone theory.

79. Arnold Schoenberg, *Theory of Harmony*, trans. Roy E. Carter (Berkeley: University of California Press, 1978), 325.

80. Ives, *Essays*, 71. Schoenberg had hoped for a time in the future when "my melodies should be known and whistled." See his 1947 letter to the conductor Hans Rosbaud, cited in William W. Austin, *Music in the Twentieth Century* (New York: W. W. Norton, 1966), 195.

Chapter 6: Ives and Berg

1. George Perle, *Twelve-Tone Tonality* (Berkeley and Los Angeles: University of California Press, 1977), 162. See also George Perle, *Serial Composition and Atonality*, 5th ed. (Berkeley and Los Angeles: University of California Press, 1981), 9.

2. Leonard Bernstein, *The Unanswered Question* (Cambridge, Mass.: Harvard University Press, 1976), 269.

3. Robert P. Morgan, "Charles Ives und die europäische Tradition," in *Bericht über das Internationale Symposion "Charles Ives und die amerikanische Musiktradition bis zur Gegenwart" Köln 1988*, ed. Klaus Wolfgang Niemöller (Regensburg: Gustav Bosse, 1990), 17–36.

4. Charles Ives, "Some 'Quarter-Tone' Impressions," in *Essays Before A Sonata, The Majority, and Other Writings*, ed. Howard Boatwright (New York: Norton, 1970), 117.

5. Charles E. Ives, *Memos*, ed. John Kirkpatrick (New York: Norton, 1972), 64.

6. These works are discussed by J. Peter Burkholder, *Charles Ives: The Ideas Behind the Music* (New Haven: Yale University Press, 1985), 49–50; idem, "The Evolution of Charles Ives's Music: Aesthetics, Quotation, Technique" (Ph.D. diss., University of Chicago, 1983), 629–44; Philip Lambert, "Compositional Procedures in Experimental Works of Charles E. Ives" (Ph.D. diss., Eastman School of Music, 1987); and J. Peter Burkholder, "The Critique of Tonality in the Early Experimental Music of Charles Ives," *Music Theory Spectrum* 12 (1990): 203–23.

7. Burkholder, "Evolution of Ives's Music," 646–47, and "The Critique of Tonality," passim.

8. Perle observes that quasi-normative procedures "play a far larger role in the 'free,' i.e., non-dodecaphonic, atonal works of Berg than they do in those of Schoenberg and Webern." George Perle, *Wozzeck*, vol. 1 of *The Operas of Alban Berg* (Berkeley and Los Angeles: University of California Press, 1980), 11.

9. Douglas Jarman, *The Music of Alban Berg* (Berkeley and Los Angeles: University of California Press, 1979), 21.

10. Perle, *Wozzeck*, 11.

11. Similarities between the musical procedures of Ives and Berg have been observed before. See, for example, Glenn Gould, "The Ives Fourth," *High Fidelity/Musical America* 15/7 (July 1965): 96–97; Nors S. Josephson, "Zur formalen Struktur einiger später Orchesterwerke von Charles Ives (1874–1954)," *Die Mu-*

sikforschung 27 (1974): 57–64; and Allen Forte, "Ives and Atonality," in *An Ives Celebration: Papers and Panels of the Charles Ives Centennial Festival-Conference*, ed. H. Wiley Hitchcock and Vivian Perlis (Urbana: University of Illinois Press, 1977), 159–86.

12. Though Ives's musical education has not always been viewed as conventional, Burkholder has shown that Ives was indeed well schooled in most of the same subjects as would be a European contemporary and that his knowledge of music was grounded in the European classics. See Burkholder, *Charles Ives*, 43–82, and the chapters in this volume by Burkholder and Nicholas Tawa.

13. Burkholder, *Charles Ives*, 49.

14. For further explication of these types of chord structures, see Philip Lambert, "Ives's 'Piano-Drum' Chords," *Intégral* 3 (1989): 1–36, and idem, "Toward a Theory of Chord Structure for the Music of Ives," *Journal of Music Theory* 37 (1993): 55–83.

15. *Charles Ives: Piano Sonata No. 2: "Concord, Mass., 1840–1860,"* 2nd ed. (New York: Associated Music Publishers, 1947), [73].

16. On Ives and Mahler, see the contribution to this volume by Robert P. Morgan.

17. Lawrence Starr offers illuminating insights into stylistic heterogeneity as a basic element of Ives's music in "Charles Ives: The Next Hundred Years— Towards a Method of Analyzing the Music," *Music Review* 38 (1977): 101–11; "Style and Substance: 'Ann Street' by Charles Ives," *Perspectives of New Music* 15/2 (Spring–Summer 1977): 23–33; and *A Union of Diversities: Style in the Music of Charles Ives* (New York: Schirmer Books, 1992).

18. Jarman, *Music of Alban Berg*, 143.

19. J. Peter Burkholder explains that Berg's stylistic evocations represent aspects of "familiarity" that contribute to the music's popular appeal. See J. Peter Burkholder, "Berg and the Possibility of Popularity," in *Alban Berg: Historical and Analytical Perspectives*, ed. David Gable and Robert P. Morgan (Oxford: Oxford University Press, 1991), 25–53.

20. George Ives's activities as director of various bands are described by Laurence David Wallach, "The New England Education of Charles Ives" (Ph.D. diss., Columbia University, 1973), 37–72, and Stuart Feder, *Charles Ives: "My Father's Song": A Psychoanalytic Biography* (New Haven: Yale University Press, 1992), 54–117. In several instances, the younger Ives recalled being associated with his father's bands in various ways; see, for example, Ives, *Memos*, 42–43.

21. For Perle's comments on op. 6, see his *Wozzeck*, 18–19. Glenn Watkins observes that the Military March from *Wozzeck* alludes to a similar use of march ideas by Mahler in *Des Knaben Wunderhorn*. See Glenn Watkins, *Soundings: Music in the Twentieth Century* (New York: Schirmer Books, 1988), 361–64.

22. Perle, *Wozzeck*, 18.

23. For more on this subject, see Philip Lambert, "Ives and Counterpoint," *American Music* 9 (1991): 119–48.

24. Perle, *Wozzeck*, 14–15, and *Serial Composition and Atonality*, 31.

25. Berg's canon is strict with regard to its rhythmic relationships between voices but inexact in certain pitch calculations. Ives's is strict in both respects.

26. On Ives's fugal writing, see his mention of "four-key fugues" in *Memos*, 38, and the analysis of *Tone Roads No. 1* in Lambert, "Ives and Counterpoint," 135–38, and Lambert, "Compositional Procedures," 261–80. The fugal section in act 2, scene 2 of *Wozzeck* is discussed by Perle, *Wozzeck*, 63–64. In *Wozzeck*, the first subject is inverted in the solo cello in mm. 319–20. In *Tone Roads No. 1*, the first subject is inverted in the bassoon in mm. 17–19.

27. Berg explains the structure of *Wozzeck* as a grouping of "character pieces" (act 1), "movements" of a "symphony" (act 2), and "inventions" (act 3). See Alban Berg, "Die musikalischen Formen in meiner Oper 'Wozzeck,' " *Die Musik* 16 (1924): 587–89; H. F. Redlich, *Alban Berg: The Man and His Music* (London: John Calder, 1957), 95; and Willi Reich, *Alban Berg*, trans. Cornelius Cardew (New York: Harcourt, Brace & World, 1965), 121.

28. The variations do not preserve aspects of rhythm, melodic shape, or phrase structure, in the conventional manner. Rather, the transposed, inverted, or retrograded pitch sequences are subject to any conceivable rhythmic, registral, and timbral realizations. See George Perle, *Lulu*, vol. 2 of *The Operas of Alban Berg* (Berkeley and Los Angeles: University of California Press, 1985), 2–3. The programmatic meanings of the variations are discussed by Brenda Dalen, " 'Freundschaft, Liebe, und Welt': The Secret Programme of the Chamber Concerto," in *The Berg Companion*, ed. Douglas Jarman (Boston: Northeastern University Press, 1989), 142–45.

29. For further discussion of *In Re Con Moto Et Al*, see Lambert, "Compositional Procedures," 351–65; and David Nicholls, *American Experimental Music, 1890–1940* (Cambridge: Cambridge University Press, 1990), 73–80.

30. In *Calcium Night Light*, the form symbolizes the approach and retreat of a parade; see Lambert, "Compositional Procedures," 160–64. Other examples of arch forms in Ives's music include the choral *Psalm 90* and *Study No. 20* for piano.

31. Robert P. Morgan, "The Eternal Return: Retrograde and Circular Form in Berg," in *Alban Berg: Historical and Analytical Perspectives*, 111–49. The other ABA forms mentioned by Morgan are in the first of the Three Pieces for Orchestra, Op. 6, and the orchestral song Op. 4, No. 3. See also Jarman's discussion of arch forms, *Music of Alban Berg*, 180–85.

32. Morgan, "Eternal Return," 124–33. Jarman finds in Berg's music "not a single major work written after the Op. 5 Clarinet Pieces," excepting the Violin Concerto, that does not include a "strict reversal of a total musical unit" in the second half. See Jarman, *Music of Alban Berg*, 185. Berg's use of palindrome in the Chamber Concerto, as well as the symbolic meanings Berg seems to have attached to this formal procedure, is discussed by Dalen, " 'Freundschaft, Liebe, und Welt.' "

33. For extensive discussion of these works, see Ulrich Maske, *Charles Ives in seiner Kammermusik für drei bis sechs Instrumente*, (Regensberg: G. Bosse, 1971), 14–15, 62, 105, 112–114, 134; Nachum Schoffman, "The Songs of Charles Ives" (Ph.D. diss., Hebrew University of Jerusalem, 1977), 46–52; idem, "Serialism in the Works of Charles Ives," *Tempo*, no. 138 (September 1981): 27–28; Thomas Dyer Winters, "Additive and Repetitive Techniques in the Experimental Works

of Charles Ives" (Ph.D. diss., University of Pennsylvania, 1986); and Lambert, "Compositional Procedures," 165–171.

34. See George Perle, "Berg's Master Array of the Interval Cycles," *Musical Quarterly* 63 (1977): 1–30, and Philip Lambert, "Interval Cycles as Compositional Resources in the Music of Charles Ives," *Music Theory Spectrum* 12 (1990): 43–82.

35. For consistency, intervals are always calculated in an "upward" direction, like the "ordered pitch-class intervals" in John Rahn, *Basic Atonal Theory* (New York: Longman, 1980), 25. That is, B–C is interval 1 and C–C♯ is interval 1, but C–B and C♯–C are both interval 11. Interval inverses, "inversions" in conventional harmonic theory, always add up to twelve: 1(m2) + 11 (M7) = 12, 2 (M2) + 10 (m7) = 12, and so forth. Informally, an inverse may be viewed as a change in direction: for example, the interval-1 cycle could generate an ascending chromatic scale, whereas its inverse, interval 11, could generate a descending chromatic scale. Similarly, an interval-7 cycle could generate a clockwise traversal of the circle of fifths, whereas its inverse interval 5 could traverse the circle counterclockwise. Interval 6 is its own inverse. In the following discussion, observations about a given cycle are usually applicable to its inverse cycle, with obvious adjustments.

36. The notable exception is the diatonic scale, which is an ordering of a seven-note portion of an interval-5 or -7 cycle, but which does not retain its original ordering in applications. The various complex reasons for the special nature of the diatonic scale are discussed by John Clough, "Aspects of Diatonic Sets," *Journal of Music Theory* 23 (1979): 45–61; Robert Gauldin, "The Cycle-7 Complex: Relations of Diatonic Set Theory to the Evolution of Ancient Tonal Systems," *Music Theory Spectrum* 5 (1983): 39–55; John Clough and Gerald Myerson, "Variety and Multiplicity in Diatonic Systems," *Journal of Music Theory* 29 (1985): 249–70; Eytan Agmon, "A Mathematical Model of the Diatonic System," *Journal of Music Theory* 33 (1989): 1–25; and Norman Carey and David Clampitt, "Aspects of Well-Formed Scales," *Music Theory Spectrum* 11 (1989): 187–206.

37. The even-odd designation comes from a labeling system whereby the numbers 0–11 are assigned to the notes of the chromatic scale starting on C (C = 0, C♯ = 1, D = 2, etc.).

38. For further discussion of Berg's whole-tone writing, see Robert Bruce Archibald, "Harmony in the Early Works of Alban Berg" (Ph.D. diss., Harvard University, 1965), 25–31, and Perle, *Serial Composition and Atonality*, 38–39. See also Janet Schmalfeldt, "Berg's Path to Atonality: The Piano Sonata, Op. 1," in *Alban Berg: Historical and Analytical Perspectives*, 79–109. Schmalfeldt's analysis places great importance on whole-tone materials, especially the "tensions that result when whole-tone and atonal materials are placed in opposition to the large-scale tonal framework" (105).

39. For further discussion of Ives's whole-tone writing, see Lambert, "Compositional Procedures," 69–83, and Burkholder, "Critique of Tonality," 207–8, 216–18. See also the analysis of "Mists" in Lambert, "Toward a Theory of Chord Structure," 72–79.

40. Mark DeVoto cites this song to illustrate chromatic "creeping," or stepwise linear motion, in the music of Berg, in "Alban Berg and Creeping Chromaticism," in *Alban Berg: Historical and Analytical Perspectives*, 57–78. See also Perle's discussion of chromatic usages in music of the period in *Serial Composition and Atonality*, 24–27.

41. The exercises with chromatic scales are notated in his father's copybook, pp. 68 and 71. See John Kirkpatrick, *A Temporary Mimeographed Catalogue of the Music Manuscripts and Related Materials of Charles Edward Ives 1874–1954* (New Haven: Library of the Yale University School of Music, 1960), 214. In *Memos*, 44, Ives recalls the youthful origins of this technique, and Kirkpatrick (44, n. 5) quotes Ives as having cited his father as a source of inspiration.

42. In *Study No. 5*, the chromatic unfoldings occur in the right hand in beats 7–20 and in the left hand in beats 25–38 (as numbered in *Charles Ives: Study No. 5 for Piano*, ed. Alan Mandel [Merion Music, 1988]). The passage from *Study No. 20* is described in Lambert, "Interval Cycles," 50–51.

43. See Archibald, "Harmony in the Early Works of Berg," 32–39, and idem, "Berg's Development as an Instrumental Composer," in *Berg Companion*, 91–121. Schmalfeldt, "Berg's Path to Atonality," 96 and 102, finds that the fourth-chords relate to the work's opening motive or *Grundgestalt*.

44. Perle, *Serial Composition and Atonality*, 24.

45. Jarman, *Music of Alban Berg*, 21. See also Archibald, "Harmony in the Early Works of Berg," 47–63.

46. Archibald, "Harmony in the Early Works of Berg," 62. Archibald also discusses the String Quartet Op. 3 in "Berg's Development as an Instrumental Composer," 96–105. For further discussion of Berg's wedges, see DeVoto, "Alban Berg and Creeping Chromaticism."

47. See Winters, "Additive and Repetitive Techniques," 24–126, and Lambert, "Compositional Procedures," 110–51.

48. For transcriptions of the triad wedges, see Burkholder, "Critique of Tonality," 215. *A Yale-Princeton Football Game* is discussed by Winters, "Additive and Repetitive Techniques," 24–25.

49. See H. Wiley Hitchcock, *Ives: A Survey of the Music* (London: Oxford University Press, 1977), 31–32. After the pattern reaches a wedge of interval 7, the process reverses and the work concludes with verses based on successively smaller intervals and contracting wedges.

50. In this passage in *Psalm 90*, both vertical and horizontal intervals are whole steps. See Winters, "Additive and Repetitive Techniques," 30–39, and Lambert, "Compositional Procedures," 154–59.

51. See Domenick Argento, "A Digest Analysis of Ives' 'On the Antipodes,'" *Student Musicologists at Minnesota* 6 (1975–76): 192–200, and Lambert, "Interval Cycles," 75–81.

52. Because Ives's melody does not strongly outline the wedge as a registral pattern, it has a more abstract relationship to the model than does Berg's version. An interpretive analytic choice determines which segment is to be considered the upper and which the lower voice, and thus whether to view it as a divergence or convergence. These matters are treated in more detail in Philip Lambert,

"Aggregate Structures in Music of Charles Ives," *Journal of Music Theory* 34 (1990): 32–36. Other music exhibiting these wedge types includes Bartók's Bagatelle for piano Op. 6, No. 2 and Nono's *Il canto sospeso*, in which the tone row is formed by a regular alternation of members of wedge voices. All these examples bring to mind J. S. Bach's E-minor organ fugue (BWV 548/2), known as the "Wedge" because of the diverging chromatic lines in its subject.

53. See Perle, "Berg's Master Array." Berg constructed a chart to illustrate a complete cyclic stacking and included it in a letter to Schoenberg. See also Perle, *Wozzeck*, 124–25.

54. For further discussion of this song, see Schoffman, "Songs of Charles Ives," 36–45, and Lambert, "Compositional Procedures," 85–93.

55. Prolongation and voice exchange are concepts from Heinrich Schenker's theories of tonal music, as presented, for example, in *Free Composition [Der freie Satz]*, trans. and ed. Ernst Oster (New York: Longman, 1979), 25–52, 84–85.

56. See Lambert, "Compositional Procedures," 165–71.

57. See Lambert, "Interval Cycles," 76–81.

58. That is, *mirror inversion*, where two melodies state the same intervals but reverse the directions. Thus, G♯–B–G (w), or "minor third up, major third down," is the inversion of E♭–C–E (x reversed), or "minor third down, major third up." Similarly, F♯–F–D (y) is the inversion of A–B♭–D♭ (z reordered).

59. The contrast with Schoenbergian operations is substantial. Whereas transposition, inversion, and retrograde all place primary importance on the adjacent intervals in a row, which are preserved or inverted, a segmental rearrangement might produce a very different intervallic succession.

60. Jarman, *The Music of Alban Berg*, 75; Perle, *Lulu*, 5. Berg's extensive use of such techniques within the first two movements of the Chamber Concerto is discussed in Philip Lambert, "Berg's Path to Twelve-Note Composition: Aggregate Construction and Association in the Chamber Concerto," *Music Analysis* 12 (1993): 321–42.

61. Several pitch structures in the Chamber Concerto are derived from letters in the names of Schoenberg, Berg, and Webern. See Jarman, *Music of Alban Berg*, 75; Perle, *Lulu*, 5; and Dalen, " 'Freundschaft, Liebe, und Welt,' " 141–45.

62. Perle, *Lulu*, 11.

63. Ives's methods are described in Lambert, "Aggregate Structures," 38–42, and Lambert, "Compositional Procedures," 212–19.

64. Berg's methods are described in Dave Headlam, "The Derivation of Rows in *Lulu*," *Perspectives of New Music* 24/2 (Spring–Summer 1985): 198–233, and idem, "Row Derivation and Contour Association in Berg's *Der Wein*," *Perspectives of New Music* 28/1 (Fall–Winter 1990): 256–92.

65. Ives, *Memos*, 104.

66. The rhythmic aspect of the "compound" is based on contrasting subdivisions of measures, as Ives explains in *Memos*, 104–5.

67. The derivation is explained in Perle, *Lulu*, 109–10. Berg's derivation is

less systematic than Ives's in that there is no consistency between vertical ordering in the chords and horizontal ordering in the melody.

68. The same ordering occurs in the piccolo, in different rhythms.

69. For example, Headlam ("The Derivation of Rows in *Lulu*") describes rows in *Lulu* that are derived by cyclically extracting "every second," "every third," or "every seventh" note from the primary row.

70. The roles of contextuality and external reference in twelve-tone music are discussed at length in Perle, *Twelve-Tone Tonality*, "Conclusion," 162–72.

71. Igor Stravinsky, *Poetics of Music*, trans. Arthur Knodel and Ingolf Dahl (Cambridge, Mass.: Harvard University Press, 1942), 64–65.

72. Perle, *Wozzeck*, 14.

73. Burkholder, *Charles Ives*, 114.

74. See Burkholder, "Evolution of Ives's Music," idem, *Charles Ives: The Ideas Behind the Music*, and idem, " 'Quotation' and Paraphrase in Ives's Second Symphony," *19th-Century Music* 11 (1987): 3–25.

75. Maynard Solomon, "Charles Ives: Some Questions of Veracity," *Journal of the American Musicological Society* 40 (1987): 443–70. Answers to Solomon's questions are coming from other sources as well. Gayle Sherwood has made significant advances toward a reliable chronology of Ives's music in "The Choral Works of Charles Ives: Chronology, Style, and Reception" (Ph.D. diss., Yale University, 1995). Her methods are those called for by Solomon: "To establish the dates of commencement and revision of Ives's works, we need to rely upon the traditional methods of historical musicology—documentary and paper studies, handwriting comparisons, and a detailed analytic reconstruction of the compositional process of each work" (Maynard Solomon, "Communication," *Journal of the American Musicological Society* 42 [1989]: 212).

Chapter 7: Ives and Stravinsky

Thanks to Rebecca Davy, Geoffrey Block, J. Peter Burkholder, and Larry Starr for their indispensable help in the preparation of this essay.

1. "I relate only from an angle to the German stem (Bach-Haydn-Mozart-Beethoven-Schubert-Brahms-Wagner-Mahler-Schoenberg)." Igor Stravinsky and Robert Craft, *Dialogues and a Diary* (London: Faber and Faber, 1963), 30.

2. Igor Stravinsky, *An Autobiography* (New York: Simon and Schuster, 1936), 118–19.

3. See Geoffrey Block's essay in the present volume; also his "Remembrance of Dissonances Past: The Two Published Editions of Ives's *Concord Sonata*," in *Ives Studies*, ed. Philip Lambert (Cambridge: Cambridge University Press, forthcoming).

4. See Sondra Rae Clark, "The Evolving *Concord Sonata*: A Study of Choices and Variants in the Music of Charles Ives" (Ph.D. diss., Stanford University, 1972); and Louis Cyr, "Writing *The Rite* Right," in *Confronting Stravinsky: Man, Musician, and Modernist*, ed. Jann Pasler (Berkeley: University of California Press, 1986), 157–73.

5. Thanks to Geoffrey Block for first pointing out the similarity between

Stravinsky's and Ives's techniques of melodic adjustment, which I believe has been noted by no other Ives scholar. See also Richard Taruskin, "Russian Folk Melodies in *The Rite of Spring*," *Journal of the American Musicological Society* 33 (1980): 502. See also the published facsimile of the *Rite of Spring* sketch book (Igor Stravinsky, *The Rite of Spring: Sketches, 1911–1913* [London: Boosey and Hawkes, 1969]).

6. J. Peter Burkholder lists fourteen techniques for recasting quotations or paraphrases into new compositions used systematically by Ives, in "The Uses of Existing Music: Musical Borrowing as a Field," *Music Library Association Notes* 50 (1994): 851–70. For discussions of folk song sources for the *Rite*, see Taruskin, "Russian Folk Songs," and Pieter C. van den Toorn, *Stravinsky and The Rite of Spring* (Berkeley: University of California Press, 1987), 4–15.

7. Ives dissects m. 124 of *Putnam's Camp* and claims that his own rhythmic experiments predate the *Rite* in his *Memos*, ed. John Kirkpatrick (New York: W. W. Norton, 1972), 138–40.

8. See this passage in the *Rite*, rehearsal numbers 64–71. Moments of imaginative orchestration strike the ear as well, such as the tone cluster in the strings, ripe with clinging harmonics, in the middle section of *Putnam's Camp* (at rehearsal letter G), which corresponds to such timbres in the *Rite* as the setting of a high soft violin harmonic against five cellos two measures after rehearsal number 12, just before the "Dance of the Adolescents."

9. Ives, *Memos*, 138.

10. Charles Ives, *Essays Before a Sonata, The Majority, and Other Writings*, ed. Howard Boatwright (New York: W. W. Norton, 1970), 99.

11. Elliott Carter, "Music Criticism," in *The Writings of Elliott Carter: An American Composer Looks at Modern Music*, ed. Else Stone and Kurt Stone (Bloomington: Indiana University Press, 1977), 313.

12. See Pieter van den Toorn, *The Music of Igor Stravinsky* (New Haven: Yale University Press, 1983), particularly pp. 63–65.

13. Ives, *Memos*, 47.

14. "This is a kind of enlarged plain chant, the fundamental of which is made of two keys." Ives, *Memos*, 178. See J. Peter Burkholder, "The Critique of Tonality in the Early Experimental Music of Charles Ives," *Music Theory Spectrum* 12 (1990): 209–15.

15. J. Peter Burkholder, *Charles Ives: The Ideas Behind the Music* (New Haven: Yale University Press, 1985), 89.

16. Thanks to Geoffrey Block for pointing out this connection of Ives and Stravinsky to the precursor both men revered so highly.

17. "Strong poets make [poetic] history by misreading one another." Harold Bloom, *The Anxiety of Influence: A Theory of Poetry* (Oxford: Oxford University Press, 1973), 5. See also Joseph N. Straus, *Remaking the Past: Musical Modernism and the Influence of the Tonal Tradition* (Cambridge, Mass.: Harvard University Press, 1990), 14–17.

18. Richard Taruskin, "Back to Whom? Neoclassicism as Ideology," *19th-Century Music* 16 (1993): 292. See also William E. Benjamin, "Tonality without Fifths: Remarks on the First Movement of Stravinsky's Concerto for Piano and

Wind Instruments," *In Theory Only* 2/11–12 (February–March 1977): 53–70 and 3/2 (May 1977): 9–33, for an illuminating discussion of Stravinsky's pandiatonicism. See van den Toorn, *Music of Igor Stravinsky*, 271-320, for extensive discussions of octatonic-diatonic "links."

19. See Burkholder, "Critique of Tonality," 209–15, for analyses of general experimental pieces by Ives.

20. These categories are derived from Stuart Feder, *Charles Ives: "My Father's Song: A Psychoanalytic Biography* (New Haven: Yale University Press, 1992), 93.

21. Only the title page of the *Schoolboy March* survives, reproduced in Feder, *Charles Ives*, 96. "Slow March" is included in Ives's *114 Songs*.

22. Feder, *Charles Ives*, 104.

23. Ibid., 38.

24. Stravinsky, *Autobiography*, 6–7.

25. Eric Walter White, *Stravinsky: The Composer and His Works* (Berkeley and Los Angeles: University of California Press, 1966), 7.

26. Stravinsky's *Autobiography* begins with a hilarious but slightly crude description of a mute villager making a song from two pitches and a rapid series of "resounding kisses" created with hand and armpit, which he describes as one of his earliest memories of sound. Stravinsky then cites his accurate recension before the age of three of a folk song he had heard a group of women sing the same day then as perhaps the first concrete evidence of his gift for music.

27. See Nicholas Tawa's essay in the present volume concerning Ives, Parker, and their contemporaries.

28. Rimsky-Korsakov's granddaughter Tatiana recounts this story in Tony Palmer's documentary film *"Once, at a Border . . . :" Aspects of Stravinsky* (1981), edited and presented by Melvyn Bragg (London Weekend Television, distributed by Kultur Video).

29. *"Once, at a Border"*

30. Feder, *Charles Ives*, 154. See also Frank Rossiter, *Charles Ives and his America* (New York: Liveright, 1975), 75–76.

31. Feder, *Charles Ives*, 161.

32. White, *Stravinsky*, 8.

33. The term "museum pieces" is borrowed from J. Peter Burkholder, "Museum Pieces: The Historicist Mainstream in Music of the Last Hundred Years," *Journal of Musicology* 2 (1983): 115–34.

34. White, *Stravinsky*, 138.

35. See Block's essay in the present volume.

36. White, *Stravinsky*, 182.

37. Burkholder, *All Made of Tunes*, 98–101.

38. For a discussion of Parker's evaluation of Ives's First Symphony, see also Tawa's essay in the present volume.

39. See Burkholder, "Uses of Existing Music," 851–70.

40. White, *Stravinsky*, 145.

41. Arthur Rubinstein, *My Many Years* (New York: Knopf, 1980), 101–2. He did play an arrangement of *Petrushka*, which Stravinsky dedicated to him.

42. Eric Salzman, liner notes to *Igor Stravinsky: Music for Piano*, Noël Lee, piano (Nonesuch LP H-71212, n.d. [1971?]).

43. *Charles E. Ives: Ragtime Dances: Set of Four Ragtime Dances for Theater Orchestra*, ed. and with a preface by James B. Sinclair (New York: Peer Music, 1990), iii–iv.

44. Burkholder, *Charles Ives*, 85. See also Charles M. Joseph, *Stravinsky and the Piano* (Ann Arbor, Mich.: UMI Research Press, 1983), 106.

45. Joseph, *Stravinsky and the Piano*, 99–100.

46. Quote from John Kirkpatrick, *A Temporary Mimeographed Catalogue of the Music Manuscripts and Related Materials of Charles Edward Ives 1874–1954* (New Haven: Library of the Yale School of Music, 1960; reprint, 1973), 86.

47. Burkholder, *Charles Ives*, 85.

48. Clayton W. Henderson, *The Charles Ives Tunebook* (Warren, Mich.: Harmonie Park Press, 1990), 95–96 and 106 (tunes H107 and H94).

49. Ives's intermingling of sacred and secular genres in the First Piano Sonata recalls medieval parodic conventions; see Dennis Marshall, "Charles Ives' Quotations: Manner or Substance?," *Perspectives of New Music* 6 (1968): 45–56; reprinted in *Perspectives on American Composers*, ed. Benjamin Boretz and Edward T. Cone (New York: W. W. Norton, 1971), 13–24.

50. Taruskin, "Back to Whom?," 293, n. 52.

51. Lawrence Morton, "Stravinsky and Tchaikovsky: *Le baiser de la fée*," in *Stravinsky: A New Appraisal of his Work*, ed. Paul Henry Lang, (New York: W. W. Norton, 1963), 47–60. Burkholder mentions Ives's use of a quotation from Tchaikovsky in the First Symphony in the present volume; see also his " 'Quotation' and Paraphrase in Ives's Second Symphony," *19th-Century Music* 11 (1987): 3–25. See also Straus, *Remaking the Past*, 54–58.

52. Gordon Cyr, "Intervallic Structural Elements in Ives' Fourth Symphony," *Perspectives of New Music* 9–10 (1971), 303.

53. Marshall, "Charles Ives' Quotations," 13–21. See Block on Beethoven and the *Concord Sonata* in his essay in the present volume.

54. Taruskin, "Stravinsky and the Painters," in *Confronting Stravinsky*, ed. Jann Pasler (Berkeley and Los Angeles: University of California Press, 1986), especially pp. 34–36. See also van den Toorn, *Music of Igor Stravinsky*, 131–33.

55. Morton, "Stravinsky and Tchaikovsky," 59–60. See also Block on Beethoven in his essay in the present volume.

56. Burkholder, *All Made of Tunes*, chap. 3.

57. Straus, *Remaking the Past*, 96.

58. Charles Rosen, *Arnold Schoenberg* (New York: Viking Press, 1975), 71–72.

59. "Beethoven frisé [curled]" is a soubriquet attributed to Stravinsky in Joseph, *Stravinsky and the Piano*, 166.

60. See Block's essay in the present volume.

61. Derived from Feder, *Charles Ives*, 325.

62. Ives, *Memos*, 138.

63. Feder, *Charles Ives*, 330.

64. According to the New York Philharmonic's Programs for the 1924–25

season, the *Rite* was first performed in North America on 3 March 1922 by the Philadelphia Orchestra, with Leopold Stokowski conducting; the New York Philharmonic first played the work on 22 January 1925, under Wilhelm Furt-wängler. Stravinsky conducted the orchestra himself on 10 January 1925, in a program including suites from *Pulcinella* and *Petrushka*.

65. On Ives, see Maynard Solomon, "Charles Ives: Some Questions of Ve-racity," *Journal of the American Musicological Society* 40 (1987), 443–70, and Fed-er's response, "Appendix A: On the Veracity of Ives's Dating of His Music," in *Charles Ives*, 351–57. On Stravinsky, see Taruskin, "Russian Folk Melodies," 501–43; see also his "Stravinsky and the Painters," 34–36, for a summary of his analysis of Stravinsky's paraphrasing of archaic Russian "calendar songs" into a "new-style octatonicism" in the *Rite*.

66. Elliott Carter, *Writings*, 48.

67. Igor Stravinsky and Robert Craft, *Expositions and Developments* (Garden City, N.Y.: Doubleday, 1962), 98.

68. Richard Crawford, *The American Musical Landscape* (Berkeley: University of California Press, 1993), 86–88 and 104–7.

69. Straus describes Stravinsky's strategies for "stripping an earlier work of expressive excess" with Harold Bloom's term *kenosis*; see *Remaking the Past*, 57–58 and 152–53. See also Joseph Straus, "Sonata Form in Stravinsky," in *Stra-vinsky Retrospectives*, ed. Ethan Haimo and Paul Johnson (Lincoln: University of Nebraska Press, 1987), 141–61.

70. Henry Cowell, "Charles E. Ives," in *American Composers on American Music*, ed. Henry Cowell (New York: Frederic Ungar, 1933), 144–45.

71. See Keith Ward's essay in this volume for more detailed explorations of commonalities between Schoenberg and Ives. Thanks to Geoffrey Block for pointing out the evolution in the critical reception of Schoenberg and Stravinsky.

72. Leonard Meyer, "The End of the Renaissance?," in *Music, the Arts, and Ideas* (Chicago: University of Chicago Press, 1967), 68–84; and Charles Hamm, "Not Yet," *Arts in Society* 4 (1967): 554–60. See Walter Jackson Bate. *The Burden of the Past and the English Poet* (Cambridge, Mass.: Harvard University Press, 1970), and Harold Bloom, *The Anxiety of Influence: A Theory of Poetry* (New York: Oxford University Press, 1975).

73. Burkholder, "Museum Pieces," and Straus, *Remaking the Past*. See Rich-ard Taruskin's review of the latter and of Kevin Korsyn, "Towards a New Po-etics of Musical Influence," *Music Analysis* 10 (1991): 3–72, in *Journal of the American Musicological Society* 46 (1993): 114–38, on their application of Bloom's "agonistic theory of poetic influence" to music. Block's essay in the current volume applies the theory to Ives's relationship to Beethoven.

74. "Late, late romanticism" is a phrase from Leonard Meyer, "A Pride of Prejudices; Or, Delight in Diversity," *Music Theory Spectrum* 13 (1991): 241.

75. Igor Stravinsky and Robert Craft, *Retrospectives and Conclusions* (New York: Knopf, 1969), 32.

Contributors

GEOFFREY BLOCK (Ph.D., Harvard) is professor of music at the University of Puget Sound. He is the author of *Charles Ives: A Bio-Bibliography* (Greenwood, 1988) and the forthcoming Cambridge Music Handbook on Ives's *Concord Sonata* for Cambridge University Press. He has also published articles on Beethoven and the Broadway musical and is currently completing a survey of Broadway from *Show Boat* to Sondheim.

ANDREW BUCHMAN has since 1986 been a member of the faculty at the Evergreen State College in Olympia, Washington, an experimental college with an interdisciplinary curriculum. In addition to his numerous compositions, he has written about Ives, Stravinsky, Sondheim, and electro-acoustic and popular music.

J. PETER BURKHOLDER is associate professor of music at Indiana University and president of the Charles Ives Society. He is the author of *All Made of Tunes: Charles Ives and the Uses of Musical Borrowing* (Yale University Press, 1995) and *Charles Ives: The Ideas Behind the Music* (Yale University Press, 1985). His articles on Ives, Brahms, musical modernism, musical borrowing, and other topics have appeared in the *Musical Quarterly, 19th-Century Music*, the *Journal of Musicology*, the *Journal of the American Musicological Society, Music Theory Spectrum*, and *Notes*, among others.

PHILIP LAMBERT is associate professor of Music at Baruch College and the Graduate Center, City University of New York. His articles on the music of Ives and Berg have appeared in *Music Theory Spectrum*, the *Journal of Music Theory, Music Analysis, American Music*, the *Journal of Musicological Research*, and *Intégral*. He is a member of the board of directors of the Charles Ives Society.

ROBERT P. MORGAN, professor of music at Yale University, is working on a book on large-scale form in nineteenth-century music. His recent publications include " 'A New Musical Reality': Futurism, Modernism, and 'The Art of Noises' " in *Modernism/Modernity* 1, No. 3 (September 1994).

NICHOLAS E. TAWA (Ph.D., musicology, Harvard) is professor emeritus of music at the University of Massachusetts, Boston. He has written eleven books and many articles on American music and music in American society. A major portion of his research has comprised the music and cultural history of New England. In recent months, he has been engaged in an inquiry involving the composer Arthur Foote and his relation to his time and place.

KEITH WARD received a bachelor of music degree from West Chester University and the M. Mus. and D. Mus. from Northwestern University. His work in Ives scholarship has included papers on the influence of New England transcendentalism on Ives's creative process and a critical edition of his piano piece *Anti- Abolitionist Riots*, forthcoming from Theodore Presser and the Charles Ives Society. He also has performed many piano pieces by Ives, including the *Concord Sonata*. He is associate professor of Music at Denison University.

Index